Numeric format specification

To format all results, type ⟨Esc⟩FORMat ⏎. To format one result, move cursor into result and type f. To return a result to global default format, move cursor into result and type d.

In this table z represents the value of the number to be displayed.

DEFAULT VALUE	OPTIONS AND MEANING
rd = d	Radix: decimal, hexadecimal, or octal
ct = 10	Complex tolerance: show as pure real if $\mathrm{Im}(z)/\mathrm{Re}(z) < 10^{ct}$; pure imaginary if $\mathrm{Re}(z)/\mathrm{Im}(z) < 10^{ct}$
im = i	Imaginary unit symbol: i or j.
et = 3	Exponential notation threshold: Show in exponential notation if $z > 10^{et}$ or $z < 10^{-et}$
zt = 15	Zero tolerance: show as zero if $z < 10^{-zt}$
pr = 3	Precision: number of decimal places displayed

Plot specification

To set global plot format, type ⟨Esc⟩PLotformat ⏎. To format one plot, move cursor into plot and type f. To use global plot format on a plot, move cursor into plot and type d.

DEFAULT VALUE	OPTIONS AND MEANING
logs = 0,0	Logarithmic axes (y first, then x): 0 for linear axis; n > 0 for logarithmic axis with n cycles.
subdivs = 1,1	Subdivisions (y first, then x): —For linear axis: number of equal subdivisions —For log axis: number of log subdivisions per cycle (1, 2, or 9)
size = 6,15	Plot size (*lines* first, then *columns*)
type = l	Plot type or types. Choose letters from the following table:

l	line
d	dots
s	step
e	error bars
b	bar chart
x	exes
X	exes with lines
p	pluses
P	pluses with lines

Plot specification *Contin.*

S0-BBX-252

o	rectangles
O	rectangles with lines
v	diamonds
V	diamonds with lines

Special characters

To use special characters, hold down the ⟨Alt⟩ key and press the appropriate letter.

SYMBOL	WHAT TO TYPE	SYMBOL	WHAT TO TYPE
α	⟨Alt-A⟩	η	⟨Alt-N⟩
β	⟨Alt-B⟩	Ω	⟨Alt-O⟩
δ	⟨Alt-D⟩	π	⟨Alt-P⟩
ϵ	⟨Alt-E⟩	θ	⟨Alt-Q⟩
ϕ	⟨Alt-F⟩	ρ	⟨Alt-R⟩
Γ	⟨Alt-G⟩	σ	⟨Alt-S⟩
Φ	⟨Alt-H⟩	τ	⟨Alt-T⟩
∞	⟨Alt-I⟩	μ	⟨Alt-U⟩
λ	⟨Alt-L⟩	ω	⟨Alt-W⟩

' (prime) . . . ` (backquote)

Predefined variables

These predefined variables have values when you start MathCAD.

VARIABLE = START VALUE	DEFINITION AND USE
π = 3.14159 ...	Pi
e = 2.71828 ...	e: the base of natural logarithms
∞ = 10^{307}	Infinity: the largest number in MathCAD
% = 0.01	Percent
TOL = 10^{-3}	Tolerance for numerical approximations
ORIGIN = 0	Vector origin
PRNCOLWIDTH = 8	Column width used for WRITEPRN
PRNPRECISION = 4	Number of decimal places used with WRITEPRN

Special keys

⟨Ctrl-Break⟩	Abort current action
⟨Esc⟩	Command by name
⟨Ctrl-⏎⟩	Text region: set wrap margin at current column. Equation region: Break equation and insert plus sign.
F10	Command menus
@	Create plot region
"	Create text region
⟨Alt-M⟩	Create matrix
f	Local format (in number or plot)
d	Restore to global default format (in number or plot)
F1	Help

Function keys

F1	help		F2	copy
		⟨Ctrl-F2⟩	incopy	
F3	cut		F4	paste
⟨Ctrl-F3⟩	incut		⟨Ctrl-F4⟩	inpaste
F5	load		F6	save
⟨Ctrl-F5⟩	search		⟨Ctrl-F6⟩	replace
F7	split		F8	switch
⟨Ctrl-F7⟩	unsplit			
F9	calculate		F10	Command menus
⟨Ctrl-F9⟩	insertline		⟨Ctrl-F10⟩	deleteline

Control keys

⟨Ctrl-A⟩	(abort—for compatibility with MathCAD Version 1)
⟨Ctrl-B⟩	**backward** (direction of motion in text)
⟨Ctrl-D⟩	(change display colors—EGA only)
⟨Ctrl-F⟩	**forward** (direction of motion in text)
⟨Ctrl-L⟩	**skipline** (skip to next line in text)
⟨Ctrl-N⟩	**justify** ("nudge")
⟨Ctrl-O⟩	**print** ("output")
⟨Ctrl-P⟩	**skipparagraph** (skip to next paragraph in text)
⟨Ctrl-Q⟩	**quit**
⟨Ctrl-R⟩	**redraw**
⟨Ctrl-S⟩	**skipsentence** (skip to next sentence in text)
⟨Ctrl-V⟩	(draw boxes around regions)
⟨Ctrl-W⟩	**skipword** (skip to next word in text)
⟨Ctrl-X⟩	**mark** (set mark in text)

Cursor keys

↑ ↓ ← →	Move one line or column in specified direction
⟨Tab⟩	In text: move forward one word. In equation or plot: move to next placeholder. Between regions: move right to next 10-character tab stop
⟨Shift-Tab⟩	In text: move back one word. In equation or plot: move to previous placeholder. Between regions: move left to next 10-character tab stop
⟨PgUp⟩	Move up 5 lines at a time
⟨PgDn⟩	Move down 5 lines at a time
⟨Ctrl-PgUp⟩	Move up 80% of page
⟨Ctrl-PgDn⟩	Move down 80% of page
⟨Ctrl-←⟩	Move left to next 10-character tab stop
⟨Ctrl-→⟩	Move right to next 10-character tab stop
⟨Home⟩	Move to previous region
⟨End⟩	Move to end of current region. If already at end, move to next region
⟨Ctrl-Home⟩	Scroll to beginning of document; move cursor to first region
⟨Ctrl-End⟩	Scroll to end of document; move cursor to last region
⏎	In text: start new line. In equation or plot: move cursor below region, even with left edge of region. Between regions: move cursor to column 0 on next line

Suffixes for numbers

SUFFIX	EXAMPLES	MEANING
i	4i	Imaginary
j	$3+1.5j \cdot 10^{-2}$	
H	0aH	Hexadecimal
h	8BCh	
O	7570	Octal
o	100o	
L	1L	Standard length unit
l	-2.54l	
M	1M	Standard mass unit
m	2.2m	
T	1T	Standard time unit
t	3600t	
Q	1Q	Standard charge unit
q	-1000q	

Valid equation forms

`expression = result`

Calculation equation.

`definable := expression`

Definition. Press colon (:) to see :=.

`variable := range`

Definition of range variable.

`definable ≡ expression`

Global definition. Press tilde (~) to see ≡.

`variable ≡ range`

Global definition of range variable.

`expression ≈ expression`

`expression > expression`

`expression < expression`

`expression ≥ expression`

`expression ≤ expression`

`expression`

Constraint in solve block. (Press ⟨Alt=⟩ to see ≈.

Press ⟨Alt-)⟩ to see ≥. Press ⟨Alt-(⟩ to see ≤.)

`Given`

Beginning of solve block.

`expression @ expression`

Plot.

In these forms:

variable is a variable name.

result is a result displayed by MathCAD.

expression is any valid MathCAD expression.

range is a range like 0, .01 ..10 (to see the .., type ;).

definable is any of the following:

- A variable name: x.
- A subscripted variable: x_i or $x_{i,j}$. Use a left bracket ([) to indicate subscript.
- A superscripted variable: $x^{<i>}$. To type a superscript, press ⟨Alt-^⟩.
- A vector or matrix of variable names: $\begin{bmatrix} x \\ y \end{bmatrix}$
- A vector or matrix of subscripted variable names.
- A function name: $f(x,y)$

Command-line options

To start MathCAD with command-line options, type this at the DOS prompt:

`MCAD options`

Options can be replaced with any combination of the following:

WHAT TO TYPE	MEANING
filename	Load filename after starting.
/A	Display mode: AT&T 6300 (640 by 400 resolution)
/Bnn	Use background color nn (requires EGA with 256K)
/C	Display mode: IBM Color/Graphics Adapter or Compaq monochrome screen
/E	Display mode: IBM Enhanced Graphics Adapter (monitor unspecified)
/EC	Display mode: IBM Enhanced Graphics Adapter and standard color monitor (640 by 200 resolution)
/EH	Display mode: IBM Enhanced Graphics Adapter and enhanced monitor (640 by 350 resolution)
/EM	Display mode: IBM Enhanced Graphics Adapter and monochrome monitor
/Fnn	Use foreground color nn (requires EGA with 256K)
/H	Display mode: Hercules Monochrome Graphics Card
/M	Start in manual calculation mode
/Rfilename	Run alternate configuration file on startup (default is MCAD.MCC)
/T	Display mode: Toshiba T3100 (640 by 400 resolution)

Built-in functions

Angles in function arguments and results are specified in radians. Complex functions return principal values.

You must type the names of built-in functions exactly as shown here: uppercase, lowercase, or mixed, as indicated.

Symbols used in this table

x, y	Real expression
z	Complex expression
n	Integer or expression returning an integer
v, vx, vy	Vector expression
M	Matrix expression
filename	Variable representing or associated with a filename
i	Range variable
var	Variable name

Trigonometric

sin(z)	Sine
cos(z)	Cosine
tan(z)	Tangent
asin(z)	Inverse sine
acos(z)	Inverse cosine
atan(z)	Inverse tangent
angle(x,y)	Angle from x-axis to (x,y)

Hyperbolic

sinh(z)	Hyperbolic sine
cosh(z)	Hyperbolic cosine
tanh(z)	Hyperbolic tangent
asinh(z)	Inverse hyperbolic sine
acosh(z)	Inverse hyperbolic cosine
atanh(z)	Inverse hyperbolic tangent

Logs and exponentials

exp(z)	e^z
ln(z)	Natural log
log(z)	Base 10 log

Bessel

Y0(x)	$Y_0(x)$
Y1(x)	$Y_1(x)$
Yn(n,x)	$Y_n(x)$
J0(x)	$J_0(x)$
J1(x)	$J_1(x)$
Jn(n,x)	$J_n(x)$

Complex

Re(z)	Real part
Im(z)	Imaginary part
arg(z)	Angle to z in complex plane

File access

READ(filename)	Value read from data file
WRITE(filename)	Value to write to data file
APPEND(filename)	Value to append to data file
READPRN(filename)	Matrix read from structured data file
WRITEPRN(filename)	Matrix to write to structured data file
APPENDPRN(filename)	Matrix to append to structured data file

Interpolation

linterp(vx,vy,x)	Linearly interpolated value at x from data vx and vy
cspline(vx,vy)	Coefficients of spline with cubic ends
lspline(vx,vy)	Coefficients of spline with linear ends
pspline(vx,vy)	Coefficients of spline with parabolic ends
interp(vc,vx,vy,x)	Cubic spline interpolated value at x from coefficients vc and data vx and vy

Fourier transform

fft(v)	Fast Fourier transform of real data
ifft(v)	Inverse transform for fft
cfft(v)	Fast Fourier transform of complex data
icfft(v)	Inverse transform for cfft

Vector

length(v)	Number of elements in v
last(v)	Index of last element in v
max(v)	Maximum element in v
min(v)	Minimum element in v

Built-in functions *Continued*

Population statistics

mean(v)	Mean of elements of v
stdev(v)	Standard deviation of elements of v
var(v)	Variance of elements of v

Linear regression

corr(vx,vy)	Correlation (Pearson's r)
slope(vx,vy)	Slope of regression line
intercept(vx,vy)	Intercept of regression line

Statistical distributions

$\Gamma(z)$	Euler's gamma function
erf(x)	Error function
cnorm(x)	Cumulative normal distribution

Matrix

rows(M)	Number of rows in matrix
cols(M)	Number of columns in matrix
tr(M)	Trace of matrix: sum of diagonal elements
identity(n)	Identity matrix of size n
$\delta(x1,x2)$	Kronecker's delta function
$\epsilon(n1,n2,n3)$	Completely antisymmetric tensor of rank 3
augment($M1,M2$)	New matrix made by combining arguments

Solving

root($expr,var$)	Value of var where $expr$ is 0
Find($var1,var2,\ldots$)	Solved values of variables
Minerr($var1,var2,\ldots$)	Variable values that minimize errors

Truncation functions

floor(x)	Greatest integer $\leq x$
ceil(x)	Least integer $\geq x$

Miscellaneous

rnd(x)	Random number between 0 and x
$\Phi(x)$	1 if $x \geq 0$, 0 otherwise
mod($x1,x2$)	Remainder on dividing $x1$ by $x2$
until($x1,x2$)	Returns $x2$ until $x1 < 0$
hist(*intervals*, *data*)	Histogram
if($c,x1,x2$)	Returns $x1$ if c is true ($c \neq 0$), x_2 otherwise (See Conditionals in the Reference Section.)

Commands *Continued*

Edit and move commands

F2	F10 E C	COPy	Copy region
F3	F10 E X	CUt	Delete region
F4	F10 E P	PASte	Insert region that was copied or cut
	F10 E S	SEParate	Separate overlapping regions
⟨Ctrl-F9⟩	F10 E I	INSertline	Insert a blank line
⟨Ctrl-F10⟩	F10 E D	DEleteline	Delete line of text or blank line in document
	F10 E G	Goto *line column*	Go to indicated position
	F10 E M	MOve *lines columns*	Scroll indicated number of positions
⟨Ctrl-F5⟩	F10 E F	SEArch *text*	Search forward or backward for text
		SEArch -*text*	
⟨Ctrl-F6⟩	F10 E R	REPlace *text text*	Replace indicated text with new text

Text commands

	F10 T W	Width *chars*	Specify width for text region; rewrap
⟨Ctrl-X⟩	F10 T M	MARk	Set beginning or end of marked text
	F10 T C	CEnter	Center line of text
⟨Ctrl-B⟩	F10 T B	BAckward	Interpret text motion commands as backward
⟨Ctrl-F⟩	F10 T F	FORWard	Interpret text motion commands as forward
⟨Ctrl-N⟩	F10 T J	Justify	Re-wrap text and realign regions with text bands

Window and page commands

F7	F10 W S	SPlit	Split screen into two windows
⟨Ctrl-F7⟩	F10 W U	Unsplit	Unsplit screen
F8	F10 W J	SWitch	Switch cursor to other window
	F10 W P	PAGelength *lines*	Set page length (use 0 for no page breaks)

Other commands

		PLotformat	Set global plot format
		SET *var value*	Set value of a system variable
⟨Ctrl-W⟩		SKIPWord	Skip a word in text
⟨Ctrl-L⟩		SKIPLine	Skip a line in text
⟨Ctrl-S⟩		SKIPSentence	Skip a sentence in text
⟨Ctrl-P⟩		SKIPParagraph	Skip a paragraph in text

Commands

Press (F10) to see command menus. Press ⟨Esc⟩ to enter commands by name.

System commands

(F1)	(F10) S H	Help	Show Help
⟨Ctrl-Q⟩	(F10) S Q	Quit	Quit MathCAD
	(F10) S D	DOs *command*	Execute DOS command
	(F10) S M	MEmory	Show available memory
⟨Ctrl-R⟩	(F10) S R	REDraw	Redraw screen
⟨Ctrl-O⟩	(F10) S P	PRInt	Print current document
	(F10) S S	SELectprinter	Select printer type
	(F10) S C	CONfigsave	Save current configuration
	(F10) S E	EXecute *filename*	Execute command file

File commands

(F5)	(F10) F L	Load *filename*	Load document file
(F6)	(F10) F S	SAve *filename*	Save document file
	(F10) F A	APpend *filename*	Append file to current document
	(F10) F F	FIlename *var file*	Associate variable with file
	(F10) F C	CLear	Clear document and reload configuration
	(F10) F R	RESet	Reset MathCAD and use system defaults

Compute commands

(F9)	(F10) C C	CAlculate	Process and calculate visible equations
	(F10) C P	PROcess	Process and calculate whole document
	(F10) C A	AUtomatic	Enter automatic computation mode
	(F10) C M	MANual	Enter manual computation mode
	(F10) C F	FORMat	Set global format for results
	(F10) C R	RAndomize *seed*	Reset random numbers
	(F10) C D	DImension	Change dimension names
	(F10) C E	EQuation (on/off)	Disable or re-enable equation
⟨Alt-M⟩	(F10) C G	MATrix *rows cols*	Create or change size of matrix (*rows* $\leq$ 5 or *cols* $\leq$ 5)

In-region commands

⟨Ctrl-(F2)⟩	(F10) I C	INCOpy	Copy marked text or part of equation
⟨Ctrl-(F3)⟩	(F10) I X	INCUt	Delete marked text or part of equation
⟨Ctrl-(F4)⟩	(F10) I P	INPaste	Paste text or part of equation previously copied or cut

The Student Edition of MathCAD®

Reference Card

Operators

Listed in order of precedence.

TO SEE THIS	TYPE THIS	OPERATOR
$(\mathbf{x})$	'x or (x)	Parentheses
$\mathbf{x_i}$	x[i	Subscript
$\mathbf{x^{<i>}}$	x⟨Alt-^⟩i	Superscript (*i*th column of matrix *x*)
$\vec{\mathbf{x}}$	⟨Alt-⟩x	Vectorize (treat operations elementwise)
$\mathbf{x!}$	x!	Factorial
$\bar{\mathbf{x}}$	x"	Complex conjugate
$\mathbf{x^T}$	x⟨Alt-!⟩	Transpose
$\mathbf{x^y}$	x^y	Power, matrix power, matrix inverse ($y = -1$)
$-\mathbf{x}$	-x	Negation
$\Sigma\mathbf{x}$	⟨Alt-$⟩x	Sum of vector elements
$\sqrt{\mathbf{x}}$	\x	Square root
$|\mathbf{x}|$	|x	Absolute value, determinant, norm
$\dfrac{\mathbf{x}}{\mathbf{y}}$	x/y	Division
$\mathbf{x \cdot y}$	x*y	Multiplication, dot product, matrix product
$\mathbf{x \times y}$	x⟨Alt-*⟩y	Cross product

TO SEE THIS	TYPE THIS	OPERATOR
$\displaystyle\sum_i \mathbf{x}$	i$x	Summation over range
$\displaystyle\prod_i \mathbf{x}$	i#x	Product over range
$\displaystyle\int_a^b \mathbf{f(x)\ dx}$	x&f(x)	Integral
$\dfrac{d}{dx}\mathbf{f(x)}$	x?f(x)	Derivative
$\mathbf{x-y}$	x-y	Subtraction
$\mathbf{x+y}$	x+y	Addition
$\mathbf{x\ ...\ +y}$	x⟨Ctrl-↵⟩y	Addition with line break
$\mathbf{x>y}$	x>y	Greater than
$\mathbf{x<y}$	x<y	Less than
$\mathbf{x \geq y}$	x⟨Alt-⟩)y	Greater than or equal to
$\mathbf{x \leq y}$	x⟨Alt-(⟩y	Less than or equal to
$\mathbf{x \neq y}$	x⟨Alt-#⟩y	Not equal to
$\mathbf{x \approx y}$	x⟨Alt=⟩y	Relational equals
$\mathbf{x,y\ ..z}$	x,y;z	Range

The Student Edition of
MathCAD® Version 2.0

Limited Warranty

Addison-Wesley warrants that the Student Edition of MathCAD ("the program") will substantially conform to the published specifications and to the documentation during the period of 90 days from the date of original purchase, provided that it is used on the computer hardware and with the operating system for which it was designed. Addison-Wesley also warrants that the magnetic media on which the program is distributed and the documentation are free from defects in materials and workmanship during the period of 90 days from the date of original purchase. Addison-Wesley will replace defective media or documentation or correct substantial program errors at no charge, provided you return the item with dated proof of purchase to Addison-Wesley within 90 days of the date of original purchase. If Addison-Wesley is unable to replace defective media or documentation or correct substantial program errors, your license fee will be refunded. These are your sole remedies for any breach of warranty.

Except as specifically provided above, Addison-Wesley makes no warranty or representation, either express or implied, with respect to this program, documentation or media, including their quality, performance, merchantability, or fitness for a particular purpose. MathSoft makes no warranty or representation, either express or implied, with respect to this program, documentation or media, including their quality, performance, merchantability or fitness for a particular purpose.

Because programs are inherently complex and may not be completely free of errors, you are advised to verify your work. **In no event will Addison-Wesley or MathSoft be liable for direct, indirect, special, incidental, or consequential damages arising out of the use of or inability to use the program, documentation or media,** even if advised of the possibility of such damages. Specifically, neither Addison-Wesley nor MathSoft is responsible for any costs including, but not limited to, those incurred as result of lost profits or revenue (in any case, the program must be used only for educational purposes, as required by your license), loss of use of the computer program, loss of data, the costs of recovering such programs or data, the cost of any substitute program, claims by third parties, or for other similar costs. In no case shall the liability of Addison-Wesley exceed the amount of the license fee and in no case shall MathSoft have any liability.

The warranty and remedies set forth above are exclusive and in lieu of all others, oral or written, express or implied. No Addison-Wesley dealer, distributor, agent, or employee is authorized to make any modification or addition to this warranty.

Some statutes do not allow the exclusion of implied warranties; if any implied warranties are found to exist, they are hereby limited in duration to the 90-day life of the express warranties given above. Some states do not allow the exclusion or limitation of incidental or consequential damages, nor any limitation on how long implied warranties last, so these limitations may not apply to you. This warranty gives you specific legal rights and you may also have other rights which vary from state to state.

To obtain performance of this warranty, return the item with dated proof of purchase within 90 days of the purchase date to: Addison-Wesley Publishing Company, Inc., Educational Software Division, Jacob Way, Reading, MA 01867.

The Student Edition of
MathCAD® Version 2.0

The electronic scratchpad for calculation and
analysis...*adapted for education*

Richard B. Anderson

 Addison-Wesley Publishing Company, Inc.

 Benjamin/Cummings Publishing Company, Inc.

Reading, Massachusetts • Menlo Park, California • New York
Don Mills, Ontario • Wokingham, England • Amsterdam • Bonn
Sydney • Singapore • Tokyo • Madrid • San Juan

The Student Edition of MathCAD is published by Addison-Wesley Publishing Company, Inc. and Benjamin/Cummings Publishing Company, Inc. Contributors included:

Alan Jacobs, Executive Editor
Dana Degenhardt, Product Development Manager
Cheryl Wurzbacher, Manager of Software Production
Mary Coffey, Software Production Supervisor
Karen Wernholm, Production Editor
Ann DeLacey, Manufacturing Manager
LuAnne Piskadlo, Media Manufacturing Supervisor
Marshall Henrichs, Corporate Art Director
Editorial Services of New England, Inc., Production Coordination
Jean Hammond, Design
CPC Type and Graphics, Composition

The Student Edition of MathCAD was developed and programmed by MathSoft, Inc. Contributors included:

Dr. Jeffrey Herrmann, Vice President of Marketing and Sales
Josh Bernoff, Director of Product Support
Kimberly Mager, Product Marketing Manager

MathSoft and MathCAD are trademarks of MathSoft, Inc. IBM, IBM PC, IBM PC/XT, IBM PC/AT, and IBM Graphics Printer are registered trademarks of International Business Machines Corporation. Hercules Graphics Card is a trademark of Hercules Computer Technology. MS-DOS is a trademark of Microsoft Corporation. The program INT10.COM is licensed from Hercules Computer Technology.

Excerpts from L.J. Krajewski and L.P. Ritzman, *Operations Management.* Reading, Mass.: Addison-Wesley Publishing Company, Inc., © 1987. Pp. 67, 68, 116, 117, 118, 316, 317, and 751. Used with permission.

Student Edition of MathCAD User's Manual
Copyright © 1989, Addison-Wesley Publishing Company, Inc.

Reference card and Reference section
Copyright © 1988, MathSoft, Inc.

It is a violation of copyright law to make a copy of the accompanying software except for backup purposes to guard against accidental loss or damage. Addison-Wesley assumes no responsibility for errors arising from duplication of the original programs.

All rights reserved. No part of this publication may be reproduced, stored in a retrieval system, or transmitted, in any form or by any means, electronic, mechanical, photocopying, recording, or otherwise, without the prior written permission of the publisher. Printed in the United States of America. Published simultaneously in Canada.

0-201-90639-2
0-201-50550-9 (5¼" disk format)
0-201-50551-7 (3½" disk format)

FGHIJ–DO–943210

Preface

Welcome to the Student Edition of MathCAD.

MathCAD is a powerful new tool for engineers, scientists, and others who use mathematics in their professional lives. Math-CAD provides technical professionals with a simple means of displaying, calculating and analyzing equations in standard math notation with the free-form ease of a blackboard or scratchpad. It can be used for a wide variety of tasks from analog design to thermodynamics, and is currently used by thousands of major U.S. corporations and educational institutions.

MathCAD

- Can type mathematical formulas, symbols, and equations into your personal computer and display them in fully expanded notation on your screen.
- Can easily evaluate complex expressions from algebra, trigonometry, calculus, statistics, and many fields of science and technology.
- Can solve simultaneous systems of equations and inequalities.
- Can prepare tabular and graphic displays of mathematical relationships.

- Can compose, save, and print mathematical documents suitable for submission in coursework and for publication.

The Student Edition of MathCAD gives students a professional tool that will benefit them throughout their college careers. Its versatility enables it to be used for classroom demonstrations, in the computer lab or on a student's own personal computer.

Objectives

The Student Edition of MathCAD allows teachers and students to perform complex calculations and mathematical analysis on a personal computer swiftly and easily. The primary objectives of this package are:

- To furnish a powerful and flexible tool for teachers and students.
- To provide a working familiarity with MathCAD's capabilities.
- To develop skill in organizing a MathCAD document.
- To make it easy for individuals or classroom groups to learn MathCAD concepts.
- To prepare students to use MathCAD effectively throughout school and, later, in their careers.

Features

To achieve these objectives, the Student Edition of MathCAD features the full mathematical power of MathCAD Version 2.0, including

- Real, complex, hexadecimal, and octal numbers.
- A wide range of mathematical operations, including summations, products, derivatives, and integrals.
- Built-in functions, including
  - trigonometric
  - hyperbolic
  - exponential
  - logarithmic

- Bessel
- complex number
- vector and matrix operations
- statistical
- regression
- linear and cubic spline interpolation
- Fourier transform

The Student Edition of MathCAD can print documents up to 80 characters wide and 120 lines long.

The Student Edition of MathCAD also includes

- An orderly sequence of MathCAD experiences designed to foster familiarity and basic skill.
- Teaching aids to facilitate both tutorial and group presentations.

Organization of This Manual

This student manual introduces MathCAD's principal features and explains the fundamentals in clear, simple language. The user who follows it through, step by step, will experience a sample of the breadth of MathCAD's applications and will gain familiarity with its commands and features.

Part One, "Getting Started," explains how to install Math-CAD on your personal computer and deal with any peculiarities that your setup may present.

"Basic MathCAD Concepts," Chapter 4, discusses

- What a MathCAD document is and how it works.
- The elements (i.e., regions, equations) that comprise a document.
- The tools (i.e., the screen, the commands) that MathCAD provides for creating and displaying documents.

Part Two, "Tutorial Lab Exercises," illustrates the breadth of MathCAD's application across the many fields that are based in mathematics.

It is important to take the time to carry out each prescribed operation *in the indicated sequence*. Do not skip around. Each exercise assumes the completion of all the earlier ones.

Each lab begins with a list of the MathCAD concepts and functions that students will practice as they work through the lab. The problem statement (itself a MathCAD document) follows. Then step-by-step instructions and representative results lead the student through the creation of a document that is the answer to the problem. Finally, a section called "Suggestions for Further Exploration" encourages the reader to use — and even go beyond — what was learned in the lab.

Each tutorial lab teaches a slightly more sophisticated approach toward the task of organizing a document. The first lab reassures students that mistakes are not generally fatal. MathCAD provides step-by-step help so students can create a logical document. Armed with this confidence, the student is ready to approach the later labs, which show how to build a document more efficiently and logically.

Differences Between the Student Edition and the Professional Version of MathCAD

The Student Edition of MathCAD is identical to the professional version, with the following exceptions:

- The Student Edition worksheet is limited to 80 columns and 120 lines, allowing approximately two printed pages for each document.
- Matrices are limited to a maximum size of $5 \times n$ or $n \times 5$.
- Sets of simultaneous equations and inequalities can be solved for at most 10 unknowns.
- The 2.0 feature "textbands" is not included.
- You cannot insert hard page breaks, although you can set page length.
- VGA cards are not supported.
- Each document printed out by the Student Edition is headed by a two-line legend identifying it as such.

Acknowledgments

My work as an author has benefitted from the contributions of many able hands, and I wish to thank all who have taken part. Some team members deserve particular mention.

I am particularly indebted to Gail Rothenberg, who brought me into this project. Her ideas and comments have been indispensable, as have the field-test reviews she obtained from John Uyemura and his students at the Georgia Institute of Technology. Gail has provided a steady, gracious hand and mind throughout the effort.

Dana Degenhardt has managed a multitude of essential details, obtaining equipment and materials, coordinating communications, and generally making the process run smoothly. She has exerted measured and effective pressure for quality and timeliness, and it has been a pleasure to work with her.

Alan Jacobs has supported the project in many ways. I've been particularly aware of his management of the central relationships between Addison-Wesley and MathSoft.

Sharon Cogdill, of Editorial Services of New England, has shown immense patience and good humor through the process of transmuting my prose to a publishable form. Without her willingness to meet at odd hours and places, we could never have met the schedule and retained anything like sanity.

Carol Munroe carried much of the burden of updating this book to reflect the improvements in MathCAD 2.0. Jeffrey Herrmann and Josh Bernoff of MathSoft, Inc., have provided crucial materials, insights, and consultations. It was their creation of an important and exciting software product with major educational potential, of course, that gave this project a reason to be.

R.B.A.

Contents

Getting Started

Part One

1 Before You Begin

This part of the book describes the contents of the Student Edition of MathCAD and the procedures for installing, starting, and ending MathCAD.

Checking Your MathCAD Package

Your package for the Student Edition of MathCAD should contain the following items:

- The User's Manual (this book)
- The System Disk, containing the MathCAD program (MCAD.EXE) and the font files MathCAD uses when it displays letters and numbers
- The Auxiliary Disk, including the MathCAD Help file, sample MathCAD documents, and the on-line directory, DIRECTRY.MCD, of these documents. Also included is a file called README.TXT that contains up-to-date release notes. (However, if your program came with a 3½″ disk, all of these files are on a single System Disk.)
- The Reference Card
- The License Agreement
- A Warranty Registration Card
- An Upgrade Rebate Coupon

Your personal computer system must be compatible with the following MathCAD system requirements:

- An IBM PC, PC/XT, PC/AT, or compatible computer, including the PS/2 series
- The operating system should be MS-DOS or PC-DOS, version 2.0 or later
- One of the following graphics adapters:
  - An IBM Color/Graphics Adapter (CGA) with color or composite monitor
  - An IBM Enhanced Graphics Adapter (EGA) with any monitor
  - A Hercules Graphics Card with monochrome monitor
  - A Toshiba T3100
  - An AT&T 6300 series (monochrome or color)
- At least 512K random access memory (RAM)
- At least one double-sided 5¼" or 3½" diskette drive (a hard-disk drive is optional)
- A coprocessor is not required, but the Intel 8087, 80287, or 80387 is supported and recommended.
- The following printers are supported:
  - IBM Graphics Printer, IBM Proprinter, and compatible printers that can print the high end of the IBM extended character set. Also use this selection for Epson and Okidata printers that are configured to emulate an IBM Graphics printer or Proprinter (including Okidata printers with "Plug 'n Play" chips).
  - Epson printers in the FX, JX, EX, LX, and LQ series.
  - Hewlett-Packard ThinkJet and QuietJet printers.
  - Hewlett-Packard LaserJet, LaserJet Plus, and LaserJet Series II printers and compatible laser printers.
  - Toshiba P351 printer and compatible Toshiba printers.
  - Okidata 90 series printers, when *not* configured as IBM Graphics Printer.
  - C.Itoh C-315 and compatible C.Itoh printers.
  - NEC P5 Pinwriter printer and compatible NEC printers in NEC mode.

- All Hewlett-Packard plotters and other plotters and devices using HPGL (Hewlett-Packard Graphics Language).

For additional information on printer compatibility, see the README.TXT file on the Auxiliary Disk.

Product Support

Neither Addison-Wesley Publishing Co., Inc. nor MathSoft provides telephone assistance to students for the Student Edition of MathCAD. Telephone assistance is provided to *registered* instructors who have adopted the Student Edition for their students.

If you encounter difficulty using the Student Edition software

- Read the section of this manual containing the information on the commands or procedures you are trying to execute.
- Use the Help screens to locate specific program or error message information.

If you have to ask your instructor for assistance, please describe your question or problem in detail. If you have a problem, write down what you were doing (the steps or procedures you followed) that caused the problem so that you can explain to your instructor what happened. Please write down the exact error message (if any) from your screen.

Typographical Conventions

You control MathCAD through the keyboard of your personal computer. In this manual, special symbols and a special typeface tell you what keystrokes to enter. For example:

Press ⏎

Type

    a:⟨Alt-P⟩r^2

Note that

- "Press" means to strike or press a single key. The name of the key you are supposed to press is specified in angle brackets (for example, ⟨d⟩, ⟨@⟩, ⟨9⟩, ⟨Esc⟩, ⟨PgDn⟩). Function keys are specified like this: ⟨F9⟩.
- "Type" means to strike or press one or more keys in sequence. Where it takes more than one character to specify a single keystroke, the necessary characters are enclosed as a group in one set of angle brackets.
- The Shift, Control (Ctrl), and Alternate (Alt) keys are used only in combination with other keys; you hold one of these special keys down while striking another key. Again, such combinations are shown in this book within angle brackets (for example, ⟨Ctrl–PgUp⟩, ⟨Alt–P⟩, ⟨Shift–Tab⟩). In general, whatever appears within a single set of angle brackets represents a single keystroke, even if it requires two or three keys to execute it.

2 Installing MathCAD

Installing MathCAD is a one-time process, unless you get new equipment. The procedures you follow depend on the kind of system you have. The three sections that follow give step-by-step instructions for installing MathCAD on

- A one-disk system (a single floppy disk drive)
- A two-disk system (two floppy disk drives)
- A hard-disk system

If your MathCAD program is on one 3½" disk, ignore the references to an Auxiliary Disk in the instructions for your system.

Installing MathCAD on a One-Disk System

You need the following items to install MathCAD:

- The MathCAD System and Auxiliary Disks.
- The DOS disk.
- One or more blank disks with sleeves and labels.

Backing Up Your MathCAD Program Diskette

Use DOS to make a backup copy of each of the MathCAD floppy diskettes. Follow these steps:

Starting Your Computer   With your computer turned off, put the DOS disk in the drive and close the door.

Turn the computer on, and wait for it either to display the date and time or to ask you for them.

If needed, type in the date in the form MM-DD-YY, and press ⏎. For example, if the date is July 15, 1989, type

07-15-89 ⏎

If needed, type in the time in the form HH:MM ⏎. For example, if the time is 1:45 p.m., type

13:45 ⏎

If you enter the date or time in the wrong form, DOS will let you try again. Once the date and time are correct, the operating system prompt (usually A⟩) appears. You are now ready to prepare new disks.

Formatting a New Disk   You need to format two disks to use as your working MathCAD System and Auxiliary disks. While you're at it, you may wish to format additional disks to store the MathCAD documents you will create; the System Disk will be too full to serve this purpose.

With the DOS disk in the drive, type

FORMAT ⏎

If you format used disks, you will lose whatever data may be stored on them.

Your screen will say, "Insert new diskette for drive A: and strike any key when ready."

Remove the DOS disk from the drive and place it in a sleeve.

Put a blank new disk in the drive and close the door.

To start formatting, press ⏎.

The message "Formatting..." appears on the screen, the red light next to the drive door goes on, and the drive makes some noise. Formatting can take as long as a minute. When it is finished, the red light goes out, and the message "Format complete" appears. DOS displays some information about the disk and asks, "Format another (Y/N)?"

Respond by typing

Y

With some versions of DOS, you have to press ⏎ after you type Y.

Remove the formatted disk and put it in its sleeve. Put a label on the disk so that you know you formatted it.

Follow the same procedure to format a second program disk and any additional data disks you want.

After you have all the formatted disks you want, respond to "Format another (Y/N)?" by typing N. The DOS prompt will appear.

Making a Backup Disk   Since a one-disk system uses the same drive mechanism for both drives A and B, DOS asks for a disk for drive A and then a disk for drive B each time it copies a file. The disk for drive A should always be the MathCAD disk being copied, and the disk for drive B should be the formatted disk on which you will make the backup copy. Before you start, label the original disk with an A and the blank disk with a B so that you will remember which disk goes in which drive.

Write on the label before you put it on the disk, otherwise you may damage the disk.

Place write-protect tabs on the original System and Auxiliary Disks. (If you have a 3½″ disk, open the write-protect window in the upper right-hand corner of the disk.) Put the MathCAD System Disk in the drive and close the door.

At the DOS prompt, type

    COPY *.* B: ⏎

The asterisk stands for any filename or file extension: *.* tells DOS to copy every file. DOS displays the name of the first file on the MathCAD System Disk and says, "Insert diskette for drive B: and strike any key when ready."

Remove the System Disk from the drive, insert the blank, formatted "target" disk, and press ⏎.

DOS copies the first file from the MathCAD System Disk to the backup disk and says "Insert diskette for drive A: and strike any key when ready." Swap the two disks again, and continue swapping them until all three files are copied.

The job is complete when DOS states the number of files it has copied.

Label the backup disk as a MathCAD System Disk. Use the name of the original disk and indicate that it is a backup copy.

Now label the original MathCAD Auxiliary Disk with an A and the second formatted blank disk with a B. Then insert the Auxiliary Disk in the drive, close the door, and type

```
COPY *.* B: ⏎
```

Swap disks as before until the copying is finished. Be sure to label the backup Auxiliary Disk.

Label one blank, formatted disk (or more, if you wish) as your MathCAD data disk.

Put the original MathCAD System and Auxiliary Disks in a safe place, and always use the backup copy to run MathCAD. If anything happens to the backup copy you are using, you will be able to make another copy from the original.

Installing MathCAD on a Two-Disk System

You will need the following items to install MathCAD:

- The MathCAD System and Auxiliary Disks.
- The DOS disk.
- Two or more blank disks with sleeves and labels.

Backing Up Your MathCAD Program Diskette

Use DOS to make a backup copy of each of the MathCAD floppy diskettes.

Starting Your Computer   With your computer turned off, put the DOS disk in drive A and close the door.

Turn the computer on, and wait for it either to display the date and time or to ask you for them. If needed, type in the date in the form MM-DD-YY, and press ⏎. For example, if the date is July 15, 1989, type

```
07-15-89 ⏎
```

If needed, type in the time in the form HH:MM ⏎. For example, if the time is 1:45 p.m., type

    13:45 ⏎

If you enter the date or time in the wrong form, DOS will let you try again. Once the date and time are correct, the operating system prompt (usually A⟩) appears. You are now ready to prepare new disks.

Formatting a New Disk   You need to format two disks to use as your working MathCAD System and Auxiliary Disks. While you're at it, you may wish to format additional disks to store the MathCAD documents you will create; the System Disk will be too full to serve this purpose.

With the DOS disk in drive A, type

    FORMAT B: ⏎

If you format used disks, you will lose whatever data may be stored on them.

Your screen should say, "Insert new diskette for drive B: and strike any key when ready."

Put a blank new disk in drive B and close the door.

To start formatting, press ⏎.

The message "Formatting..." appears on the screen, the red light next to the drive door goes on, and the drive makes some noise. Formatting can take as long as a minute. When it is finished, the red light goes out, and the message "Format complete" appears. DOS displays some information about the disk and asks, "Format another (Y/N)?"

Respond by typing Y.

With some versions of DOS, you have to press ⏎ after you type Y.

Remove the formatted disk from drive B and put it in its sleeve. Put a label on the disk, so that you know you formatted it.

Follow the same procedure to format the second blank disk and any additional data disks you want.

After you have all the formatted disks you want, respond to "Format another (Y/N)?" by typing N. The DOS prompt will appear.

Making Backup Disks   Place write-protect tabs on the original System and Auxiliary Disks. (If you have a 3½″ disk, open the write-protect window in the upper right-hand corner of the disk.) Put the MathCAD System Disk in drive A and close the door.

Put a formatted, blank disk in drive B and close the door.

At the DOS prompt, type

    COPY *.* B: ⏎

DOS copies the files from the System Disk in drive A to the formatted blank disk in drive B. The asterisk stands for any filename or file extension; *.* tells DOS to copy every file. DOS displays the names of the files as it copies them. When it has finished, it tells you the number of files it has copied, and the A⟩ prompt reappears on the screen.

Remove the System Disk from drive A and the backup System disk from drive B.

Label the backup System disk. Use the name of the original disk and indicate that this is a backup copy.

Now put the MathCAD Auxiliary Disk in drive A and close the door.

Put a second formatted blank disk in drive B and close the door. Type

    COPY *.* B: ⏎

Remove the Auxiliary Disk from drive A and the backup Auxiliary disk from drive B. Label the backup Auxiliary disk, and indicate that this is a backup copy.

Label one blank, formatted disk (or more, if you wish) as your MathCAD data disk.

Put the original MathCAD System and Auxiliary Diskettes in a safe place, and always use the backup copy to run MathCAD. If anything happens to the backup copy you are using, you will be able to make another copy from the original.

Installing MathCAD on a Hard-Disk System

If you have a hard-disk system, you probably want to copy MathCAD onto the hard disk. Once it is there, you will be able to start and run MathCAD and store the documents you create without having to handle diskettes.

These instructions assume that you have DOS on your hard disk and that your hard disk is designated as drive C. If this is not the case (or if you are not sure), ask your dealer or the technical resource person at your school for assistance. If your computer is on and displays the C⟩ prompt, you can skip over the "Starting Your Computer" section.

Starting Your Computer

Turn the computer on, and wait for it either to display the date and time or to ask you for them.

If needed, type in the date in the form MM-DD-YY, and press ⏎. For example, if the date is July 15, 1989, type

> 07-15-89 ⏎

If needed, type in the time in the form HH:MM ⏎. For example, if the time is 1:45 p.m., type

> 13:45 ⏎

If you enter the date or time in the wrong form, DOS will let you try again. Once the date and time are correct, an operating system prompt appears that includes the letter C. You are now ready to create a subdirectory for MathCAD.

Creating a Subdirectory for MathCAD

Directories let you organize the files on your hard disk into groups. It is a good idea to have a subdirectory that contains only the MathCAD files. For MathCAD to run properly, the main system files must all be in the same directory. It is usually convenient to keep your MathCAD documents in the same directory as the program, although you can put them elsewhere if you want.

Create a MathCAD directory on drive C by typing

```
C: ⏎
MD \ MCAD ⏎
```

Change to the MCAD directory by typing

```
CD \ MCAD ⏎
```

Place write-protect tabs on the original System and Auxiliary Disks. (If you have a 3½″ disk, open the write-protect window in the upper right-hand corner of the disk.) Insert the MathCAD System Disk in drive A, and close the door. Make sure that you are in the MCAD directory and that the DOS prompt is displayed on the screen.

Copy all the files from the System Disk to the MCAD directory on the hard disk:

```
COPY A:*.* ⏎
```

DOS copies files from the MathCAD System Disk to the hard disk in the MCAD subdirectory. An asterisk stands for any filename or file extension: *.* tells DOS to copy every file. DOS lists the files as it copies them to the hard disk. After all the files are copied, a message tells you the number of files copied, and a C⟩ prompt appears on the screen.

Remove the System Disk from drive A and store it safely.

If you have an Auxiliary Disk, place it in drive A. Copy all of the files from the Auxiliary Disk to the MCAD directory on the hard disk by typing

```
COPY A: *.* ⏎
```

Remove the Auxiliary Disk from drive A and store it safely.

MathCAD is now installed on your hard disk.

3 Starting and Ending MathCAD

Once you have installed MathCAD on a working copy of the program disk, or on your hard disk, you can start up MathCAD and use it as many times as you wish.

As with the installation procedures, the startup procedures differ depending on your storage equipment.

Running MathCAD from a Diskette

If your computer is off, insert the DOS disk in drive A, close the door, and turn the computer on. Provide date and time information, if necessary.

If your computer is on, and if it displays the DOS prompt A⟩, insert the MathCAD System Disk in Drive A.

Type:

    MCAD ⏎

You will see the startup screen and the MathSoft and Addison-Wesley logos (see Figure 1).

You are now ready to type entries into your first MathCAD document.

Remember that you will need to exchange the System Disk for the Auxiliary Disk each time you wish to get help by pressing F1 .

< Ctrl-Q > is equivalent to
< Esc > Quit ⏎.

When you are ready to leave MathCAD, press ⟨Ctrl–Q⟩.

Running MathCAD from a Hard Disk

Once you have installed MathCAD on your hard disk, you can run it by following these steps.

Turn your computer on (if necessary).

To make sure the hard disk (Drive C) is the default drive, type

    C: ⏎

Switch into your MathCAD subdirectory (if you have named it something other than MCAD, use that name instead). Type

    CD ＼ MCAD ⏎

Then type

    MCAD ⏎

You will see the startup screen and the MathSoft and Addison-Wesley logos (see Figure 1).

When you are ready to leave MathCAD, press ⟨Ctrl–Q⟩ or type

    ⟨Esc⟩Quit ⏎

Command-Line Options for Starting MathCAD

Normally, you start MathCAD by typing

    MCAD ⏎

at the DOS prompt.

**Slash Options for
Graphics Cards**

MathCAD attempts to identify the graphics card in your system and to run in a mode appropriate to that card. If MathCAD does not recognize your graphics card, or if you want to force MathCAD to run in a different graphics mode or with different colors, you can use **slash options** on the command line. You

Figure 1

```
▌ine File◂                                              0      0   auto
```

```
M a t h   S o f t              Addison Wesley  ▲   Student Edition
                                               ▼ ▼
Σ  +  ∫  =  ÷  σ

MathCAD 2.06 Copyright 1986 1987 1988 MathSoft Inc. Press [F1] for help.
```

can also use slash options to start MathCAD in automatic or
manual recalculation mode. To run MathCAD with slash options, at the DOS prompt type

MCAD */options*

where */options* represents any combination of the following options:

/A   AT&T 6300 (640×400 resolution)

/C   Color/Graphics Adapter. This mode also works on graphics
cards that emulate the IBM Color/Graphics adapter, including the Enhanced Graphics Adapter and the Professional
Graphics Adapter. The display is black and white with
640×200 resolution.

/E   Enhanced Graphics Adapter (EGA). This mode forces Math-
CAD to recognize the Enhanced Graphics Adapter in your
system. MathCAD determines whether you are using a
monochrome or a color monitor and how much memory is on
your EGA and runs accordingly, using the highest possible
resolution (see /EC, /EM, and /EH, below).

/EC   EGA, standard color monitor. This option runs MathCAD on
an EGA at a resolution of 640×200, the standard resolution
of a Color/Graphics Adapter. This is similar to /C, but with
eight colors.

/EH   EGA, Enhanced Color Display. This option runs in high-resolution mode on enhanced color display using eight colors. It requires an EGA with 256K on-board memory. If you attempt to use this mode on a 64K EGA, you will not be able to see the traces on graphs. On a 64K EGA with a color display, use /E or /EC.

/EM   EGA, monochrome monitor

/H   Hercules Monochrome Graphics Card

/T   Toshiba T3100 (640×400 resolution)

In addition, the option /R *filename* allows you to run an alternate configuration file on Startup. (The default file is MCAD.MCC.)

MathCAD also includes options for selecting foreground and background colors on an Enhanced Graphics Adapter with 256K on-board display memory. By default, on a 256K EGA, MathCAD uses white characters on a dark blue background. You can use slash options for display colors in addition to the ones listed above, all on the same command line. The syntax for setting foreground and background colors is

```
MCAD /Fnn /Bnn
```

Here, *nn* is a code for one of the 64 colors that a 256K EGA can represent. /F specifies the foreground color; /B specifies the background color.

To determine the code for the color you desire, use this chart:

32	Red
16	Green
8	Blue
4	Intense Red
2	Intense Green
1	Intense Blue

To choose a color, sum the numbers from the chart for the base colors that mix to create the desired color. For example, to run MathCAD with an intense red (4) background and a yellow (red + green = 32 + 16 = 48) foreground, type

```
MCAD /F48 /B04
```

Loading a File While Starting MathCAD

MathCAD normally starts with an empty screen. You can start MathCAD, however, and immediately begin working on an existing document by putting the filename on the command line when you start MathCAD:

MCAD *filename* (↵)

MathCAD will start by loading the MathCAD document whose name is *filename*, if it exists. If you don't specify an extension, MathCAD assumes the filename ends in the extension .MCD.

Choosing a Calculation Mode at Startup

For files that call for time-consuming calculations, you may want to load the file in manual calculation mode. To load the file without processing any equations, tables, or plots, specify /M on the command name along with the filename:

MCAD /M *filename* (↵)

This starts MathCAD, puts MathCAD into manual calculation mode, and loads the indicated file.

4

Basic
MathCAD Concepts

This chapter introduces a number of MathCAD's basic features and operations, along with a few simple examples. By the time you've followed the steps in this section, you'll be ready to move on to the more advanced Tutorial Lab Exercises.

A MathCAD Document

The Student Edition of MathCAD lets you compose a **document** or **worksheet** up to 80 columns wide and 120 lines long. On this document, you can

- Formulate a wide variety of mathematical concepts and relationships
- Display these concepts and relationships as equations, tables, plots, and text labels

You can also

- Store a MathCAD document as a file on a floppy diskette or hard disk
- Recall a stored document for further work or display
- Print a document on any of the dot matrix or laser printers that MathCAD supports
- Append one document to another to make one long document out of several shorter ones

Regions

A MathCAD document is made up of **regions**, plus varying amounts of empty space around them. MathCAD manipulates three kinds of regions: **equation**, **plot**, and **text regions**.

Each region occupies a rectangular area of the document. MathCAD will display the boundaries of the regions; pressing ⟨Ctrl–V⟩ will turn the boundary lines on or off.

You can put a region of any kind in any unoccupied location on your document. Once you have created a region, you can delete it (by pressing F3), move it (cut with F3 and paste with F4), or duplicate it (copy with F2 and paste with F4). If regions overlap, you can separate them by typing ⟨Esc⟩ SEParate.

The MathCAD Screen

At the beginning of a MathCAD session, the **screen** shows you the top portion of a blank document. On the screen, you edit the various regions that make up your finished document.

The Cursor

The flashing underscore near the top of the screen is the **cursor**. When you type, MathCAD inserts text or equations at the cursor. You can move the cursor around the document with the arrow keys. Other special keys let you move it more rapidly.

See the Reference Card under Cursor Keys for more details.

When the cursor enters an existing region, MathCAD assumes that it is there to edit that region and displays information, normally hidden, that helps with the editing process. In equation and plot regions the cursor itself even changes from the flashing underscore to one of two **edit cursor** forms. Since the cursor behaves differently in each of the three kinds of regions, it helps to know where it is at all times.

Equation Regions

Equation regions contain the mathematical meat of a Math-CAD worksheet. Unless you signal otherwise, MathCAD assumes that any new region you start is an equation region.

Plot Regions	**Plot regions** contain graphic displays of relationships that you have formulated in earlier equation regions.
	To tell MathCAD that you're starting a new plot region, move the cursor to an empty space between regions where you want to put the upper left-hand corner of the new region.
	Then type an at sign (@).
	A small, empty plot will appear on the screen, with rectangular placeholders for you to replace with axis labels and, optionally, with scale limits.
	For an example of a simple MathCAD plot, see Figure 12 on page 47.
Text Regions	**Text regions** have no mathematical significance. They serve as labels to explain the meaning of your document.
	Type a double quotation mark (") in empty territory to signal to MathCAD that you want to make a new text region.
The Message Line	The inverse video stripe near the top of the screen is the **message line**. It shows, from left to right:
	The Current Filename When you read a document in from disk, the name of the file from which you read it becomes the **current filename** and appears at the left end of the message line.
	When you write a document to disk, the name you supply becomes the new current filename.
	Since you have thus far done neither, the message line shows "no file."
	Messages From time to time, MathCAD will ask you questions, offer you options, and deliver other messages. When you start a MathCAD session, the space reserved for this purpose, in the middle of the message line, is blank.

The Cursor Position Indicator   Near the right end of the message line appear the numbers of the line and column where the cursor is now located. This information comes in handy when, for example, you want to move the cursor quickly to a particular point on the document, or when you want to tell MathCAD what portion of the document to print out.

The space available for your MathCAD document is longer than the screen you see. Press the down arrow key ($\boxed{\downarrow}$) to move the cursor down; you will see the left-hand number change. Now press the right arrow key ($\boxed{\rightarrow}$), and the right-hand number will change. Use the up ($\boxed{\uparrow}$) and left ($\boxed{\leftarrow}$) arrow keys to move the cursor back to the upper left-hand corner. If you move the cursor past the bottom of the screen, the display will **scroll** up, with new lines appearing at the bottom and the uppermost ones disappearing, until you reach the document length limit (120 lines) that is built into the Student Edition of MathCAD.

In the horizontal direction, however, you see the entire line. The Student Edition of MathCAD does not scroll horizontally.

If you attempt to type after column 79, the message "Region out of bounds" will appear. Anything you type after the message appears will not be entered.

The Calculation Mode Indicator   MathCAD lets you choose whether to run through the calculations you've ordered

- Each time you move the cursor out of a region where you've changed something (**automatic mode**)

or

- Only when you tell it to (**manual mode**)

Unless you specified otherwise when you started MathCAD, you are in automatic mode, as indicated by "auto" on the message line. To change from automatic to manual mode, press

$\boxed{\text{F10}}$ CM

To return to automatic mode, press

$\boxed{\text{F10}}$ CA

Figure 2

```
↓a:fig2.MCD↓                                    0    0   auto
```

$$163 \cdot 25 + \frac{1}{2} \cdot 22 \cdot 25^2 = 1.095 \cdot 10^4$$

In either mode, the indicator reads "WAIT" while calculations are being performed. You can interrupt a long calculation by pressing ⟨Ctrl–Break⟩.

Example 1: A Simple Calculation

(F10) CM is equivalent to <Esc>MANual.

(F10) CA is equivalent to <Esc>AUTOmatic.

Here is a simple example to help you get some practice making MathCAD work.

Suppose you're a rocket expert (or a freshman physics student), and you want to calculate the distance s that a rocket travels

- While accelerating from $v_0 = 163$ meters per second
- With acceleration of $a = 22$ meters per second per second
- Over a period of $t = 25$ seconds

If you know the formula that governs this motion

$$s = v_0 t + \frac{1}{2} a t^2$$

you might take out your trusty pocket calculator to

- Multiply 163×25, and store the result.
- Square 25, multiply it by 22, divide the product by 2, and add the result to the previously stored quantity.

Or, since you have MathCAD loaded into your personal computer, you can simply type in the equation in the order that the formula suggests. Use the following sequence of keystrokes:

```
163*25+1/2*22*25^2=
```

Figure 2 shows the result.

You wouldn't normally use a program as powerful as Math-CAD to perform such a simple calculation, but doing so demonstrates some of MathCAD's features.

- MathCAD displays equations just as you would write them on a piece of paper.

- MathCAD understands the **precedence rules** for mathematical operators. It knows, for example, to do the exponentiation (squaring t, in the example) before the multiplication and division, and all those before the addition.
- As soon as you type the "equals" sign, MathCAD calculates and displays the result, unless you've already told it to wait.
- As you type each operator (in the example, *, +, /, *, and ^), MathCAD shows a small rectangle called a **placeholder**. Placeholders hold spaces open for numbers you haven't yet typed. As soon as you type a number, it replaces the placeholder in the equation. The placeholder that appears at the end of the equation is used for unit conversions. You can ignore it for now; units come up for discussion later.

Equations

In recreating Figure 2, you entered your first MathCAD **equation**. Before trying a more interesting example, you need to understand a bit more about MathCAD equations and calculation.

Parts of an Equation

MathCAD equations are made up of numbers, variables, operators, and parentheses.

Numbers   MathCAD uses the following types of numbers:
- **Floating point numbers**, such as 6 or -3.14159.
- **Imaginary numbers**. To enter an imaginary number, follow it with i or j. For example, 1i or -2.5j. You can't use i or j alone to represent the imaginary unit; you must always type 1i or 1j.

The unnecessary 1 will disappear when you move the cursor out of the region.

- **Octal integers**. To enter a whole number in octal, follow it with the letter o or O. For example, -705o. Octal numbers are limited to 32-bit integers.
- **Hexadecimal integers**. To enter a whole number in hexadecimal, follow it with h or H. To represent digits above 9, use the uppercase or lowercase letters A through F. For

example, 10AE9h. Hexadecimal numbers are limited to 32-bit integers.

- **Dimensional values**, numbers that are associated with one of the MathCAD dimensions:
  - length ($1L \equiv 1$ unit of length)
  - mass ($1M \equiv 1$ unit of mass)
  - time ($1T \equiv 1$ unit of time)
  - charge ($1Q \equiv 1$ unit of charge)

  MathCAD uses these dimensions to keep track of units for dimensional analysis and unit conversions. For example, the MathCAD equation

  ```
  ft := 1L
  ```

  defines feet (ft) as the basic unit of length on the current worksheet.

  You can assign dimensional values such as 42.5 ft to a variable. You can also define other units in terms of feet; for example

  ```
  yd := 3 ft
  ```

  Dimensional values can be expressed explicitly by typing any number (even zero) followed by an uppercase or lowercase L, M, T, or Q. Thus a yard (yd) could also be defined here as

  ```
  yd := 3L
  ```

- **Exponential notation**. To enter very large or very small numbers in **exponential** (standard scientific) **notation**, just multiply a number by the power of 10. For example, to represent the number 3×10^8, type

  ```
  3*10^8
  ```

Variables MathCAD **variable names** must start with a letter, followed by any combination of letters, numbers, underscores, periods, or percentage signs. You can also use certain Greek letters and the infinity sign. (See the Reference Card for instructions on how to enter these characters in a document.) Variable names cannot include spaces or special characters. MathCAD distinguishes uppercase from lowercase letters in variable names: *diam*, for example, is a different variable from *Diam*.

Operators   The MathCAD Reference Card lists the 29 mathematical **operators** that are incorporated into Math-CAD. It also shows the keystrokes you have to type to enter each one.

Operators are symbols for mathematical actions or relationships, such as

+	Addition
−	Subtraction
*	Multiplication
/	Division
\	Square Root
>	Greater than
<	Less than

The operators appear on the Reference Card in precedence order, that is, MathCAD performs operations that appear higher on the list before it performs lower ones.

Parentheses   When you want MathCAD to carry out an operation in an order other than the standard precedence order, you say so with parentheses.

MathCAD lets you enter parentheses either by typing them in one at a time or, if you type an apostrophe, MathCAD will display a pair of parentheses and let you insert material between them.

Kinds of Equations

See Equation Solving in the Reference Section for another special kind of equation in MathCAD

MathCAD uses two main kinds of equations: calculation equations and definition equations. There are also two types of definition equations, local and global. You tell MathCAD which kind you're entering by your choice of the "equals sign" that you type in:

> =   Calculation Equation
> :   Local Definition Equation
> ~   Global Definition Equation

Calculation Equations   Figure 2 showed you an example of a **calculation equation**. You formulated an expression and followed it with an equals sign (=), and MathCAD displayed the numerical value of the expression.

Since MathCAD responds in this way, you'll find it convenient to read the equals sign not as "equals," but rather as "calculate and display."

Definition Equations   Before MathCAD can calculate a result, however, it has to know the meaning of everything in the calculation equation. That is, each symbol in the equation has to be defined

- Within MathCAD
- On the worksheet, via a **global definition equation**
- At an earlier point on the worksheet, via a **local definition equation**. "Earlier," to MathCAD, means "above and to the left."

When you tell MathCAD to calculate, it starts at the upper left-hand corner and continues from left to right, top to bottom, just as you read a page of a book.

The calculation in Figure 2 contains only numbers (**constants**) and standard arithmetic operators. Since MathCAD knows these already, you don't have to precede this calculation equation with any definition equations.

Example 2: Using Formulas

The next example will consist of several definition equations and one calculation. We will use MathCAD to calculate the distance covered on uniformly accelerated motion from the gen eral **formula**:

$$s = v_0 t + \frac{1}{2} a t^2$$

This formula contains three symbols (v_0, t, and a) that Math-CAD has no way of knowing about. You will have to define them on the worksheet so that MathCAD comes to the definitions before it has to use them.

As a first step, start with a clean MathCAD document, using ⟨Esc⟩ to signal to MathCAD that you want to issue a command.

Type

    ⟨Esc⟩clear ⏎

MathCAD asks, "Changes not saved. OK to discard?"

Type

    Y ⏎

Now, define t, the elapsed time, and a, the acceleration.

Type

    t:25 ⏎

Type

    a:22 ⏎

Since this is a local definition equation, it is entered with a colon instead of an equals sign. That's how MathCAD knows that this is a local definition, not a command to calculate and display.

MathCAD displays the local definition with

    :=

so that you can distinguish the two equation types at a glance.

Now, define the initial velocity v_0:

Type

    v.0:163 ⏎

Note that you tell MathCAD about the subscript zero in v_0 with a period. This works for a subscript that is an integral part of the variable name. (Subscripts that vary over a range are handled in a different way and will be discussed later.)

So far, you've defined only the constants, giving each just one of the very large number of possible values it could have. Now, you are ready to define the formula itself.

Type

```
s:v.0*t+1/2*a*t^2 ⏎
```

Then type ⟨Ctrl–V⟩.

The result should look something like Figure 3.

The final command (⟨Ctrl–V⟩) drew boxes around the regions. You won't want to do this all the time, but it's useful at this point because it emphasizes the separate regions that you've created.

Now that everything is defined by definition equations, you're ready to enter your second calculation equation, a much more powerful one than the first.

First, unclutter the worksheet by turning off the boxes:

Type ⟨Ctrl–V⟩.

Now for the calculation, type

```
s= ⏎
```

Figure 4 shows the result.

Now you are going to edit some of the equations on your worksheet. To make sure it will be easy to get back to this document, save it to disk.

Press F6.

Figure 3

```
↓a:fig3.MCD↓                                          0      0   auto

t := 25

a := 22

v    := 163
 0

            1   2
s := v   ·t + ─·a·t
      0      2
```

MathCAD responds (in the message line) by asking for a filename under which to save this document.

Type

    ROCKET ⏎

MathCAD now saves this document as ROCKET.MCD in your current directory and shows the new filename on the message line.

Example 3: Editing Equations

There is nothing magical about the particular numbers you have assigned so far. Suppose, for example, that you want to know how far the rocket went during the first 11 seconds of the 25-second period. To find out, all you have to do is to **edit** the appropriate part of the worksheet, deleting the 25 and replacing it with 11. This simple task will illustrate MathCAD's powerful features for editing equations.

In the practice exercises that follow, it will be easy to make mistakes that scramble the display. Since you're only now learning the editing features that will make it easy for you to unscramble it, you may need to rely on the programmer's parachute: your backup file. You have saved the unedited version of this file as ROCKET.MCD, and you can always get it back by typing

    F 5 ROCKET ⏎ y ⏎

Positioning the Cursor   The first step is to put the cursor where you want it. That sounds easy, and it is, as long as you remember two principles.

Figure 4

```
↓a:fig4.MCD↓                                    0    0   auto

t := 25

a := 22

v   := 163
 0

          1   2
s := v  ·t + -·a·t
      0       2
              4
s = 1.095·10
```

Principle 1. MathCAD can't edit a blank space. In order to edit anything in a MathCAD equation region, you have to put the cursor on something, either

- On a character

or

- On some part of the extended display that certain operators (like division, square root, summation, and integral) create

Principle 2. Remember the keystroke sequence. It may seem that you're editing the screen display, but that's only indirectly true. In fact, you're editing the sequence of keystrokes with which you entered the equation. You can't see that sequence, but MathCAD remembers it.

Let's give it a try:

With the arrow keys, move the cursor into the region where you defined $t := 25$.

Appending   As soon as the cursor enters the equation region, it changes from its familiar underscore form to a symbol that resembles a backward L. This is the **append cursor**. Its vertical bar shows where any characters you type will be appended.

Move the append cursor until it encloses the "5" of "$t := 25$" in its angle.

This brings up a third principle:

Principle 3. The editing cursor is said to be "on" the character or other display element that is enclosed in its angle. If the angle of the cursor is empty, the cursor is on a blank space, which, by Principle 1, it can't edit.

Now that the cursor is on the "5," you are ready to append keystrokes after it.

Type

    abcd

Not a surprising result: "25" has become "25abcd."

Deleting   To get back to where you were before, delete the new characters.

Type

    〈Bksp〉〈Bksp〉〈Bksp〉〈Bksp〉.

The number should be back to 25. If not, reload (F 5) the backup file ROCKET. Try adding a minus sign after the 25, and see what happens.

Type

    −

Type

    〈Bksp〉

Now, try putting new characters in the middle of the existing material. First move the append cursor to enclose the "2" in "t := 25."

Type

    abcd

Type

    〈Del〉〈Del〉〈Del〉〈Del〉

Note that 〈Bksp〉 and 〈Del〉 act identically in equation editing: either one deletes the character on which the cursor is located.

Inserting an operator between the 2 and 5 is equally easy.

Type

    −

Type

    〈Del〉〈Del〉

Inserting

Type

    〈Ins〉

The cursor flips over from the backward L shape of the append cursor and assumes an L shape. This is the **insert cursor**. Again, the horizontal part of the cursor tells you where it is, and the vertical part tells you where new material will be entered.

Move the cursor one space back, so that it is sitting on the blank space before "25."

Type

    abcd

Since the angle of the cursor is empty, MathCAD tells you that it "Can't edit blank space."

The append cursor works fine for putting operators in the middle or at the end of a string of characters. But when, as in this case, you want to add an operator at the beginning of the string (that is, before the cursor position), you have to call on another MathCAD feature.

The ⟨Ins⟩ key toggles between the append and insert modes whenever the cursor is in an equation region. Using these two types of cursors, you will be able to take full advantage of MathCAD's editing capabilities.

Switching to insert mode doesn't move the cursor off its blank space; you still have to put it on the character before which you wish to insert.

Press the right arrow key.

Type

    –

Type

    ⟨Bksp⟩

Note that ⟨Bksp⟩ or ⟨Del⟩ erases the character on which the cursor is located.

In append mode, the character most recently appended sits under the cursor and, therefore, is the first to be erased.

In insert mode, however, the character most recently inserted sits to the left of the cursor and, therefore, is not in position to be erased.

Example 4: Editing Complicated Equations

So far, you have edited a simple numerical string within the underlying keystroke sequence, using the append and insert cursors, ⟨Bksp⟩, and ⟨Del⟩ to add and delete characters.

Armed with these basics, you are ready to practice editing a more complicated equation display.

First, clear the screen and enter a more challenging expression.

Type

⟨Esc⟩clear 〔↵〕
y 〔↵〕

It is all right to discard what you have been working on; you will call it back from the disk file ROCKET.MCD after you finish this exercise.

This is the bell curve of the normal distribution.

Now you will enter a more complicated formula.

Type

N:20 〔↵〕
i:0;2*N 〔↵〕
x[i:4*i/N−4 〔↵〕
y[i:1/(2*⟨Alt-P⟩))*e-(x[i^2/2) 〔↵〕

The result should look like Figure 5.

Save this document as PRACTICE.MCD, so that you can get back to it easily.

Type

〔F 6〕 PRACTICE 〔↵〕

Figure 5

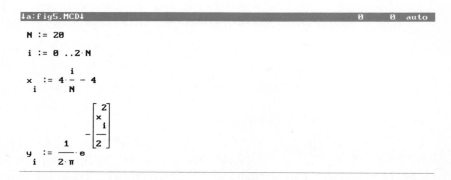

Editing Operators   Notice how the mathematical operators (/, *, ^, −) and the parentheses in the keystroke sequence direct the organization of the main formula in this document in accordance with the standard mathematical rules of precedence.

Segments of the sequence that lie between operators (but do not include them) are easy to edit with the append and insert cursors, as you did before. You can edit the operators and parentheses, too, but you have to keep the underlying keystroke sequence firmly in mind (Principle 2).

It is also frequently easier to delete an operator than to put it back the way it was.

Editing Parentheses   Try deleting the second pair of parentheses in the formula — the pair that follows the minus sign and surrounds the exponent.

Move the cursor (either append or insert) to any part of either parenthesis; make sure some portion of the parenthesis lies within the angle of the cursor.

Press ⟨Bksp⟩.

By deleting one parenthesis, we have deleted both. The formula is now different — the exponent used to be divided by two; now the whole exponential expression is. The parentheses we deleted were there to keep that factor of 1/2 in the exponent where it belonged. Now put the parentheses back.

Move the cursor to the minus sign in the formula. Press ⟨Ins⟩, if necessary, to create the insert (L-shaped) cursor so you can insert a parenthesis before the "x". Since there's a blank on the screen there, the append cursor would not let you do this.

Type

(

This does only half of the job. If you take the cursor out of the equation region now (try it, if you wish), MathCAD will tell you that you've created an unmatched parenthesis.

Now move the cursor to the "2" after which you want to insert the other parenthesis.

Type

)

You should be back where you started. If you get lost, just reload PRACTICE.MCD and start over.

Deleting an Operator   Deleting an operator is just like deleting any other symbol, except that it tends to make more of a difference in the screen display.

Move the append cursor to the multiplication symbol that appears just before the "e" in the formula, and press ⟨Del⟩ (or ⟨Bksp⟩).

You should see a hollow rectangle, which represents a placeholder for a missing operator. Now press ⟨Del⟩ once more.

The resulting display looks drastically changed. If you move the cursor outside the region, MathCAD will display an error message indicating that an operator is missing. You have changed the underlying keystroke sequence so that "e" follows directly after ")" — and the result is not a meaningful expression.

Inserting an Operator   You can insert an operator, just as you can insert any other symbol, often with dramatic results. As always, particularly when inserting, you have to be very careful to have the right editing cursor in the right place.

Move the editing cursor so that its vertical bar rises between the closing parenthesis and the "e."

Type

*

to put the multiplication sign back where it was before.

Now insert a more complicated operator, a summation.

With the append cursor on the multiplication sign (raised dot) that you just restored, type

    $

This time, the resulting expression is legitimate, although a rectangular placeholder indicates that you still have to specify the variable over which the summation is to run.

Practice adding and deleting various elements of the formula until you feel confident in your ability to edit MathCAD equations.

Global Definitions   Not all MathCAD definitions have to appear before the equations that use them. Global definitions are the exception to the rule. A global definition applies to the whole document, regardless of where it appears in the document. Global definitions are the only definitions that apply upward as well as downward.

In carrying out the computational instructions in a document, MathCAD passes through the entire document twice. On its first pass, it interprets all the global definitions in the order in which they are specified. When it returns to pick up the local definitions on the second pass, therefore, the global definitions are already specified.

Most keyboards put the tilde (~) and the backquote (') on the same key.

Just as you type in a colon to tell MathCAD that it's getting a local definition equation, you signal a global definition equation with a **tilde** (~) in the place of an equals sign. MathCAD displays a "triple equals sign" ($\equiv$) in a global definition. We will use global definitions in the next exercise.

Example 5: Units

Now you are going to put **units** into your calculations to gain access to some of MathCAD's most useful features.

The time variable t in the ROCKET worksheet created in Example 2 isn't just 25, of course, it's 25 seconds.

In MathCAD, units behave like variables. To attach units to a quantity, you simply multiply the quantity by the units. Type

    (F 5) ROCKET (↵)
    y (↵)

Move the cursor to the "5" in the entry "t := 25."

Type

    *sec (↵)

The result (Figure 6) is a bit startling.

You have to define units, just as you do other variables in MathCAD, before you can use them.

MathCAD defines all units in terms of four basic dimensions:

1L   Length
1M   Mass
1T   Time
1Q   Charge

By entering the definitions of units (usually globally), you can choose whatever system of measurement you wish: MKS (meter-kilogram-second), CGS (centimeter-gram-second), or U.S. Customary (foot-pound-second).

Move to the end of the last region in your worksheet by pressing ⟨Ctrl–End⟩.

Go beyond that by pressing (↵).

<aside>
If you should wish to change the M, L, T, and Q labels, the DImension command

⟨Esc⟩DImension

or

(F10)CD

will let you do so.
</aside>

Figure 6

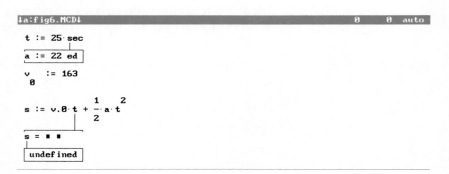

40 Getting Started

Type

> sec ~ 1T ⏎

Now *t* is defined, and its error message has vanished (Figure 7).

Your screen display probably shows some gaps now where the error message used to be. This can also happen when regions expand or move or otherwise come to overlap each other. The cure is simple.

Press ⟨Ctrl–R⟩ to redraw the screen.

Since *t* is now the only variable with units in the formula for *s*, MathCAD warns that you are trying to add together two terms, one with units of "sec" and the other with units of "sec²."

To fix this incompatibility, you need to get the rest of the definitions on the screen; the only other basic unit that needs definition is the length unit.

The original statement of the problem in Example 1 specified that you were working in meters (m).

Type

> m ~ 1L ⏎

Move the cursor to the beginning of the third region by pressing ⟨Home⟩ four or five times.

Figure 7

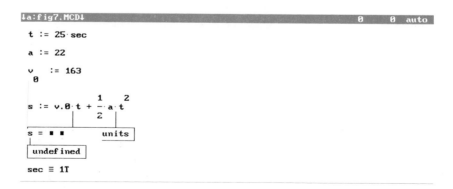

With the arrow keys, move the cursor to the "3" in "v.0:163."

Type

    *m/sec ⏎

Now move to the second "2" in "a := 22," and type

    *m/sec^2 ⏎

Finally, you are rid of error messages (Figure 8).

Everything seems to be working, although the screen is a bit crowded. Clean it up now, before moving on.

First, it may help to redraw the screen to fill in any gaps that previous manipulations may have created.

Press ⟨Ctrl–R⟩.

Move the cursor to the second region ("a := 22.m/sec²"), and press F3.

To cut, press F3. To paste, press F4.

The region vanishes from the screen, but don't worry: you've moved it into a temporary storage area called the **cut buffer**. Let's put (**paste**) it in a more convenient place

Move the cursor to the top row of the worksheet, to the right of what is there already. Leave some horizontal space for a better appearance.

Figure 8

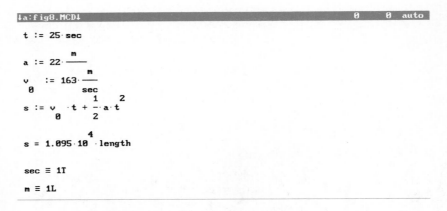

Press $\boxed{F4}$.

Now cut ($\boxed{F3}$) and paste ($\boxed{F4}$) other regions, as you like, until you have a pleasing arrangement.

The SEParate command provides a way to space out overlapping regions. It is issued in either of the following ways:

⟨Esc⟩SEP $\boxed{↵}$

or

$\boxed{F10}$ ES

SEParate simply moves each region down far enough to eliminate any overlap.

If gaps show in some regions because they used to overlap with others, issue the REDraw command by pressing ⟨Ctrl–R⟩.

Figure 9 shows one way you might arrange this worksheet.

The first time MathCAD calculates a result with units, it displays the **dimensionality**, rather than the actual units. To show why this is, and what you can do with it, add in some alternative unit definitions.

Press ⟨Ctrl–End⟩ to move to the bottom of the worksheet.

In a convenient location, type in the units conversion factors:

mi ~ 1609*m $\boxed{↵}$
hr ~ 3600*sec $\boxed{↵}$

Rearrange ($\boxed{F3}$, $\boxed{F4}$) these new regions, if you wish.

Figure 9

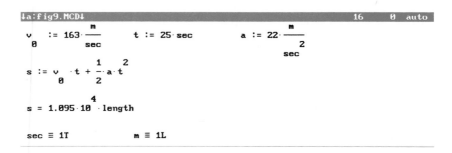

Move the cursor into the region that contains your calculation equation (s=) and then to the rectangular placeholder that appears at the end of that region.

Type

    mi ⏎

As long as you have supplied the definitions, the units conversion (Figure 10) will be automatic.

Finally, you can improve the clarity of your worksheet by adding some labels.

Recall that you type

    "

to start a text region.

You can insert a blank line for labels at the top of the worksheet by typing

    ⟨Ctrl-Home⟩ ⟨Ctrl-F9⟩

Then type

    "Time elapsed: Acceleration: Initial velocity: (↓)

Add enough spaces so that each phrase labels the variable defined below it. You will need to use the cursor keys, rather than ⏎, to leave a text region. You can tell when the cursor is no longer inside the text region because the quotation marks indicating its beginning and end will be hidden.

Figure 10

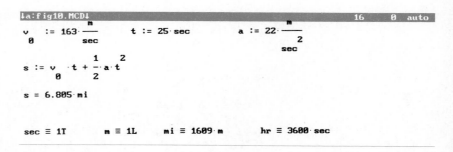

Move the cursor to the blank space next to the formula for *s* and type

> "Distance formula ⬇

Next to the region where the final value of s is displayed, type

> "Distance traveled by rocket ⬇

Finally, move to the blank line just above your definitions of units and type

> "Units used in this example: ⬇

Now your worksheet should look something like Figure 11. You may want to save this final version for further experimentation on your own.

Example 6: Graphing

For the final example of this chapter, you will use MathCAD to draw a simple plot.

Suppose you want to graph the function

$$f(x) = \cos(2x) + 2\cos(x)$$

The natural approach is to let *x* take on a range of values. For example, suppose we want our graph to include points for values of *x* between 0 and 4π. To have enough points for a smooth

Figure 11

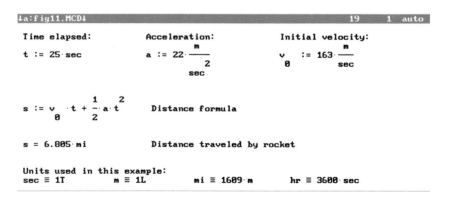

curve, let's include all the numbers 0, 0.1, 0.2, 0.3, and so on, up to 4π. MathCAD will do this if you type

```
N:4*⟨Alt-P⟩ ⏎
x:0,0.1;N ⏎
```

This defines x as a **range variable**, a variable that runs through all the values in a fixed set every time it is used. Note that you type a comma before the second value in the list, and a semicolon before the last value. In this case, the first value for x will be 0, the second value 0.1, and then the difference or increment of .1 will continue to be added to x until the values would exceed the upper limit $N=4\pi$.

To see some of the values for x, type

```
x=
```

Check that the values for x are what you expected. Because the table would have over a hundred values, only the first part of it is printed out. To erase the table, just press F3.

Now define your function $f(x)$ by typing

```
f(x):cos(2*x)+2*cos(x) ⏎
```

To create a plot region, type

```
@
```

The location of the cursor determines the upper left-hand corner of the region. Now use the tab key to enter x as the label of the horizontal axis and $f(x)$ as the label of the vertical axis as follows.

```
x⟨Tab⟩⟨Tab⟩⟨Tab⟩f(x) ⏎
```

Observe how the cursor jumps around the rectangular placeholders along the axes. The placeholders for the largest and smallest values to be represented on each axis are still blank, so MathCAD will choose appropriate limits for you. This is a very convenient, although slower, option called **autoscaling**.

Now wait for the plot to appear.

In order to make the plot larger, change its **format** specification. Put the cursor on any portion of the plot and type

f

On the message line, use the cursor to replace the entry

size=5, 15

by

size=15, 40

and press

Finally, add the line $y=0$ (the x-axis) to the plot to serve as a baseline. Move the cursor to the end of the expression $f(x)$ at the left side of the graph, and type

,0

In general, several expressions can be listed, separated by commas, to be plotted along the y-axis.

Your final version of the graph should look like Figure 12.

Already MathCAD has moved far beyond what you can conveniently do on your pocket calculator. A discussion of the commands that are available to you follows. Then you'll be ready to go on to the Tutorial Lab Exercises.

Figure 12

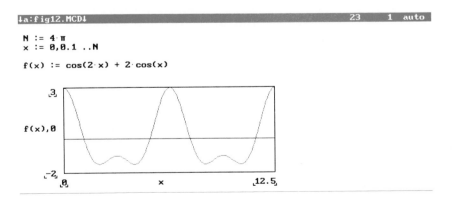

MathCAD has some 53 **commands**. You'll use some of them all the time, and they'll become very familiar. Others you'll use less often, and you'll find it convenient to consult the reminders that the MathCAD system provides:

- On-screen **command menus**, discussed in the next section, group the commands logically.
- MathCAD's Help facility, invoked by pressing F1, gives you reminders right on the screen.
- The Reference section of this manual lists all the commands in functional groups, with a brief explanation of each.
- The Reference Card provides a convenient table, showing all the ways that you can issue each command.

This chapter has discussed only a few of the most common commands, as the examples brought them up. The Tutorial Lab Exercises will explain a broader set of commands in more depth. The Reference section is your best source for an exhaustive treatment of the MathCAD commands.

You can issue commands in three ways: via the command menus, directly by name, and with special command keys.

Command Menu

When you press the F10 key, MathCAD offers you a menu of logical command groups (submenus) on the message line. Press enter to see System submenu, then the right and left arrow keys to see the other submenus.

- **System commands** provide access to DOS, to available memory, and to MathCAD's Help facility, and let you redraw the screen, print a document, and exit from Math-CAD.
- **File commands** allow you to load and save documents from and to disk storage, to combine a stored document with the one currently in memory, to change the current filename, and to clear the worksheet.
- **Compute commands** govern mathematical computations, specifying how and when to carry them out.

- **Edit/Move commands** move the cursor and regions around the document.
- **In-Region** commands allow you to copy and move parts of regions, such as expressions or marked text.
- **Text commands** facilitate the editing of text regions.
- **Window/Page commands** open and close windows and control the positioning of page breaks in printed output.

Move the message-line cursor (the highlighted segment of the inverse-video message line) to the right and to the left with the arrow keys; the submenus appear on the screen.

When you have determined which submenu contains the command you want to issue, select that submenu in either of two ways:

- Type the first letter of the submenu's name (S, F, C, E, I, T, or W).

or

- Move the message-line cursor to the submenu with the right- and left-arrow keys, and press ⏎.

In either case, the selected submenu appears in pull-down format, with its first command highlighted. To select the desired command, do one of the following.

- Type the first letter of the command.

or

- Use the up- and down-arrow keys to highlight the command, then press ⏎.

While you are learning MathCAD, you'll find the menus convenient. They will also be valuable later when you cannot remember the name of a command you rarely use.

The menus do slow down the process of issuing commands, however, as you search for the command you want. After you select from a pull-down menu, moreover, MathCAD has to pause to redraw the screen.

Issuing Commands by Name

Once you're a practiced MathCAD user, you'll find yourself issuing most commands either by name or via the special command keys.

To issue a command by name, simply press ⟨Esc⟩, and then type in enough characters of the command name so that Math-CAD can tell which command you mean. Figure 13 lists the 53 MathCAD commands, displaying in upper case the characters that you actually have to type.

Special Command Keys

You can issue some of the most frequently used MathCAD commands by pressing special keys, as Figure 14 shows.

You issue the ⟨Ctrl–⟩ commands by holding down the ⟨Ctrl⟩ key while pressing the other key or keys.

Note that ⟨Ctrl–Break⟩, ⟨Ctrl–D⟩, and ⟨Ctrl–V⟩ can only be issued as ⟨Ctrl–⟩ commands.

⟨Ctrl–Break⟩ interrupts calculation, printing, or other continuing activities. (⟨Ctrl–A⟩ has the same function, but does not work in all cases.)

⟨Ctrl–D⟩ changes background display colors on computer setups that include an IBM Enhanced Graphics Adapter. Each time you press ⟨Ctrl–D⟩, MathCAD changes the screen background color, until you get back to the original color (blue).

Figure 13

APpend	FIlename	MATrix	SAve
AUtomatic	FORMat	MEmory	SEArch
BAckward	FORWard	MOve	SELectprinter
CAlculate	Goto	PAGelength	SEParate
CEnter	Help	PASte	SET
CLear	INCOpy	PLotformat	SKIPLine
CONfigsave	INCUt	PRInt	SKIPParagraph
COPy	INPaste	PROcess	SKIPSentence
CUt	INSertline	Quit	SKIPWord
DEleteline	Justify	RAndomize	SPlit
DImension	Load	REDraw	SWitch
DOs	MANual	REPlace	Unsplit
EQuation	MARk	RESet	Width
EXecute			

⟨Ctrl–V⟩ draws boxes around the current regions.

Other keys have special functions.

Cursor Movement Keys Several keys move the cursor around without affecting the contents of the region that the cursor occupies.

The keystrokes shown in Figure 15 work the same way in both text and equation regions.

Figure 16 lists some keys that make it easy to jump from one region to another.

Finally, Figure 17 lists other keys that act differently in different kinds of regions.

Figure 14

F1	Help		
F2	COPy	⟨Ctrl–F2⟩	INCOpy
F3	CUt	⟨Ctrl–F3⟩	INCUt
F4	PASte	⟨Ctrl–F4⟩	INPaste
F5	Load	⟨Ctrl–F5⟩	SEArch
F6	SAve	⟨Ctrl–F6⟩	REPlace
F7	SPlit	⟨Ctrl–F7⟩	Unsplit
F8	SWitch		
F9	CAlculate	⟨Ctrl–F9⟩	INSertline
F10	**menus**	⟨Ctrl–Break⟩	**abort**
		⟨Ctrl–A⟩	**abort** (effective in most cases)
		⟨Ctrl–B⟩	BAckward
		⟨Ctrl–D⟩	**change colors**
		⟨Ctrl–F⟩	FORWard
		⟨Ctrl–L⟩	SKIPline
		⟨Ctrl–N⟩	Justify
		⟨Ctrl–O⟩	PRInt
		⟨Ctrl–P⟩	SKIPParagraph
		⟨Ctrl–Q⟩	Quit
		⟨Ctrl–R⟩	REDraw
		⟨Ctrl–S⟩	SKIPSentence
		⟨Ctrl–V⟩	**draw boxes**
		⟨Ctrl–W⟩	SKIPWord
		⟨Ctrl–X⟩	MARk

Three commands, Goto, SEArch and MOve, also move the cursor. Invoke the Goto command by typing either

⟨Esc⟩ Goto ⌨

or

[F10] EG

You can then supply a line and column number to move to.

The SEArch command works the same way as Goto, but it allows you to search for a string of characters. Invoke SEArch by typing either

⟨Esc⟩ SEArch

or

[F10] EF

Figure 15

Arrow keys: (↑) (↓) (→) (←)	Move one space in the specified direction.
⟨Ctrl–Right⟩ ⟨Ctrl–Left⟩	Move right or left to next 10-character tab stop.
⟨PgUp⟩ ⟨PgDn⟩	Move up 5 lines. Move down 5 lines.
⟨Ctrl–PgUp⟩ ⟨Ctrl–PgDn⟩	Move up 80% of page. Move down 80% of page.

Figure 16

⟨Home⟩	Move to previous region.
⟨End⟩	Move to end of current region, or if you are at the end of a region, to the beginning of the next region.
⟨Ctrl–Home⟩	Move to first region in document.
⟨Ctrl–End⟩	Move to last region in document.

If you put a minus sign in front of the string, MathCAD will search backwards (upward) through the document.

The MOve command, invoked by typing either

> ⟨Esc⟩MOve n ⏎

or

> F10 EM

scrolls the display n rows up ($-n$ scrolls it n rows down), leaving the cursor at the same spot on the screen. If you enter the command without specifying n, the message line will display two zeros for you to edit: the first for the number of lines (n) to scroll, and the second for the number of columns. Do not change the second zero to another number: the Student Edition of MathCAD doesn't scroll horizontally, and you will only get an error message.

Figure 17

Key	In Text Regions	In Equation Regions	Between Regions
⟨Tab⟩	Move forward one word.	Move to next operator.	Move right to next tab stop.
⟨Shift–Tab⟩	Move back one word.	Move to previous operator.	Move left to next tab stop.
⏎	Start a new line.	Move to the first line below the region, even with left edge of region.	Move to the beginning of the next line.

Keys that Create Regions   As noted earlier, there are two keys that have special functions in the spaces between regions.

The double quote (") creates a new text region.

The at sign (@) creates a new plot region.

Local Formatting   When you want to adjust the format of local displays (tables and plots), the f-key takes on special meaning. When you put the cursor into the display and type

    f

you gain access to the format options. The Reference Card summarizes these options, and the Tutorial Lab Exercises illustrate them.

Non-Keyboard Characters   Mathematics requires (and MathCAD supplies) a number of characters and symbols (particularly mathematical operators) that do not appear on the keyboard of a personal computer. The Reference Card provides a convenient list of the keystrokes to use to enter these characters and symbols into your worksheet. The Reference Section of this manual also lists these keystrokes.

Tutorial Lab Exercises

Part Two

The five tutorial lab exercises that follow are based on real applications from physics, statistics, electrical engineering, and pure mathematics.

Even if these are not among your own fields of interest and knowledge, please follow the development of each lab, step by step. Otherwise, you'll miss the introduction of important aspects of MathCAD.

Once you have understood MathCAD's power and logic, you'll find it easy and exciting to create your own applications in the areas that interest you most.

1 Earth Satellite Motion

This first lab exercise comes from physics, but its practical implications extend into communications and space science as well.

In this exercise, you will practice:

- Organizing a MathCAD document
- Entering a MathCAD expression
- Moving regions around by
  - Copying, cutting and pasting
  - Inserting and deleting blank lines
- Specifying data
  - Individually
  - In tables of evenly spaced or arbitrarily chosen values
  - With units
- Displaying calculated results individually, in tables, with units, and in various formats
- Labeling a MathCAD document with text regions.
- Using split-screen windows
- Displaying relationships with line plots
- Finding the root of an expression
- Creating a user-defined function

Figure 18 states the problem for this exercise in MathCAD format.

Before you evaluate an algebraic expression on your old-fashioned scratchpad, you have to know what each of its elements means. MathCAD operates under the same logical rule: it requires a **definition** of everything in the expression: variables, constants, and operators.

The meaning of all the usual mathematical operators (like $+$, $-$, $*$, and $/$) is built into MathCAD. Some standard constants (π, in particular) are also predefined.

You have to supply everything else.

Entering a MathCAD Expression

Figure 18 provides a simple formula for calculating the period of a satellite's orbital motion given its radius.* The period is the amount of time that the satellite takes to travel all the way around its orbit and to return to its starting point. Part A of the problem asks that you evaluate that formula for orbits at four different altitudes.

For this exercise, you will start with the formula and depend on MathCAD to guide you through the steps you must follow. The next time around, with this practice behind you, you can try to define the elements of a document in their logical order. It is useful to go through it this way once so you will gain confidence in MathCAD's ability to lead you by the hand when you make mistakes.

Enter the formula by typing the following keystroke sequence:

Period:2*⟨Alt-P⟩/r.E*∖(Radius^3/g) ⏎

*For a derivation of this formula, see Thomas and Finney, *Calculus and Analytic Geometry,* 7th ed. (Addison-Wesley, 1988), pp. 827–836).

$$g = \frac{Gm_E}{r_E^2}$$

where m_E is the mass of the earth.

Error messages will appear on the screen; we'll deal with them soon.

Note that you type in the elements of the formula very much as you read them:

Period is defined as two times π divided by r_E times the square root of (the radius cubed divided by g).

```
↓a:fig18.MCD↓                                              0      0   auto
```

MathCAD Tutorial Lab Exercise #1:   Earth Satellite Motion

As long as a satellite is much smaller than the earth around
which it revolves, its motion depends neither on its size nor on
its mass.   Whether a speck of cosmic trash or a giant space
station, it follows from Kepler's Third Law that its speed and
period in circular orbit may be computed from the size of the
orbit alone.   Given the following values and definitions...

$$ft \equiv 1L \qquad mi \equiv 5280 \cdot ft \qquad sec \equiv 1T \qquad hr \equiv 3600 \cdot sec$$

Acceleration of gravity: $\qquad g \equiv 32.174 \cdot \dfrac{ft}{sec^2}$

Mean equatorial radius of the Earth $\qquad r_E := 3963 \cdot mi$

Satellite's altitude above the surface of the Earth $\qquad Altitude := 1000 \cdot mi$

Orbital radius (distance from the center of the earth) $\qquad Radius := Altitude + r_E$

... the satellite's orbital period is given by $\qquad Period := 2 \cdot \dfrac{\pi}{r_E} \cdot \sqrt{\dfrac{Radius^3}{g}}$

A.   Compute the orbital period (in hours) for satellites in
     orbits 1000, 2000, 5000, and 10000 miles above the
     earth's surface.

B.   Compute escape velocity (the horizontal speed an object
     must reach at the surface of the earth in order to enter
     earth orbit).   HINT:
     $$Speed := 2 \cdot \pi \cdot \frac{Radius}{Period}$$

C.   Plot orbital period against altitude.   From the graph,
     estimate the altitude (in miles) of the geostationary
     orbit, in which a satellite takes exactly one day to
     circle the earth and therefore appears (from the earth)
     to stand still.

D.   From the formulas, compute the altitude of the
     geostationary orbit to the nearest mile.

Earth Satellite Motion   59

MathCAD then puts them on the screen in full traditional mathematical display format.

Most keystrokes put their corresponding characters on the screen. Some symbols needed on the screen do not appear on the keyboard, of course, and you have to get used to a few substitutions.

Use a colon (:) for "is defined as." (Do not confuse the colon with the equals sign, which you enter as a command to calculate and display one or more results.)

Use an asterisk (*) for "times" (multiplication).

Use ⟨Alt–P⟩ for $\pi = 3.1415...$.

Use a slash (/) for "divided by."

Use r.E for r_E, the radius of the earth. You enter a **subscript** with a period when, as in this case, the subscript is an integral part of the symbol and doesn't represent a range of numbers.

Use a backslash (\ ) for "the square root of."

Use a caret (^) for "raised to the power of."

See the MathCAD Reference Card and the Reference Section of this book for a complete list of special keystroke definitions.

MathCAD responds that it needs a definition for r_E (which it displays as r.E until the definitional issue is resolved). Your screen should look like Figure 19.

The problem statement (Figure 18) provides a definition for r_E, the radius of the earth: it is 3,963 miles.

Figure 19

Moving Regions Around

You have to type each definition into your worksheet before (that is, above or to the left of) the formula that needs it, unless you make it a global definition, as discussed earlier.

Since the formula is at the top of the document, you will have to make room for the definitions either by cutting and pasting regions, or by inserting and deleting blank lines.

Cutting and Pasting Regions

With only one region on the worksheet, one way to create blank space at the top is to pick up the existing region and move it down, using MathCAD's cut-and-paste functions.

F3 is equivalent to <Esc> CUt.

Move the cursor into the region you want to move, and press F3.

F4 is equivalent to <Esc> PASte.

Next, move the cursor to the position that you would like the upper left-hand corner of the region to occupy, and press F4.

F2 is equivalent to <Esc> COPy.

You can also test the closely related COPy command now. Put the cursor in the region you want to move and press F2, then move the cursor to a blank area, and press F4 to paste in a copy.

If you left one or more blank lines at the top of your worksheet, you'll now have room to insert the required definition.

Move the cursor to a convenient empty location in the blank area you have just created, and type in the value of r_E, as provided.

The keystroke sequence is

```
r.E:3963*mi ⏎
```

Cutting, Copying, and Pasting Pieces of Regions

You can also move numbers, names, or expressions around your MathCAD document in much the same way you cut and paste whole regions, except that you cut with ⟨Ctrl–F3⟩ (or the INCUt command) and paste with ⟨Ctrl–F4⟩ (or the IN-Paste command).

When you press ⟨Ctrl–F3⟩, whatever the cursor is on vanishes from the screen and goes into the cut buffer. Then, when you move the cursor to the desired new position and press ⟨Ctrl–F4⟩, the item reappears.

If the cursor is on a name or a number when you press ⟨Ctrl–F3⟩, the name or number moves to the buffer. If it's on an operator, the whole expression that that operator controls moves to the buffer.

If you want to put an item into the cut buffer without erasing it from its point of origin, use ⟨Ctrl–F2⟩ (or the INCOpy command) to copy it.

Put the cursor in various places in the definition of *Period* that is on your screen, and press ⟨Ctrl–F3⟩⟨Ctrl–F4⟩ in each position, until you get the feel of how to grab the pieces of a region to move or copy them.

Inserting and Deleting Blank Lines

The other way to create blank space is to insert blank lines. It's easier than moving several regions one by one, but you have to wait for MathCAD to redraw the screen after each line you insert.

< Ctrl–F9 > is equivalent to < Esc > INSertline.

Move the cursor to the top of the worksheet, and insert several blank lines by pressing ⟨Ctrl–F9⟩ several times.

< Ctrl–F10 > is equivalent to < Esc > DEleteline.

Now delete as many of these blank lines as you want, by pressing ⟨Ctrl–F10⟩ once for each deletion.

You may want to leave some room at the top of the worksheet. Your screen should look something like Figure 20 now, indicating that you still have some defining to do.

Figure 20

Copy the definition for "mi" into your worksheet, using the tilde ($\sim$) keystroke to get the "triple equals sign" global definition operator. The keystroke sequence is

```
mi~5280*ft ⏎
```

As a block, the global definitions can appear either above or below the local definitions. Within the global group, however, any definition that depends on another must follow it.

Note that MathCAD incorporates units into an expression by multiplication.

Since MathCAD doesn't know "ft" either, you will also have to copy its definition. "1L" is MathCAD's way of indicating the basic length definition; you are using the U.S. Common system of measurement:

```
ft~1L ⏎
```

With r_E defined, we have reached the stage, illustrated in Figure 21, at which MathCAD reminds us that we also haven't defined the radius of the satellite's orbit.

Make room, if necessary, above and below the definition of r_E by moving the cursor to the line where you wish to create blank space, and by pressing $\langle$Ctrl–F9$\rangle$ one or more times.

Figure 21

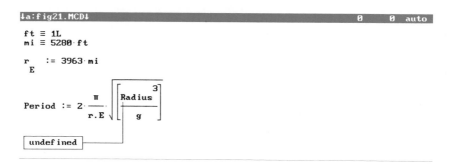

Copy the definitions for sec, *g*, *Altitude*, and *Radius* from Figure 18. The keystrokes are as follows:

```
sec~1T (J)
g~32.174*ft/sec^2 (J)
Altitude:1000*mi (J)
Radius:Altitude+r.E (J)
```

Radius has to be defined below r_E; MathCAD will remind you if you put it in the wrong place.

If you have done it right, you should be free of MathCAD error messages, and your display should look something like Figure 22.

Displaying an Individual Result

Now that the formula has the information it needs, you are ready to calculate the orbital period. First, get one value of the *Period*, corresponding to one specific orbit size.

Below the formula, at the bottom of the display, simply enter the "calculate and display" command via the equals sign. Type

```
Period= (J)
```

Figure 22

```
↓a:fig22.MCD↓                                            0      0   auto

ft ≡ 1L              mi ≡ 5280·ft          sec ≡ 1T

r    := 3963·mi
 E

Altitude := 1000·mi

Radius := Altitude + r
                      E
              ft
g ≡ 32.174·  ----
              2
             sec
                          ┌─────────
                          │       3
                   π      │ Radius
Period := 2· -----   ·   │ -------
                   r      │    g
                   E      √
```

The result appears to the right of the equals sign, as shown in Figure 23. It is correct, although not yet in the form you want. You'll want to fix it up in two respects: in its units and in its formats.

Specifying the Units of Calculated Results

MathCAD displays "time" — the dimensionality of the orbital period — rather than a specific unit. The cursor sits on top of a rectangular placeholder following the result, inviting you to specify the units you want.

With the cursor at the placeholder, type

> sec ⏎

and there's your answer: 7.101×10^3 seconds!

That's a lot of seconds. Maybe you'd rather see the answer in some other unit — hours, or even days. It is easy to add these new units to the document.

Type in the definitions for hours and days, as shown in Figure 24. The keystrokes are

> hr ~ 3600*sec ⏎
> day ~ 24*hr ⏎

Figure 23

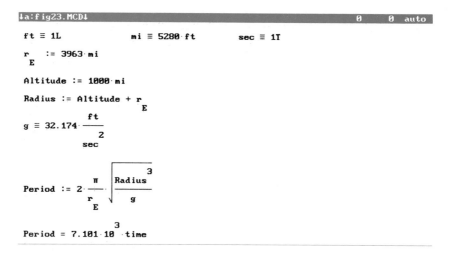

ft ≡ 1L   mi ≡ 5280·ft   sec ≡ 1T

r_E := 3963·mi

Altitude := 1000·mi

Radius := Altitude + r_E

$g \equiv 32.174 \cdot \dfrac{ft}{sec^2}$

$Period := 2 \cdot \dfrac{\pi}{r_E} \cdot \sqrt{\dfrac{Radius^3}{g}}$

$Period = 7.101 \cdot 10^3 \cdot time$

Repeat the "calculate and display" command two more times, specifying "hr" for the units the first time, and "day" the second time, and spacing out the requests horizontally for a manageable display.

To do this, you could retype the word "Period" twice, but let's try another way. Remember that the In-Region commands allow us to copy, cut, and paste parts of regions, including names, numbers, and expressions.

First, move the cursor to the word "Period" and press

$$\langle \text{Ctrl-}\boxed{\text{F 2}}\,\rangle$$

<Ctrl-$\boxed{\text{F 2}}$> is equivalent to <Esc> INCOpy

The words "Expression copied" on the message line tell you that a copy of that name has been stored in the cut buffer.

Then move the cursor below the new unit definitions and type

$$\langle \text{Ctrl-}\boxed{\text{F 4}}\,\rangle =$$

Figure 24

```
↓a:fig24.MCD↓                                          0      0   auto
ft ≡ 1L              mi ≡ 5280·ft          sec ≡ 1T

r    := 3963·mi
 E


Altitude := 1000·mi

Radius := Altitude + r
                      E
          ft
g ≡ 32.174·———
           2
          sec

                         3
                  π  │Radius
Period := 2·———   │———
              r  √   g
              E
                   3
Period = 7.101·10  ·sec

hr ≡ 3600·sec        day ≡ 24·hr

Period = 1.973·hr

Period = 0.082·day
```

< Ctrl-F4 > is equivalent to < Esc >
INPaste

The cursor should now be on the placeholder of a new display. Type

hr ⏎

Finally, to display the period in days as well, simply type

⟨Ctrl-F4⟩ = day ⏎

The result should resemble Figure 23.

Display Format for Calculated Results

Rather than show the result in standard scientific notation (7.101×10^3) you might want to translate it to an equivalent form (7101, for example).

Move the cursor onto the number you wish to reformat (that is, the period in seconds). Type

f

In the message line at the top of the screen, edit the display specifications. To do this, use the right and left arrow keys to move the cursor to the immediate right of each group of characters that you want to change. Erase the old entry with backspaces, and type in the desired characters.

The backspace key works this way in text regions as well as on the message line.

Change "pr" ("precision" — that is, decimal places) from 3 to 0, so that the result will be a whole number.

Change "et" (exponential threshold) from 3 to 5 (or higher), so that it will not be displayed in exponential format.

At this point, you can either press ⏎ to execute the format changes you have made, or press ⟨Esc⟩ to return to the previous format.

Press ⏎.

You will see a small dot in front of 7101·sec, showing that the number has been formatted locally. This local format can be changed back to the global (default) format at any time if you put the cursor on the number and type

d

Figure 25 shows the result.

Figure 25

ft ≡ 1L   mi ≡ 5280·ft   sec ≡ 1T

r_E := 3963·mi

Altitude := 1000·mi

Radius := Altitude + r_E

$g \equiv 32.174 \cdot \dfrac{ft}{sec^2}$

$Period := 2 \cdot \dfrac{\pi}{r_E} \cdot \sqrt{\dfrac{Radius^3}{g}}$

Period = ·7101·sec

hr ≡ 3600·sec   day ≡ 24·hr

Period = 1.973·hr

Period = 0.082·day

Preserving a MathCAD Document

You can make a permanent, retrievable record of your Math-CAD document in two ways: you can **save** it to disk, and, if your computer system has the necessary hardware, you can print it out.

Saving a MathCAD Document to Disk

F6 is equivalent to < Esc > SAve.

To save your version of the resulting document to disk, press ⎡F6⎤.

The message line asks for a filename. Name your file

    PERIOD1

We will be using this document again.

If you want to save your document files on a disk drive other than the one that contains the MathCAD Program and Help files (MCAD.EXE and MCAD.HLP), simply specify the letter designation of the desired drive with the filename, for example

    b:period1

To avoid typing "b:" before every filename, you can change MathCAD's default drive to b: by typing

⟨Esc⟩DOS ⏎
b: ⏎

Once you've done this, however, MathCAD will look on drive b: for any disk files it needs to consult, including DOS and Help.

Printing a MathCAD Document

If you have a compatible printer attached to your computer, print this document.

Try the following command.

⟨Esc⟩PRInt ⏎

Depending on how MathCAD has been set up on your machine, the first time you try to print a document, you may receive a message telling you that no printer has been selected. If this happens, type

⟨Esc⟩SELectprinter

Remember that all command names may be shortened. You can simply type ⟨Esc⟩SEL.

Select the printer designation that matches your equipment using the cursor arrows to move down the menu, then type

⏎ ⟨Esc⟩PRInt ⏎

Accept (with a ⏎) MathCAD's offer to print the whole document.

Accept (with a ⏎) the printer device that MathCAD proposes, unless your system requires something different.

As with many functions of the program, MathCAD gives you three ways to order a printout. You could have selected "print" from the system menu by typing

F10 SP

or

⟨Ctrl-O⟩

instead of

⟨Esc⟩PRInt ⏎

But the $\boxed{\text{F10}}$ SP form takes longer, because MathCAD must redraw the screen before proceeding to identify your printer.

The printers that MathCAD supports are listed in Part One, "Getting Started."

When you want to print a document that extends over more than one page of hard copy, the PAGelength command lets you set page breaks and see them on the screen. To set the page length at *nn* lines, type

    ⟨Esc⟩PAGelength *nn* $\boxed{\text{⌐}}$

or select "Page Length" from the System Command menu and specify *nn*.

You can use the COPy ($\boxed{\text{F 3}}$) and PASte ($\boxed{\text{F 4}}$) commands to move plots and regions off the page breaks shown on the screen as dotted lines, before printing.

When you are setting the page length, remember that the Student Edition of MathCAD prints a two-line header on each page.

Displaying Multiple Results in Tables

You have now calculated the orbital period of a satellite at an altitude of 1,000 miles; this is the first of the four answers that Part A requires. For the other three altitudes, you need only change the value of the *Altitude* variable from 1,000 miles to 2,000, 5,000, and 10,000 miles and MathCAD will automatically calculate the corresponding values of *Period*.

Move the cursor to the right of the number (1000) that you specified for *Altitude*. Press the backspace key four times to delete the number, and then type

    2000 $\boxed{\text{⌐}}$

in its place.

You could submit four separate printouts in response to Part A. It is tidier and more professional, however, to combine the four calculations into a set of parallel tables. This requires several changes to the worksheet of Figure 25, which you saved as PERIOD1.

Turning Automatic Calculation On and Off

You don't really have to switch to manual calculation, but it makes the editing go faster if you don't have to wait for Math-CAD to calculate everything every time you press ⏎ or in some other way leave a region.

Select the MANual command from the Compute Commands menu by typing

> F10 CM

The word "Auto" will disappear from the end of the message line. MathCAD will now wait to execute calculations until you tell it to calculate.

MathCAD provides two distinct manual calculation commands:

- The function key F9 or the command

    ⟨Esc⟩CALculate ⏎

  tells MathCAD to perform the calculations required to update the results that are now visible on the screen.
- The PROcess command

    ⟨Esc⟩PROcess ⏎

  orders up a complete recalculation of everything in the document.

The CAlculate command usually takes less time to execute, but it does not update portions of the document that lie below the display that is currently visible. If you were to print the document after pressing F9, the lower part of the document might not reflect recent changes.

Setting Up a Subscript Range

Since we want *Periods* that correspond to four *Altitudes*, we need to set up an index that runs from 1 to 4.

Near the top of the worksheet, define the **index variable** k. The keystroke sequence is

> k:1;4 ⏎

The semicolon tells MathCAD that you are setting up a range variable.

Setting Up an Input Table

An input table is just like an ordinary variable definition (for example, Altitude := 1000 * mi), except that it contains several values. Instead of giving *Altitude* only one value, an input table lets you give four values to $Altitude_k$, one for each value we have assigned to the index k. The subscript tells MathCAD how many values to ask for.

Move the cursor to the current definition of *Altitude*. Delete it with (F3), add some extra lines by pressing ⟨Ctrl–(F9)⟩ four or five times, and to replace it, type

        Altitude[k:1000*mi,

Note the comma at the end of the sequence; it tells MathCAD to draw a box for you to fill with the next number

        2000*mi,

Fill the input table, putting

        5000*mi,

and

        1000*mi ⏎

in the final two positions. Each entry ends with a comma except the last. Since you don't need another box at that point, the final entry ends with ⏎.

When you want to save MathCAD-generated data to disk, or when you have data already saved to disk (generated by MathCAD or by some other program), you can use MathCAD's data file functions (READ, WRITE, APPEND, READPRN, WRITEPRN, and APPENDPRN) to associate MathCAD variables with the contents of disk files. See the Reference Section for details.

| Changing Variables from Single-Valued (Scalar) to Multiple-Valued (Vector) | *Radius*, *Altitude*, and *Period* are all variables in the current worksheet. Each is a **scalar variable**, that is, it can take on only one value at a time. We'll now change each one to a subscripted vector variable so that it can take on the four values that the problem specifies. |

Radius, *Altitude*, and *Period* are all variables in the current worksheet. Each is a **scalar variable**, that is, it can take on only one value at a time. We'll now change each one to a subscripted vector variable so that it can take on the four values that the problem specifies.

Begin by changing *Radius* each time it occurs on the worksheet to "*Radius$_k$*."

With the arrow keys, move the cursor to the immediate right of the "s" in "Radius."

Type

    [k

Also change *Altitude* to *Altitude$_k$* and *Period* to *Period$_k$*, where they appear.

Requesting Tabulated Results

You tell MathCAD to calculate and display the four values of *Period$_k$* the same way you asked earlier for the single value of *Period*.

After (below or to the right of) all the definitions, simply type

    Period[k= ⏎
    (F 9)

You have to press (F 9), the CAlculate command key, because you turned automatic calculation off. Now you have all four values in a table, as in Figure 26.

Again, you'll want to clean up the units. In tables, you don't normally want to see units repeated in every cell. You would rather have the units appear once, as part of the table label, and only have numbers in the cells.

As it turns out, MathCAD provides a rather elegant way to do just that. Since units in MathCAD are factors like any other, you can get rid of them by division. And since MathCAD presents division in fractional form, you can get a cleanly labeled

Figure 26

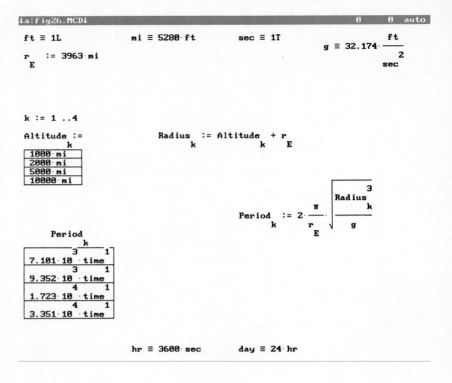

a:fig26.MCD 0 0 auto

$ft \equiv 1L$ $mi \equiv 5280 \cdot ft$ $sec \equiv 1T$ $g \equiv 32.174 \cdot \frac{ft}{sec^2}$

$r_E := 3963 \cdot mi$

$k := 1 .. 4$

$Altitude_k :=$ $Radius_k := Altitude_k + r_E$

1000·mi
2000·mi
5000·mi
10000·mi

$$Period_k := 2 \cdot \frac{\pi}{r_E} \cdot \sqrt{\frac{Radius_k^{\,3}}{g}}$$

$Period_k$
$7.101 \cdot 10^3 \cdot time^1$
$9.352 \cdot 10^3 \cdot time^1$
$1.723 \cdot 10^4 \cdot time^1$
$3.351 \cdot 10^4 \cdot time^1$

$hr \equiv 3600 \cdot sec$ $day \equiv 24 \cdot hr$

table by simply dividing the output variable name by the units that you chose.*

---

*Consider the algebraic equation that the first entry in the table implies:

$$Period_k = 7.101 * 10^3 * sec$$

Now, divide each side of the equation by "sec":

$$\frac{Period_k}{sec} = 7.101 * 10^3$$

The right side of this equation is close to what you want in the table, and the left side makes a label for the table.

Move the cursor to the subscript k in the calculation request ($Period_k =$) you just entered, and insert

```
/hr ↵
F 9
```

Now clean up the table entry format, as before.

Put the cursor inside the table, and type

```
f
```

to adjust the local format.

If necessary, change the "pr=0" to "pr=3" in the message line.

Next, since you are interested in the relationship between *Altitude* and *Period*, put a table of $Altitude_k$ next to the $Period_k$ table. Use F 3 and F 4 (CUt and PASte) to move the $Period_k$ table over to the right, if you like, then type

```
Altitude[k/mi= ↵
F 9
```

Press ↵.

Put the cursor inside the table and type

```
f
```

Set pr=0 and et=5.

Figure 27 shows the result.

Finishing Touches: Labeling a MathCAD Document with Text Regions

You are now ready to put the finishing touches on the Math-CAD document that you can submit as a solution to the problem posed in Part A of this exercise. To give the final product your own personal style, use F 3 and F 4 to move the regions around, and insert text regions where they can clarify the problem and its solution.

To insert a text region, move the cursor to the place where you want to put the upper left corner of the region, and type a double quote (").

Figure 27

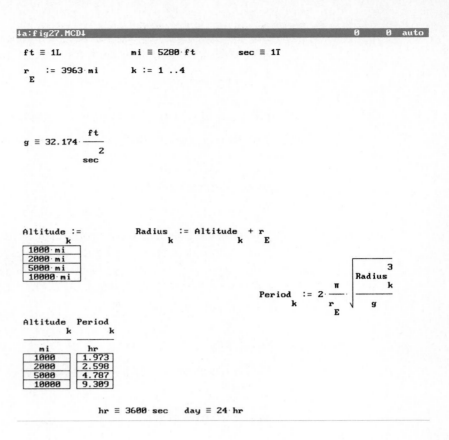

MathCAD responds with two double quotes; whatever you type between them will appear on the screen as text.

⟨Ctrl–↵⟩ is equivalent to ⟨Esc⟩ Width.

The first double quote sets the location of the upper lefthand corner of the text region. When you press ⟨Ctrl–↵⟩ at the end of the first line, you set the width of the region. Use the space bar *before* hitting ⟨Ctrl–↵⟩ if you want blank space at the right of that line, or if you want the region to be wider than the length of its first line.

Once the width of the region is set, MathCAD wraps text automatically within it as you continue typing. Optionally, you can press ⏎ to start a new line (that is, insert a **hard line break**, indicated on the screen by an arrow) within the text region.

Leave the region by using the arrow keys.

If you want to change the width of a text region, put the cursor in it and type

⟨Esc⟩Width

The message bar will tell you the width of the current region and invite you to change it, if you want. When you are finished, press ⏎ to execute the change or ⟨Esc⟩ to leave the width as it was.

Just as you can **copy**, **cut** and **paste** regions to arrange them on your document, you can copy, cut and paste segments of text with the In-Region Commands: INCOpy, INCUt and INSert-line, which you have already used for cutting and pasting expressions in equation regions.

- Move the cursor to the beginning of the piece of text you want to move.
- Press ⟨Ctrl–X⟩ or type

  ⟨Esc⟩MARk ⏎

  to mark the spot.
- Move the cursor to the end of the text segment to be moved and press ⟨Ctrl–X⟩ again. MathCAD will highlight the segment that you have selected.
- Type ⟨Ctrl–F3⟩ or

  ⟨Esc⟩INCUt ⏎

  to cut the marked text, removing it from the screen and storing it in the cut buffer.
- Finally, move the cursor to the place (within the same text region or another) where you wish to paste the text segment, and press ⟨Ctrl–F4⟩ or ⟨Esc⟩INPaste ⏎

If you want to copy a text segment without erasing it, use ⟨Ctrl–F2⟩ (or ⟨Esc⟩INCOpy) to store the marked text, and then paste it where you want it with ⟨Ctrl–F4⟩ (or ⟨Esc⟩ INPaste).

Remember that your printer can probably accommodate only 80 columns — 65 or so with adequate margins. The line and column numbers displayed at the right of the message line can help you keep your display within printable bounds.

Figure 28 shows one possible way to polish up this document. Feel free to copy it for practice, or to improve on it as you see fit.

Figure 28

```
↓a:fig28.MCD↓                                          0      0   auto
```

A. Compute the orbital period (in hours) for satellites in orbits
1000, 2000, 5000, and 10000 miles above the earth's surface.

   First, set up the units that the computation will require:

         ft ≡ 1L   mi ≡ 5280·ft   sec ≡ 1T   hr ≡ 3600·sec

   Next, set up the four altitude values as an input table, and
specify the remaining constants and formulas:

         $k := 1 .. 4$ $\text{Altitude}_k :=$ Satellite's altitude
                                                                above the surface of
                              | 1000·mi | the earth
                              | 2000·mi |
                              | 5000·mi |
                              | 10000·mi |

         $r_E := 3963 \cdot mi$ Mean equatorial radius
                                                          of the earth

         $\text{Radius}_k := \text{Altitude}_k + r_E$ Orbital radius (distance
                                                          from the center of the
                                                          earth)

         $g \equiv 32.174 \cdot \dfrac{ft}{sec^2}$ Acceleration of gravity

         $\text{Period}_k := 2 \cdot \dfrac{\pi}{r_E} \cdot \sqrt{\dfrac{\text{Radius}_k{}^3}{g}}$ Orbital period

   Finally, compute the orbital period in hours for each of
the four specified altitudes:

                    Altitude_k Period_k

                         mi   hr
                      | 1000 | | 1.973 |
                      | 2000 | | 2.598 |
                      | 5000 | | 4.787 |
                      | 10000 | | 9.309 |

78   Tutorial Lab Exercises

Press F6 to save your version to disk, typing in

> LAB1A ↵

when the message line asks for a filename.

This worksheet, when printed out, is suitable for submission to your instructor.

Using Split-Screen Windows to Borrow Regions from Another Document

Part B of the problem asks you to calculate the speed at which an object on the surface of the earth escapes into orbit. This is, of course, the orbital speed of a satellite with zero altitude (assuming, implausibly, that it wouldn't bump into tall buildings or mountains). Figure 29 displays a MathCAD analysis that does this calculation.

You will now prepare a worksheet like Figure 29, making as much use as possible of the work you already did to produce Figure 25.

The formula and definitions of Part A contain most of the material required for Part B. Since the question calls for a single number, we want the scalar version of the formula, which appeared in Figure 25, and which you saved earlier in a diskette file named PERIOD1.

Rather than reenter everything from scratch, you can borrow selected contents of an earlier worksheet in either of two ways:

- You can simply load the old file (F5) and edit it directly, throwing away what you don't need. This is a good approach to use when you're starting a new document.
- You can split the screen (F7) and cut and paste the regions of interest from one window into the other. This is usually the best approach when you are in the middle of a document and realize that you need something you've already saved in another context.

Since the first approach would exercise only skills that you have already practiced, we'll take the second one here.

Figure 29

↓a:fig29.MCD↓   0   0   auto

B.   Compute escape velocity (the horizontal speed that an object
must reach at the surface of the earth in order to enter earth
orbit.

Units: ft ≡ 1L   mi ≡ 5280·ft   sec ≡ 1T   hr ≡ 3600·sec

$$g \equiv 32.174 \cdot \frac{ft}{sec^2}$$ Acceleration of gravity

$$r_E := 3963 \cdot mi$$ Mean equatorial radius
                                                   of the earth

Altitude := 0·mi   Altitude above the surface
                                                   of the earth

$$Radius := Altitude + r_E$$ Orbital radius (distance
                                                   from the center of the
                                                   earth)

$$Period := 2 \cdot \frac{\pi}{r_E} \cdot \sqrt{\frac{Radius^3}{g}}$$ Orbital period

    Compute orbital speed by dividing the length (circumference)
of the orbit by the time the satellite spends in covering that
distance:

$$Speed := 2 \cdot \pi \cdot \frac{Radius}{Period}$$ Orbital speed

$$Speed = 17691 \cdot \frac{mi}{hr}$$ Escape velocity (orbital
                                                   speed at zero altitude)

Type

⟨Esc⟩MANual □

to turn off automatic calculation and avoid a lot of unhelpful
error messages.

Clear the screen by typing

⟨Esc⟩CLear □

Move the cursor about halfway down the screen; a couple of
⟨PgDn⟩ will do the trick. Wherever you put the cursor, the
screen will split.

F7 is equivalent to < Esc > SPlit.

Press F7 to split the screen into two windows.

F8 is equivalent to < Esc > SWitch.

Press F8 to toggle the cursor between the windows.

With the cursor in the bottom window, press F5, and instruct MathCAD to load PERIOD1.MCD. When you are prompted, tell MathCAD that it is all right to clear the current document out of memory.

Jump from one region to another with < Home > and < End >.

With the cursor in the bottom window, where the old document is displayed, move it to a region that you want to copy into the new document. Press F2 to copy it into the cut buffer memory without erasing it.

Press F8 again to switch the cursor to the top window. Move the cursor to the place where you want to put the region, and press F4.

When you have pasted in all the regions you need:

- Put the cursor in the top window (F8), if necessary.
- Type

    F6 LAB1B ↵

    to save its contents as a new diskette file named LAB1B.

< Ctrl–F7 > is equivalent to < Esc > Unsplit.

Press ⟨Ctrl–F7⟩ to unsplit the screen. Do not save the contents of the bottom window; you called up the old file only to draw from it, not to change it.

Create your own version of the worksheet in Figure 29. Save it again (as LAB1B). Print it, and keep it with the LAB1A sheet for submission.

Displaying Relationships with Plots

Part C of the lab calls for a plot of *Period* against *Altitude*. Again, much of the material in the earlier worksheets can be recycled to help set up the plot. This time, recall and revise an earlier document.

Load (F5) the file that you previously saved under the name of LAB1A. It had approximately the contents of Figure 28.

F10 CM is equivalent to
< Esc > MANual.

Turn off automatic calculation if it is on. Type

F10 CM

Delete (F3) the regions you won't need for this problem, keeping the definitions of units, k, r_E, $Radius_k$, g, and $Period_k$.

Unless it is a straight line, a plot with only four points would not be very smooth. The range variable k will therefore need more values; 31 (from 0 to 30) will do.

Move the cursor just to the right of the "4" that set the range of k before; backspace to erase the number, and replace it with "30." Similarly, change the "1" to "0" (zero).

Change the definition of $Altitude_k$. You now want 30 evenly spaced altitudes to plot. Spread them out, one each 1,000 miles.

Enter a new definition for $Altitude_k$, using the keystrokes

```
Altitude[k:k*1000*mi
```

In the geostationary orbit, a satellite goes around the earth in just 24 hours. If it is moving due east, it appears from the earth to stand still.

To pinpoint the altitude of the geostationary orbit, it will help to plot a horizontal line at $Period = 1$ day, along with the curve reflecting the relationship between $Altitude$ and $Period$. Where the line and the curve cross, you will find the geostationary altitude.

Set up an array named $Geostat_k$, and set each of its values to one day. Type

```
Geostat[k:1*day
```

Figure 30 displays one form that the response to Part C might take.

Now, finally, you are ready to order up the plot.

Move the cursor below the definitions, and press

@

Figure 30

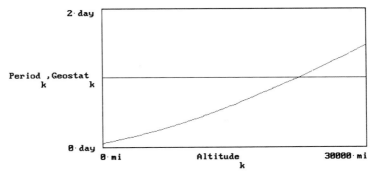

```
C.  Plot orbital period against altitude.  From the graph, estimate the
    altitude of the geostationary orbit.


ft ≡ 1L      mi ≡ 5280·ft      sec ≡ 1T      hr ≡ 3600·sec      day ≡ 24·hr

                                                         ft
Acceleration of gravity                      g ≡ 32.174·────
                                                          2
                                                         sec

Mean equatorial radius                       r    := 3963·mi
of the Earth                                  E

Set up a range of                            k := 0 ..30
satellite altitudes above
the surface of the Earth:                    Altitude   := k·1000·mi
                                                     k
Orbital Radius                               Radius   := Altitude  + r
(distance from Earth's                             k          k     E
center):
                                                              _____
                                                             /       3
                                                            / Radius
                                                      π    /        k
Satellite orbital period:                    Period  := 2·───  /  ─────────
                                                   k       r  √      g
                                                            E

Period for a geostationary orbit:            Geostat  := 1·day
                                                    k
```

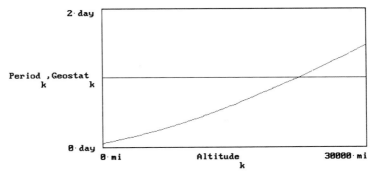

```
2·day ┌─────────────────────────────────────┐
      │                                      │
      │                                      │
      │                                      │
Period ,Geostat                            ╱ │
     k       k │──────────────────────────╱──│
      │                               ╱       │
      │                          ╱            │
      │                    ╱                  │
 0·day │_____╱_____│
      0·mi        Altitude         30000·mi
                      k
```

The geostationary orbit appears to lie between 20000 and 25000 miles
above the surface of the earth.

MathCAD responds by drawing a small plot, surrounded on the left and bottom by rectangular placeholders. They are there to invite you to label the horizontal (x) and vertical (y) axes, and, optionally, to provide the highest and lowest values to be plotted along each axis. To do this, fill in the six labels that define the plot.

<Tab> cycles the cursor around the six placeholders.

Move the cursor to the middle placeholder along the bottom, and type

```
Altitude[k
```

In the same fashion, label the *x*-axis origin (the left placeholder along the bottom) as

```
0*mi
```

Label the right end of the *x*-axis origin (the rightmost placeholder along the bottom) as

```
30000*mi
```

(reflecting the *Altitude* which corresponds to *k*=30, its highest value). If you don't supply axis limits, MathCAD will set reasonable ones, which you can change as you like.

Label the *y*-axis (the middle placeholder along the bottom) with the names of both of the result variables, inserting the keystrokes

```
Period[k,Geostat[k
```

Label the *y*-axis origin (the bottom placeholder along the left) as

```
0*day
```

Label the top of the *y*-axis as

```
2*day
```

(as a guess; you can always change it if it turns out not to be large or small enough).

Press F9 to tell MathCAD to run the calculations and plot the graph.

Now you need only adjust the size of the graph and tidy up the document.

Move the cursor into the plot area, and type

```
f
```

MathCAD responds by displaying the plot-formatting parameters at the top of the screen. You don't need logarithmic scales ("log") or grids ("subdivs"). The "type=1" plot that you get by default serves your purpose. But the plot is too small.

Edit the "size=rows, cols" part of the format specification and press F9, repeating this action until you are satisfied with the size of the plot. Figure 30 shows a plot with size=16,50.

Finally, look at the plot to estimate the altitude of the geostationary orbit, indicated by the x-axis value of the point where the two curves cross. At the scale illustrated in Figure 30, you can make only a crude guess, as indicated.

Create, save as LAB1C, and print your own version of the worksheet that corresponds to Part C.

By experimenting with the scales of the x- and y-axes of the plot, however, you can refine your estimate substantially.

Change the upper limit of $Altitude_k$ on the x-axis to "20000* mi" and the lower limit to "25000*mi".

Figure 31 shows the result of this closer look at the most interesting part of the plot.

Continue narrowing both the x- and y-ranges, until you get to the point where the whole x-axis range would amount to less than the 1,000-mile space between adjacent values of $Altitude_k$. At this point, the plot doesn't work any longer.

If you wish, change the definition of $Altitude_k$ to provide a finer grained view of the range of interest. You might enter, for example,

```
Altitude[k:22000*mi+k*20*mi
```

Finding the Root of an Expression

Part D of the lab asks for a direct calculation of the altitude of the geostationary orbit "from the formulas." The most straightforward way to do this would be simply to:

- Solve the *Period* formula for *Radius*.
- Plug

```
Period:1*day
```

into the resulting expression.

Figure 31

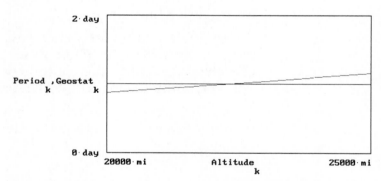

C. Plot orbital period against altitude. From the graph, estimate the
    altitude of the geostationary orbit.

ft ≡ 1L   mi ≡ 5280·ft   sec ≡ 1T   hr ≡ 3600·sec   day ≡ 24·hr

Acceleration of gravity

$$g \equiv 32.174 \cdot \frac{ft}{sec^2}$$

Mean equatorial radius
of the Earth

$$r_E := 3963 \cdot mi$$

Set up a range of
satellite altitudes above
the surface of the Earth:

$$k := 0 \ .. 30$$

$$Altitude_k := k \cdot 1000 \cdot mi$$

Orbital Radius
(distance from Earth's
center):

$$Radius_k := Altitude_k + r_E$$

Satellite orbital period:

$$Period_k := 2 \cdot \frac{\pi}{r_E} \cdot \sqrt{\frac{Radius_k^{\ 3}}{g}}$$

Period for a geostationary orbit:

$$Geostat_k := 1 \cdot day$$

The geostationary orbit appears to lie between 20000 and 25000 miles
above the surface of the earth.

- Evaluate it.

However, this method wouldn't teach you anything new about
MathCAD. Instead, then, let's use MathCAD's ability to calculate the roots of mathematical expressions.

For convenience, piggyback LAB1D on LAB1C, which contains much of the setup you will need.

Reload (F5) LAB1C, if it isn't still on the screen.

Make space at the bottom of the sheet by deleting (F3) the plot, the $Geostat_k$ definition, and the associated labels.

Applying the MathCAD Root Function

As you know, when the value of an expression depends entirely on the value of a variable, the expression is called a **function** of that variable. For example,

$$Altitude = Radius - r_E$$
$$= Radius - 3,963 \text{ miles}$$
$$= f(Radius)$$

A value of the variable for which the function is zero is called a **root** of the function. For example,

$$Radius = 3,963 \text{ miles}$$

is a root of the function.

To use the MathCAD root function, set up a name for the root value you want to calculate, and enter your best guess at it. For your current purposes, a crude guess from the plot on Figure 30 will do.

Your guess does not have to be particularly close: the closer it is to the actual value, the more rapidly MathCAD can calculate the root, but if there is only one root, any number will do. For functions that can have many roots, like sine curves, the accuracy of the guess can become more important.

Type

```
Geo:20000*mi  ↵
```

Creating a User-Defined Function

Now set up the function whose roots interest you. In this case, you want a function of the geostationary altitude *Geo* that will be zero when *Period* is one day. The formula for *Period* that we have been using all along makes this easy, and the appropriate function is shown in Figure 32.

Figure 32

D. From the formulas, compute the altitude of the geostationary orbit
    to the nearest mile.

$ft \equiv 1L$ $mi \equiv 5280 \cdot ft$ $sec \equiv 1T$ $hr \equiv 3600 \cdot sec$ $day \equiv 24 \cdot hr$

Acceleration of gravity

$$g \equiv 32.174 \cdot \frac{ft}{sec^2}$$

Mean equatorial radius
of the Earth

$$r_E := 3963 \cdot mi$$

Set up a range of
satellite altitudes above
the surface of the Earth:

$$k := 0 \; .. \; 30$$

$$Altitude_k := k \cdot 1000 \cdot mi$$

Orbital Radius
(distance from Earth's
center):

$$Radius_k := Altitude_k + r_E$$

Satellite orbital period:

$$Period_k := 2 \cdot \frac{\pi}{r_E} \cdot \sqrt{\frac{Radius_k^3}{g}}$$

Compute Geo, the altitude of
the geostationary orbit:

1. Make a guess from the graph
    in Figure 1.13:

$$Geo := 20000 \cdot mi$$

2. Set up a function of
    altitude that is zero when
    Period is one day:

$$f(Geo) := 2 \cdot \frac{\pi}{r_E} \cdot \sqrt{\frac{\left[Geo + r_E \right]^3}{g}} - 1 \cdot day$$

3. Apply the root function:

$$Geo := root(f(Geo), Geo)$$

$$Geo = 22291 \cdot mi$$

Satisfy yourself that you understand how this function was
derived.

Enter the function as shown; the keystroke sequence is

    f(Geo):2*⟨Alt-P⟩/r.E*\((Geo+r.E)^3/g)-1*day

Invoke the root function itself.

Type

    Geo:root(f(Geo),Geo)

And finally, tell MathCAD in the usual way that you want a calculated result.

Type

Geo=⏎

Clean up the worksheet, save (F6) it as LAB1D, and print and submit it.

Suggestions for Further Exploration

1. Extend your table of orbital altitudes and periods (Figure 27), and add a parallel table of orbital speeds.

2. Plot *Period* versus *Speed*, and comment on the relationship, which holds for planets and small moons in the solar system, too. With some elaboration, it also holds for systems like the earth and its moon, whose mass is not negligible.

2

Distribution of a Sum of Random Numbers

The second lab exercise illustrates some fundamental concepts of statistics. MathCAD provides special statistical functions and utilities that make it easy to simulate and investigate many kinds of random processes.

Here you will have a chance to test out a prediction of statistical sampling theory.

If you add together random numbers, each uniformly distributed over the range from zero to one, the sum will not be distributed uniformly; instead, it will tend to pile up in the middle of its possible range.

The theory predicts not only that this bunching up will happen, but also

- Where the pile will be centered (the mean of the distribution of the sums)
- How much the pile will spread out (the standard deviation)
- Just how the mean and standard deviation will depend on n, the number of random numbers added together to form each sum

This lab exercise illustrates the application of several important MathCAD capabilities:

- The random number function
- The summation function
- Vectors
- Statistical functions

- The histogram function
- Plots formatted as stairsteps and bar charts
- Data-file management
- Command files
- Using DOS from within MathCAD

Figure 33 states the problem in MathCAD format.

Organizing a MathCAD Document

In Tutorial Lab #1, you approached the organization of your document somewhat backwards, to illustrate the ways in which MathCAD can lead you by the hand to a logical presentation. It worked, but you spent a lot of time moving things

Figure 33

```
↓a:fig33.MCD↓                                              0      0 calc F9
MathCAD Tutorial Lab Exercise #2:

DISTRIBUTION OF A SUM OF RANDOM NUMBERS


        A number selected at random from a uniform distribution
between zero and one is equally likely to have any value in that
range.   The sum of two such numbers can take on any value from
zero to two, but it is more likely to lie close to the midpoint
of that range than to either end.   The more random numbers you
add together, the more strongly their sum gravitates toward the
middle of its possible range.

        Sampling theory predicts that a sum of n random numbers,
sampled from a uniform distribution between zero and one, will be
normally distributed, with
```

$$mean = \frac{n}{2}, \quad and \quad dev = \sqrt{\frac{n}{12}}$$

```
        Prepare a MathCAD document that examines this distribution
empirically:

        A.   Set up ranges for n and for m, the number of sums to be
             computed.

        B.   Write a formula to compute the m sums and to store them
             in a vector.

        C.   Compute the mean and standard deviation of the sums, and
             compare them with the theoretical values.

        D.   Display the distribution of the sums in a histogram.
```

around. With that experience behind you, you can now set up this second lab more efficiently.

A properly organized MathCAD document follows this logical sequence of definition and display:

- **Text headers and labels** (in a convenient order, since they don't participate in calculations)
- **Definitions**
  - **Units** (usually defined globally, since they don't change within a document)
  - **Variables** to which units attach
  - **Ranges** over which variables vary
  - **Vectors** in which to store ranges of values
  - **Formulas** that govern relationships among variables
- **Displays**, which often require new variables, ranges, and vectors

This statistical application calls for the following definitions:

- Units — none; we aren't using units here
- Variables
  - n, the number of random numbers to be added together to form each sum
  - m, the number of sums to be calculated
- Ranges
  - $i := 1 .. n$
  - $j := 0 .. m - 1$
- Vectors — initially, only one: SUM_j, the vector of m sums whose distribution we are examining
- Formulas
  - A summing formula, to tell MathCAD to figure the sums and store them in SUM_j
  - Theoretical mean and standard deviation as functions of n (provided in the problem statement)
- Displays
  - Comparisons between empirical and theoretical means and standard deviations
  - Histogram(s), displaying the empirical distribution for various values of n and m, and in selected levels of detail

Follow this sequence to enter the elements of your document in the proper logical order.

First, start off with a clean slate.

Be sure that you've saved ($\boxed{F6}$) what you were working on most recently if you want to be able to retrieve it later on.

Type

$\boxed{F10}$ FC

to clear the worksheet. Answer with

y $\boxed{\lrcorner}$

if MathCAD asks you whether it's OK to clear.

Turn off automatic calculation, so you do not clutter up the screen with error messages if you happen to enter something in the wrong sequence.

Type

$\boxed{F10}$ CM $\boxed{\lrcorner}$

You will want to head this document with text — a brief restatement of the problem, perhaps some personal identification, and explanatory comments as needed. Now is not really the time to compose this material, but leave some space for it. While you can always make blank space by inserting lines or by moving regions around, it is much quicker to start part of the way down the page.

Press

⟨PgDn⟩

Ranges and Range Variables

When you give MathCAD a formula and ask for a value, MathCAD carries out the calculation once and displays the result.

Often, you need to repeat a calculation a number of times. Here, for example, you need to tell MathCAD to calculate n random numbers, and then to add them up. Do so by setting up a range variable or **index variable** named i, specifying that it take on each value from 1 to n, in turn.

Type

    i:1;n ⏎

Similarly, you want the summing procedure repeated m times, requiring another range variable. Call this one j.

Type

    j:0;m–1 ⏎

If you had not turned off automatic calculation, MathCAD would have reminded you by now that you haven't yet defined m and n. Do that now, making sure to define each before its first use.

Move the cursor to a position above or to the left of the definition of i, and type

    n:10 ⏎

This specifies that ten random numbers are to be added to create each sum. You will ultimately want to sum larger groups of numbers. For debugging purposes, however, it will save time to use small values of m and n. Each time we press ⎡F9⎤ to command MathCAD to calculate, it has to generate $m \times n$ random numbers and add them up in m groups of n. Unless m and n are small, this can take a significant amount of time.

Move the cursor to a position above or to the left of the definition of j, and type

    m:20 ⏎

Your worksheet should look something like Figure 34. Again, you have set m low so that each run doesn't take much time, but with a small sample size, we won't see the distribution clearly. We'll increase it later, when we're willing to wait for MathCAD to process a large sample.

Figure 34

```
↓a:fig34.MCD↓                                    0     0   auto

  n := 10
  i := 1 ..n
  m := 20
  j := 0 ..m - 1
```

The function rnd(x) supplies a random number, sampled from a uniform distribution ranging between zero and x. Each time you use the function, you get a newly generated random number. For example if you define a vector named *RAND* with 20 members as

```
k:0;19 ↵
RAND[k:rnd(4)
```

MathCAD fills the vector with 20 numbers, each of which is equally likely to take on any value between 0 and 4.

To see some random samples, enter the definitions above, and then type

```
RAND =
```

Press [F 9] several times (move the cursor to rnd (4), if necessary) and watch how the display changes as each new set of 20 numbers is calculated.

Strictly speaking, of course, rnd provides a **pseudorandom number**, calculated from a formula. It acts like a random number for ordinary computational purposes, with one very convenient exception: you can get exactly the same pseudorandom sequence as many times as you wish. Genuine random numbers, of course, can't be predicted or replicated in this manner.

For many purposes, you want independent sequences of random numbers — sequences that do not overlap and that act like separately drawn random samples. That is what happens unless you instruct MathCAD otherwise.

MathCAD has inside it, in effect, an indefinitely long series of pseudorandom numbers. Each time you ask for a random number, you get the next one in the series unless you tell MathCAD to jump to some other point. You may want to start at a brand new place and get random numbers you've never used before. Or you may wish to go back for another look at a random sequence you used earlier.

MathCAD resets the rnd generator and starts the sequence over when you first start MathCAD, or when you issue the RAndomize command. To practice issuing the RAndomize command, move the cursor into the region containing the rnd(x) function.

Press ⟨Esc⟩, then type

    RAndomize ⏎

Press ⏎ again to accept the default seed value. When you are finished experimenting with $RAND_k$, delete these regions using ⟨F3⟩.

From this point on, until you randomize again or leave Math-CAD, random numbers generated by rnd will follow the same sequence as when you started up MathCAD.

You can start the sequence from a different point by specifying a number with the RAndomize command. For example, type

    ⟨Esc⟩RAndomize 25 ⏎

Each time you start with the same numeric argument, the sequence starts from the same place.

Vectors and Vector Variables

MathCAD's statistical functions operate on data stored in vectors. A MathCAD vector is a one-dimensional list of values assigned to a single **vector variable**.

You will now set up, for example, a vector variable named SUM. The dollar sign ($) keystroke invokes the MathCAD summation function. With j taking on each value from 0 to $m-1$, the vector SUM contains m numbers, from SUM_0 to SUM_{m-1}, each of which is a sum of n random numbers.[1]

---

[1]MathCAD's vectors and consequently its statistical routines (means, variances, standard deviations) are set up to begin with vector element zero. If you were to set up the index j to run from 1 to m, rather than from zero to $m-1$, each statistical computation would start with an empty "element zero" and thus be thrown off. However, it is possible to change this convention by redefining the system variable ORIGIN to 1 instead of 0.

With the cursor below the definition of the range variable *j*, type

```
SUM[j:i$rnd(1) ↵
```

The worksheet should now look roughly like Figure 35.

The *m* numbers in *SUM* comprise the set of data whose distribution you are investigating. Each time you run the computational machinery (F9), you get a new set of $m \times n$ random numbers and therefore a new set of *m* sums.

The Built-In Statistical Functions

The next task (Part C) is to compare

- the empirical mean and standard deviation as calculated from the actual random numbers you have placed into *SUM*

to

- the theoretical statistics predicted by the formulas given in the problem statement.

You will now define these formulas on the worksheet, so that you'll only need to invoke their names in order to calculate their values.

With the cursor anywhere below the definition of *n*, type

```
mean.theory:n/2 ↵
stdev.theory:\(n/12) ↵
```

Figure 35

```
↓a:fig35.MCD↓                                    0      0    auto

n := 10
i := 1 ..n
m := 20
j := 0 ..m - 1

        ___
SUM  := \        rnd(1)
        /
        ‾‾‾
         i
    j
```

You now have everything you need to compare the empirical and theoretical statistics.

With the *m* sums safely stored in the vector named *SUM*, you need only call on MathCAD's built-in statistical functions to calculate the desired empirical mean and standard deviation.

Now that you have finished moving regions around, turn the automatic calculation back on.

Type

    〈Esc〉AUtomatic ⏎

To command MathCAD to calculate and display, use the equals sign.

Below all the definitions, type

    mean(SUM)= ⏎
    stdev(SUM)= ⏎

Similarly, you can order up the theoretical values of the same statistics.

Near the value of mean (*SUM*) that you just displayed, type

    mean.theory= ⏎

And near the displayed value of stdev(*SUM*), type

    stdev.theory= ⏎

The resulting display should look something like Figure 36.

Figure 36

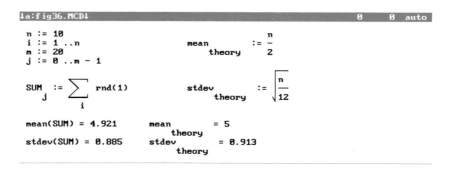

To see the new empirical values for mean(SUM) and stdev (SUM), press $\boxed{\text{F9}}$.

The Histogram Function

Theoretically, the sums that you have stored in the vector SUM should be distributed normally — that is, in accordance with the familiar bell curve illustrated in Figure 37.

MathCAD's histogram function provides a way to draw a picture of the actual distribution so you can compare reality with expectation.

The histogram function requires a vector of real numbers containing the data whose distribution you want to display. You have this: it is the vector named SUM. The index of the data vector has to begin with zero, as you have specified. The highest index, therefore, has to be $m-1$, one less than the number of data elements .

The histogram function also requires another vector of real numbers defining the boundaries of the intervals, or bins, into which you want MathCAD to sort the m sums which make up the vector SUM.

Figure 37

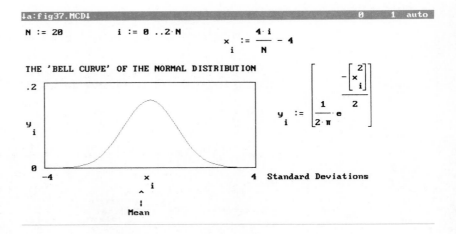

If we wanted, for example, to look at a range of sums from $MINSUM = 0$ to $MAXSUM = 10$, and to divide that range into $N = 2$ bins,

- Each bin would be five units wide.
- We'd need three boundaries to define the two bins, as Figure 38 shows.

In general, the width of each bin is

$$\frac{MAXSUM - MINSUM}{N}$$

and the number of boundaries is $N + 1$.

Setting up the interval definition array (label it $BINS_I$) can be a bit tricky. Step by step:

- Decide how many intervals you want to show on your histogram plot: call this number N, and set it equal to n for the moment. You can change it later, when you want to look at the distribution from different angles. Type

    N:n

- Define an index I, running from zero to N, to label the $N + 1$ interval boundaries. Type

    1:0;N

- Choose $MINSUM$, the starting point for the first interval that you want to display. This can be the smallest possible value of $BINS$ (that is, zero), if you wish, but you are free to locate your window on the SUM distribution anywhere you want. Type

    MINSUM:0

Figure 38

	MINSUM		5		MAXSUM
	0		5		10
	|————————		———————|	————————	|
		bin 1		bin 2	
boundary:	1		2		3

- Choose *MAXSUM*, the ending point for the last interval to be displayed. Again, this can be the highest possible value (*n*) or any smaller value greater than *MINSUM*. Type

  MAXSUM:n $\boxed{\lrcorner}$

- Set up the *BINS* array of $N + 1$ interval boundaries from $BINS_0 = MINSUM$ through $BINS_N = MAXSUM$. Type

  BINS[I:MINSUM+I*(MAXSUM−MINSUM)/N $\boxed{\lrcorner}$

- Finally, invoke the MathCAD histogram function. Type

  FREQS:hist(BINS,SUM) $\boxed{\lrcorner}$

This procedure issues the following commands to Math-CAD:

- Set up vector called *FREQS*, running from $FREQS_0$ to $FREQS_{N-1}$, containing one member for each of the *N* bins defined by the boundaries listed in the vector called *BINS*.
- Count the members of *SUM* that fall into each of the bins. Store each count in the corresponding member of *FREQS*.

Your worksheet should now resemble Figure 39.

Figure 39

```
↓a:fig39.MCD↓                                                    0      0   auto

n := 10
i := 1 ..n                              mean            :=   n
m := 20                                      theory          2
j := 0 ..m − 1


SUM   :=  ∑   rnd(1)          stdev           :=   ╱ n
     j    i                        theory          √ 12


mean(SUM) = 4.921     mean            = 5
                           theory
stdev(SUM) = 0.885    stdev           = 0.913
                           theory
N := n                MINSUM := 0

I := 0 ..N            MAXSUM := n

                            MAXSUM − MINSUM
BINS   := MINSUM + I ─────────────────────
     I                          N

FREQS := hist(BINS,SUM)
```

The next time you calculate ($\boxed{\text{F 9}}$), the m values of SUM_j will be sifted into the N bins you have just defined.

One step remains before you can see the distribution in a plot.

You cannot ask MathCAD to plot $FREQS_I$, because the range I has $N + 1$ members, one too many. It would try to evaluate $FREQS_N$ and become terminally bewildered. So, we have to define a second index J, running from 0 to $N-1$, to label the N intervals.

Type

```
J:0;N-1 ↵
```

Now, at last, you are ready to create a histogram plot that will stretch across the entire possible range of the SUM distribution. From this plot, you will have a good interocular indication of the tendency of sums of random numbers to cluster around the middle of their range.[2]

To maximize the range of the vertical scale, let max(v), another of MathCAD's built-in statistical routines, supply the maximum frequency that it finds in the $FREQS$ vector.

Move the cursor below the definitions and type

```
Max:1+max(FREQS) ↵
```

You add one to leave a bit of space at the top of the plot. Now, order up the plot itself.

Type @.

Use the ⟨Tab⟩ key to jump around among the six square placeholders.

Label the x-axis (horizontal) as $BINS_J$, running from zero to n:

Type

```
BINS[J
```

---

[2]"Interocular" means "evident at first glance," that is, it hits you "right between the eyes." This is, believe it or not, a highly respectable expression in statistical circles.

in the middle of the x-axis,

```
MINSUM
```

at the left, and

```
MAXSUM
```

at the right.

Label the y-axis (vertical) as *FREQS_J*, running from zero to *Max*:

Type

```
FREQS[J
```

in the middle of the y-axis,

```
0
```

at the bottom, and

```
Max
```

at the top.

With the cursor inside the plot area, type

```
f
```

and adjust the format of the plot.

Change "Type" from l to s to get the stairstep pattern of a histogram.

Adjust the size of the plot to suit your taste, and press ⏎

Figure 40 shows a plot with "size"=6,60.

Press [F9] to command MathCAD to carry out the calculations and to draw the picture. The result should resemble Figure 40. The picture in Figure 40 shows the distribution in the context of its total range. It shows that the sums do indeed cluster in the middle of the range, as the theory predicted. The comparison of empirical and theoretical means and standard deviations also bears out this theory.

Figure 40

```
n := 10
i := 1 ..n                          mean        :=  n
m := 20                                 theory      ─
j := 0 ..m - 1                                      2
```

$$SUM_j := \sum_i rnd(1) \qquad\qquad stdev_{theory} := \sqrt{\frac{n}{12}}$$

```
mean(SUM) = 4.921        mean        = 5
                             theory
stdev(SUM) = 0.885       stdev       = 0.913
                             theory
```

```
N := n                    MINSUM := 0

I := 0 ..N                MAXSUM := n

                          MAXSUM - MINSUM
BINS  := MINSUM + I ·────────────────────
    I                           N

FREQS := hist(BINS,SUM)

J := 0 ..N - 1

Max := 1 + max(FREQS)
```

The stairstep display that you get with Type=s is the same as a bar chart with the bars running together. If you prefer space between the bars, choose Type=b.

Also, we have chosen the endpoints for each axis explicitly. Another option, called **autoscaling**, is to have MathCAD find appropriate limits automatically. To test this, erase some or all of the four axis limits and examine the new plot.

There is a lot more that this worksheet can show you. But before starting on the variations, clean up the layout and supply labels that make the logic easier to follow. Figure 41 shows one possible arrangement. The lines in the comparison table are

Figure 41

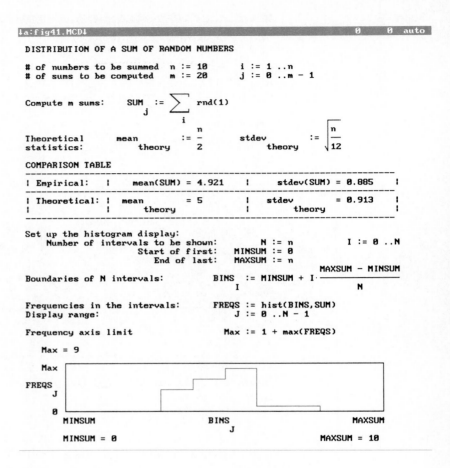

DISTRIBUTION OF A SUM OF RANDOM NUMBERS

\# of numbers to be summed $n := 10$ $i := 1 .. n$
\# of sums to be computed $m := 20$ $j := 0 .. m - 1$

Compute m sums: $SUM_j := \sum_i rnd(1)$

Theoretical   mean$_{theory} := \dfrac{n}{2}$ stdev$_{theory} := \sqrt{\dfrac{n}{12}}$
statistics:

COMPARISON TABLE

| Empirical: | mean(SUM) = 4.921 | stdev(SUM) = 0.885 |

| Theoretical: | mean$_{theory}$ = 5 | stdev$_{theory}$ = 0.913 |

Set up the histogram display:
    Number of intervals to be shown: $N := n$ $I := 0 .. N$
                Start of first: $MINSUM := 0$
                End of last: $MAXSUM := n$

Boundaries of N intervals: $BINS_I := MINSUM + I \cdot \dfrac{MAXSUM - MINSUM}{N}$

Frequencies in the intervals: $FREQS := hist(BINS, SUM)$
Display range: $J := 0 .. N - 1$

Frequency axis limit $Max := 1 + max(FREQS)$

   Max = 9

MINSUM = 0   MAXSUM = 10

only text regions. Feel free to invent a better arrangement of your own.

You might choose, for example, to use MathCAD's matrix definition capability to create a table that puts the two versions of each statistic close together for easy comparison. This is a pretty trivial application of a powerful feature; we'll do a lot more with matrices in Tutorial #5.

To set up a matrix, type

⟨Alt-M⟩

and then supply the desired numbers of rows and columns (two of each, in this case). MathCAD provides a 2×2 table of place-holders for you to replace with numbers or expressions.

Type

Statistics: ⟨Alt-M⟩⟨Bksp⟩⟨Bksp⟩⟨Bksp⟩2 2 ⏎
mean(SUM)⟨Tab⟩mean.theory⟨Tab⟩
stdev(SUM)⟨Tab⟩stdev.theory ⏎
Statistics=

In this keystroke sequence, you need to type the three ⟨Bksp⟩s only if numbers appear in the message line to indicate the size of the matrix. If they don't, and you backspace anyway, no harm will be done. Be careful to hit ⏎ only where it says to do so; the first part of the sequence appears as three lines only so it will fit on the page. Also be sure to leave a space between the two numbers.

Figure 42 shows the result: rather more compact and easier to achieve than the table in Figure 41.

Save as FIG41.MCD (F5) and print (F10 SP) your version of this worksheet.

Figure 42

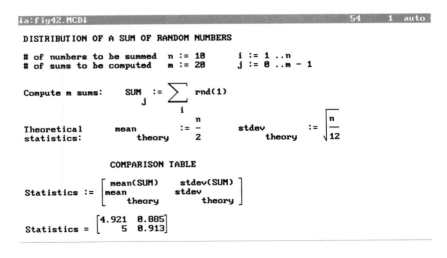

Does the picture in Figure 41 look like the classic bell-curve normal distribution? The empirical and theoretical statistics match up reasonably well, but the histogram is too lumpy to yield any comfortable conclusions.

With only 20 sums in the *SUM* vector, it's hard to get a very detailed picture of the shape of the distribution. They all fall roughly in the middle of the range, and the tallest of the bars are the middle ones, but you'd have to look hard and stand back to judge this picture as bell-shaped.

You can sharpen the picture by boosting any of three parameters:

- m, the sample size (that is, the length of the *SUM* vector).
- n, the number of random numbers being added together into each SUM_j.
- N, the number of intervals (that is, slicing the picture more finely).

We'll leave these improvements as exercises; you'll find them at the end of the tutorial.

Managing Data Files

Each time that you've computed the mean and standard deviation of m sums and n random numbers, they have come out reasonably close to the values that statistical theory predicts. If you run (that is, replicate) such an experiment a number of times, you can collect a sample of means and a sample of standard deviations and study their distributions to see just how tightly they cluster around their theoretical values. Computers are very good at this sort of repetitious work, and Math-CAD offers some convenient features for automating it.

Start by stripping down for heavy work:

Load ($\boxed{F5}$) your version of Figure 41, if it isn't already loaded.

If you haven't saved it already; save it as FIG41.MCD:

$\boxed{F6}$ FIG41 $\boxed{↵}$

Now save it again, this time with the filename REPLIC.MCD:

> $\boxed{\text{F 6}}$ REPLIC $\boxed{\,\lrcorner\,}$

This changes the default filename for future saves, so that you won't inadvertently overwrite your own saved version of the Figure 41 worksheet.

CUt all but the top few regions, so that your worksheet looks approximately like Figure 43.

Set up variables *Mean* and *Stdev* to hold the current mean and standard deviation values. Type

> Mean:mean(SUM) $\boxed{\,\lrcorner\,}$
> Stdev:stdev(SUM) $\boxed{\,\lrcorner\,}$

Then tell MathCAD to display the newly calculated values of *Mean* and *Stdev*. Type

> Mean= $\boxed{\,\lrcorner\,}$
> Stdev= $\boxed{\,\lrcorner\,}$

Save the result as REPLIC.MCD:

> $\boxed{\text{F 6}}$ $\boxed{\,\lrcorner\,}$ y $\boxed{\,\lrcorner\,}$

Now tell MathCAD to write *Mean* to a disk file named MEANS.DAT, and to write *Stdev* to another file named STDEVS.DAT, so that you can call them back for further analysis whenever you wish:

The READ, WRITE and APPEND functions use a .DAT filename extension by default.

> WRITE(MEANS):Mean $\boxed{\,\lrcorner\,}$
> WRITE(STDEVS):Stdev $\boxed{\,\lrcorner\,}$

Figure 43

> ↓a:fig43.MCD↓   0   0   auto
>
> TESTING THE STATISTICAL BEHAVIOR OF SUMS OF RANDOM NUMBERS
>
> # of numbers to be summed   n := 10   i := 1 ..n
> # of sums to be computed   m := 20   j := 0 ..m - 1
>
> $$\text{SUM}_j := \sum_i rnd(1)$$

Figure 44

TESTING THE STATISTICAL BEHAVIOR OF SUMS OF RANDOM NUMBERS

```
# of numbers to be summed    n := 10    i := 1 ..n
# of sums to be computed      m := 20    j := 0 ..m - 1
```

$$\text{SUM}_j := \sum_i \text{rnd}(1)$$

```
Mean := mean(SUM)              Mean = 4.921
Stdev := stdev(SUM)            Stdev = 0.885

WRITE(MEANS) := Mean
WRITE(STDEVS) := Stdev

Readmean := READ(MEANS)        Readstdv := READ(STDEVS)
Readmean = 4.921               Readstdv = 0.885
```

If you've had automatic calculation turned on all this time, you may have noticed the little red light on your disk drive glowing for a moment as you pressed ⏎ at the end of each WRITE entry. If not, it will happen when you press F9 or when you tell MathCAD to PROcess the worksheet. So far, that's your only evidence that MathCAD has in fact created the two files and written a number to each.

To get more direct evidence, read the numbers back with new variable names, and display them:

```
Readmean:READ(MEANS) ⏎
Readmean= ⏎
Readstdv:READ(STDEVS) ⏎
Readstdv= ⏎
```

The result should resemble Figure 44.

Now command the MathCAD to process your worksheet with a fresh batch of random numbers:

```
F10 PROcess ⏎
```

A new pair of numbers appears in the display regions of your worksheet and is written to MEANS.DAT and STDEV.DAT.

The second number that was written to each disk file was written right over the previous one, erasing it. At other times, that may be what you want, but now you're trying to compile an accumulating list of means and standard deviations. The solution is to change WRITE to APPEND when you add new values to the file.

The APPEND function acts the same way WRITE does, except that it leaves what is already in the file alone and tacks on the new entry at the end of the file. The result will be a growing list of means in MEANS.DAT and a parallel list of standard deviations in STDEVS.DAT.

One more change is in order. As it stands now, each of the two READ functions will fetch only the first number from its file, since that's all it needs in order to fulfill its mission of assigning a value to *Readmean* and to *Readstdev*.

You want to know about the whole list of numbers that has accumulated in each file, not just the first one. MathCAD's READPRN function reads an entire vector or matrix from a file that is structured into rows and columns. To READPRN, the lists of numbers in MEANS.DAT and STDEVS.DAT look just like vectors. So CUt ($\boxed{\text{F 3}}$) the regions that contain your READ functions, and replace each with the analogous READ-PRN function.

Type

```
MEANS:READPRN(MEANS.DAT) ⏎
MEANS= ⏎
STDEVS:READPRN(STDEVS.DAT) ⏎
STDEVS= ⏎
```

If you had told MathCAD to READPRN a file named MEANS without specifying the .DAT extension, it would look for MEANS.PRN. The WRITEPRN function assigns .PRN by default to the structured files it creates. You can override this default extension by supplying the complete filename in the READPRN function call.

Now tell MathCAD to process the worksheet four times.

Type

$\langle$Esc$\rangle$PROcess ⏎
$\langle$Esc$\rangle$PROcess ⏎
$\langle$Esc$\rangle$PROcess ⏎
$\langle$Esc$\rangle$PROcess ⏎

and watch what happens.

After four replications of the experiment, you should have something like Figure 45.

Now that you've seen how it works, you don't really need to display the two lists at each iteration. You're interested in the distribution of the randomly varying means and standard deviations, not in the individual numbers. You'd like to see, in fact, the mean and standard deviation of the means and standard deviations. Set up a compact display for these statistics.

To save time; turn off automatic calculation:

$\langle$ESC$\rangle$MANual ⏎

Figure 45

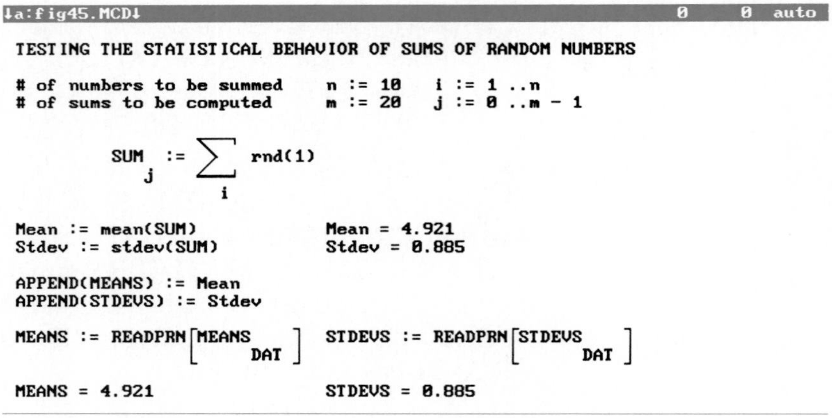

```
↓a:fig45.MCD↓                                           0      0   auto
TESTING THE STATISTICAL BEHAVIOR OF SUMS OF RANDOM NUMBERS

# of numbers to be summed    n := 10    i := 1 ..n
# of sums to be computed     m := 20    j := 0 ..m - 1

              SUM   :=  ∑   rnd(1)
                 j       i

Mean  := mean(SUM)           Mean = 4.921
Stdev := stdev(SUM)          Stdev = 0.885

APPEND(MEANS) := Mean
APPEND(STDEVS) := Stdev

MEANS := READPRN⎡MEANS  ⎤    STDEVS := READPRN⎡STDEVS  ⎤
                ⎣    DAT⎦                     ⎣     DAT⎦

MEANS = 4.921                STDEVS = 0.885
```

CUt the two bottom regions of the current worksheet (MEANS= and STDEVS=), and add regions as follows:

```
length(MEANS)= ⏎
MM:mean(MEANS) ⏎
MM= ⏎
SM:stdev(MEANS) ⏎
SM= ⏎
MS:mean(STDEVS) ⏎
MS= ⏎
SS:stdev(STDEVS) ⏎
SS= ⏎
```

Label and arrange them to suit yourself; Figure 46 shows one possible arrangement.

When you process (or if you have left automatic calculation on) with empty or near-empty data files, you'll get a lot of error messages until MEANS.DAT and STDEVS.DAT each contains two or three entries. Just ignore them and process again:

Figure 46

```
↓a:fig46.MCD↓                                            0      0   auto

TESTING THE STATISTICAL BEHAVIOR OF SUMS OF RANDOM NUMBERS

# of numbers to be summed    n := 10    i := 1 ..n
# of sums to be computed     m := 20    j := 0 ..m - 1
```

$$SUM_j := \sum_i rnd(1)$$

```
Mean := mean(SUM)           Mean = 4.921
Stdev := stdev(SUM)         Stdev = 0.885

APPEND(Means) := Mean
APPEND(Stdevs) := Stdev

MEANS := READPRN⌈Means   ⌉   length(MEANS) = 11
                ⌊    dat ⌋

Mean of means:     MM := mean(MEANS)    MM = 4.941
Stdev of means:    SM := stdev(MEANS)   SM = 0.157

STDEVS := READPRN⌈Stdevs  ⌉
                 ⌊    dat ⌋

Mean of stdevs:    MS := mean(STDEVS)   MS = 0.903
Stdev of stdevs:   SS := stdev(STDEVS)  SS = 0.041
```

MathCAD is just reminding you that you have to have at least two numbers in order to compute a standard deviation.

Each time that you process the file from now on, you'll see the length of the MEANS vector increase by one. STDEVS will grow too, of course, but we haven't asked to see it.

The four summary statistics *MM*, *MS*, *SM*, and *SS* also change at each replication. The changes tend to get smaller, though, since each new entry represents a smaller fraction of the growing vector and therefore has less influence on the total picture.

It's easy to get plots that show just how these means and standard deviations converge toward a single value.

First, add APPEND functions to the current worksheet to save the four statistics in new disk files:

```
APPEND(MM):MM ⏎
APPEND(SM):SM ⏎
APPEND(MS):MS ⏎
APPEND(SS):SS ⏎
```

This is your final statistical experiment generation worksheet. It should resemble Figure 47. By varying *n*, and *m*, you can investigate the distributions of different arrangements of sums of random numbers. By changing the definition of the *SUM* vector you can use the same general format to simulate much more complex statistical processes.

Save the final worksheet.

Type

```
F6 exprmnt ⏎
```

To start the six data files off on the same footing, go to DOS and delete what has already accumulated in MEANS.DAT and STDEVS.DAT:

```
⟨Esc⟩DOS ⏎ ⏎
del means.dat ⏎
del stdevs.dat ⏎
exit ⏎ ⏎
```

Each time you want to start a new series of experimental replications, you'll have to empty out MEANS.DAT and STDEVS.DAT, and also MM.DAT, SM.DAT, MS.DAT, and SS.DAT in this manner. For the moment, you don't have to bother with the last four: with automatic calculation off, they won't be created until the first time you process the worksheet.

Put fifty numbers into each file by processing the EXPERMNT worksheet fifty times:

⟨Esc⟩PROcess 🠔

⟨Esc⟩PROcess 🠔

.

.

.

⟨Esc⟩PROcess 🠔

Once again, be prepared at the outset for a barrage of error messages as MathCAD encounters empty vectors and can't compute the statistics you have ordered.

Figure 47

```
↓a:fig47.MCD↓                                              0     0   auto

TESTING THE STATISTICAL BEHAVIOR OF SUMS OF RANDOM NUMBERS

# of numbers to be summed     n := 10    i := 1 ..n
# of sums to be computed      m := 20    j := 0 ..m - 1


         SUM    :=  ∑   rnd(1)
             j       i


Mean := mean(SUM)             Mean = 4.921
Stdev := stdev(SUM)           Stdev = 0.885

APPEND(Means) := Mean
APPEND(Stdevs) := Stdev

MEANS := READPRN⎡Means  ⎤    length(MEANS) = 12
                ⎣    dat ⎦

Mean of means:    MM := mean(MEANS)    MM = 4.94
Stdev of means:   SM := stdev(MEANS)   SM = 0.15

STDEVS := READPRN⎡Stdevs  ⎤
                 ⎣     dat ⎦

Mean of stdevs:   MS := mean(STDEVS)   MS = 0.902
Stdev of stdevs:  SS := stdev(STDEVS)  SS = 0.039

APPEND(MM) := MM    APPEND(SM) := SM
APPEND(MS) := MS    APPEND(SS) := SS
```

Now save the EXPERMNT.MCD worksheet one more time, and clear the decks for a new worksheet. (Saving the worksheet is not really necessary — it hasn't changed since you first saved it — but it's wise to be compulsive about saving your work.)

Type

```
(F6) (↵)y(↵)
⟨Esc⟩CLear (↵)
```

In this display worksheet, redefine *MM*, *MS*, *SM*, and *SS* as vectors, rather than as variables as you did before. Fill each vector from the corresponding data file and display each statistic's convergence toward its theoretical value.

Use READPRN to read the MM.DAT data file, put its contents into a vector named *MM*, check its length, and set up a range variable, *k*, to index the members of *MM*:

```
MM:READPRN(MM.DAT) (↵)
K:length(MM) (↵)
k:0;K-1 (↵)
```

Read the other three data files, and set up a shorter range variable for the standard deviations, which are meaningful only for vectors longer than one number:

```
MS:READPRN(MS.DAT) (↵)
SM:READPRN(SM.DAT) (↵)
SS:READPRN(SS.DAT) (↵)
j:0;K-2 (↵)
```

Finally, set up a plot for each of the four vectors:

```
@k⟨Tab⟩⟨Tab⟩⟨Tab⟩MM[k (↵)
@j⟨Tab⟩⟨Tab⟩⟨Tab⟩SM[j (↵)
@k⟨Tab⟩⟨Tab⟩⟨Tab⟩MS[k (↵)
@j⟨Tab⟩⟨Tab⟩⟨Tab⟩SS[j (↵)
```

The result, after processing, should look like Figure 48. The four summary statistics level off fairly quickly: after perhaps twenty replications, you get a pretty good idea of where they're going to end up. To put a number on each, it helps to zoom in on the display.

Put a duplicate of each plot to its right. The easiest way is to place the cursor in the plot region, press (F2), move the cursor to the place where you wish to locate the copy, and press (F4).

Now choose vertical axis limits on the copy that narrow down the field of view to the immediate area of convergence; type these in place of the limits that MathCAD provided automatically.

Finally, add a reference grid: move the cursor into the region of the new plot, type

f

Figure 48

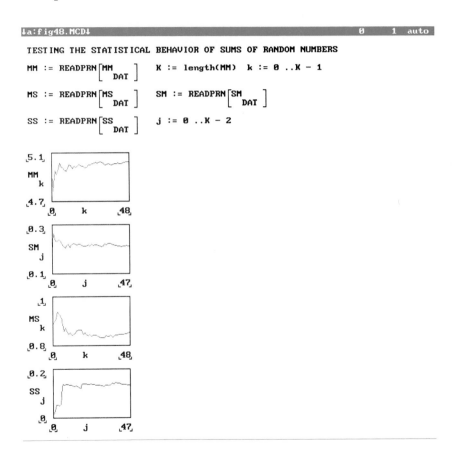

and change Subdivs=1,1 to Subdivs=10,1 in the message line at the top of the screen.

SAve ($\boxed{F6}$) the current worksheets as DISPSTAT.MCD.

Type

$\qquad$ $\boxed{F6}$DISPSTAT $\boxed{\downarrow}$

After processing, the result should look something like Figure 49.

Figure 49

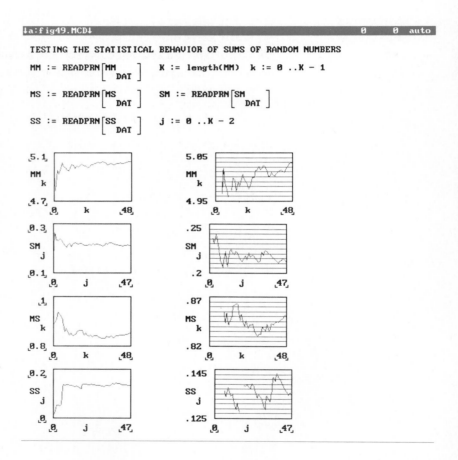

MM, the mean of the means, appears to be creeping up on its expected value of 5.00. *SM*, the standard deviation of the means, pretty clearly lies between 0.21 and 0.225. *MS*, the mean of the standard deviations, looks as if it will come out somewhere between 0.83 and 0.86. And *SS*, the standard deviation of the standard deviations, is wiggling around between 0.127 and 0.143.

You can have as much more precision as you want, of course; your patience imposes the only real limit.

Command Files

The basic statistical simulation worksheet EXPRMNT.MCD saves you some writer's cramp by automatically recording the results of a series of experimental trials, but you're still stuck with the tedious task of telling MathCAD to process each replication.

MathCAD's command file capability provides a way to automate this repetitious job. A MathCAD command file is an ordinary ASCII text file that consists of a series of MathCAD commands. When you issue the EXecute command and specify the name of the command file, MathCAD acts just as if you had issued the stored series of commands one at a time.

Let's modify EXPRMNT.MCD so that a command file will tell MathCAD to process it over and over.

Retrieve the basic simulation worksheet, if you saved it earlier as REPLIC.MCD. Or if not, retrieve EXPRMNT.MCD and CUt ((F 3)) all the regions below the two APPEND lines. The results should look like Figure 49a.

Now create a very simple command file named LOOP.MCC that processes the worksheet and loops back upon itself. It will contain just these two lines:

```
PROcess
execute loop
```

The first line processes the worksheet; the second reloads LOOP.MCC and starts it over in an infinite loop.

A command file can't include any file-access functions (READ, WRITE, APPEND, READPRN, WRITEPRN, APPENDPRN). A command file can contain any direct MathCAD command — any command that you normally issue after pressing ⟨Esc⟩. You can create it with any text editor, word processor, or other device that writes ASCII files.

A DOS Shell

Even without leaving MathCAD, DOS gives you at least two ways to create a command file: edlin and copy. We'll use copy here.

Issue the DOS command to gain access to DOS, and then press ⏎ again to set up a DOS shell.

Type

⟨Esc⟩DOS ⏎ ⏎

Your current DOS prompt appears.

Without the second ⏎ after ⟨Esc⟩DOS, you would have returned automatically to MathCAD after invoking a single DOS command. The second ⏎ sets up a DOS shell within which you can issue as many DOS commands as you like, ending with the exit command.

Figure 49a

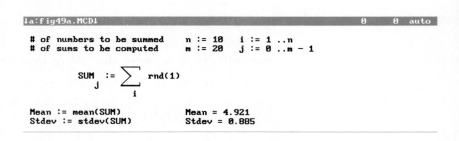

```
↓a:fig49a.MCD↓                                      0     0   auto

# of numbers to be summed    n := 10   i := 1 ..n
# of sums to be computed     m := 20   j := 0 ..m − 1

        SUM  := ∑ rnd(1)
           j     i

Mean  := mean(SUM)          Mean = 4.921
Stdev := stdev(SUM)         Stdev = 0.885
```

At the DOS prompt, copy your command file from the console (your PC keyboard) to a file named LOOP.MCC:

```
copy con: loop.mcc ⏎
process ⏎
calculate ⏎
execute loop ⏎
<Ctrl-Z> ⏎
```

If you make a mistake while typing a line, just use ⟨Bksp⟩ and fix it. But once you've pressed ⏎ at the end of a line, you have to go back and repeat the whole copy process to repair any errors.

Look at the result by typing the command file to your monitor screen:

```
type loop.mcc ⏎
```

Now return to MathCAD

```
exit ⏎ ⏎
```

The second ⏎ here (in response to MathCAD's prompt — actually, any ordinary keystroke will do) completes the exit command and puts you back where you were before your excursion into DOS. You'll have to wait a few moments while MathCAD reloads.

Execute the command file:

```
<Esc>EXecute loop ⏎
```

You will have to copy the *Mean* and *Stdev* numbers off the screen, since they are no longer being saved to a disk file.

When you have written down all the means and standard deviations that you care to collect, interrupt the loop.

Type

```
<Ctrl-Break>
```

Now, if you like, you can type the numbers you collected into ASCII files and read them in for further MathCAD processing using the READ and READPRN functions.

1. Try $m=200$, $m=1,000$ and $m=5,000$ (and some patience) to get smoother bell curves than the one in Figure 41.

2. Try making each of the $m=200$ sums out of $n=50$ random numbers, rather than $n=10$, for a finer grained picture.

3. with $n=10$ and $m=200$, break the display down into finer intervals by setting $N=100$.

4. Zoom in for a closer look by setting $n=50$, $m=200$, $N=n$, $MINSUM=20$, and $MAXSUM=30$.

5. Modify your worksheet FIG41.MCD to investigate the distribution of n ratios of random numbers between 1 and 2. Display the histogram and comment on the distribution.

3 Signal Processing

Electrical engineers devise sophisticated ways to make electromagnetic signals (like radio, television and telephone signals) carry more and more information with greater reliability. Complex signal processing schemes, well beyond the scope of this manual, respond to the challenges of noisy environments, a crowded transmission spectrum, power limitations, and jamming.

Figure 50 shows a pattern that is fairly typical of the waveforms that communications engineers have to work with. At first glance, it is not easy to see any order in all these wiggles, or how one might use them to transmit and receive information.

As it turns out, this waveform is made up of three simple components. MathCAD knows how to sort these components out and to make sense of them. This lab exercise illustrates the process of putting such a waveform together and taking it

Figure 50

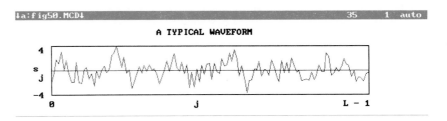

apart again, in order to demonstrate the breadth of Math-CAD's range of applications, as well as these features, which you have not yet encountered.

- The fast Fourier transform.
- Built-in trigonometric functions.
- Complex numbers.
- Numerical display format: zero tolerance.
- Graphic options.
  - Subdivisions (grid lines).
  - Error bars.

Figure 51 presents the problem in MathCAD format.

Figure 51

```
↓a:fig51.MCD↓                                    0      0    auto
```

MathCAD Tutorial Lab Exercise #3: SIGNAL PROCESSING

Modern electronic communications technology transmits information by means of complex waveforms. A single signal can carry multiple messages. Sophisticated coding can provide for security and enhance resistance to jamming and to degradation in the (omni)presence of noise.

Simulate and analyze a composite waveform on a MathCAD worksheet:

A. Set up a vector of time intervals over which to display the waveform. As the Fast Fourier Transform function requires, give it a length of

$$L := 2^m$$

where m is an integer.

B. Compose a waveform consisting of two superimposed sine waves, each with unit amplitude, and with additive noise of uniform frequency spectrum. Set it up so that you can easily adjust the frequencies of the two signals and the amplitude of the noise.

Note: with j := 0 ..L − 1 and frequency = a, one such sine wave is described by the formula:

$$\sigma_j := \sin\left[\frac{2 \cdot \pi \cdot a \cdot j}{L}\right]$$

C. Plot the waveform over its time domain.

D. Apply the Fast Fourier Transform to obtain an analysis of the frequency spectrum of the waveform. Display the spectrum as a plot in the frequency domain.

A few definitions will be helpful to begin with.

A **waveform** is the shortest representative sample of a repetitive wave pattern. If you think of the wave as a string of identical beads stretching forward and backward in time, then the waveform is one typical bead.

A **sine wave** is the smooth, wiggly curve that the sine function $\sin(x)$ generates. It is zero when its **argument** x is zero, and then again when x reaches π (pi= 3.14159...), and again each time x is equal to a multiple of π. See Figure 52.

The **amplitude** of the wave is the size of its wiggles — how far they deviate from zero. Figure 52 illustrates a sine wave with **unit amplitude**, that is, it oscillates between $+1$ and -1.

The wave's **frequency** is the number of times it repeats itself per unit time. If the plot in Figure 52 covers a total of one second, then it shows a frequency of 6 Hz (Hertz, or cycles per second). If the time span is one millisecond, then the figure indicates a frequency of 6 kHz.

To complete the description of a sine wave, you also have to specify its **phase** — the time (between $t = 0$ and $t = 2\pi$) at which the curve first crosses the x-axis on its way up. The wave in Figure 52 has a phase of zero. The cosine curve looks just like a sine curve, except that it starts out at 1 rather than at 0. You can think of it as a sine curve with phase $= \frac{3\pi}{2}$.

Fourier's theorem says that any waveform, even a messy one like the one in Figure 50, can be analyzed into a sum of simple sine waves, each with its own frequency, amplitude, and phase.

Figure 52

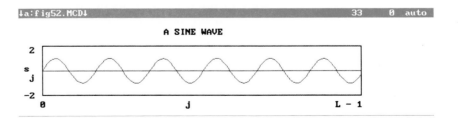

The Fourier transform, available in MathCAD, performs this analysis. Given data on the amplitude of the waveform at each of L evenly spaced points, it determines amplitude and phase for each of $\frac{L}{2}$ component sine waves, likewise spread out evenly in a **frequency spectrum**.

You can think of the frequency spectrum as a mathematical rainbow. Just as water droplets in the air break up white light into its component colors (frequencies) and spread them out to view, the Fourier transform displays the frequencies that add up to make a complex waveform.

If you were to compute the Fourier transform of the sine wave in Figure 52, you would expect it to show zero everywhere except for a spike at frequency = 6. At the other extreme, the Fourier transform of pure noise would show a contribution from each possible frequency, with the amplitudes of the component sine waves varying randomly in the vicinity of the overall noise amplitude, and with their phases varying randomly over the entire range from 0 to 2π.

All the information in the waveform is also contained in the frequency spectrum. The inverse Fourier transform, also available in MathCAD, turns the spectrum back into the waveform, without any loss of detail.

For a vector of real values, MathCAD's Fourier transform is fft(vector), and its inverse is ifft(vector). If your waveform includes complex values, the corresponding functions are cfft (vector) and icfft(vector).

Organizing the MathCAD Document

As you have seen, a bit of advance planning can save a lot of subsequent reorganization in a MathCAD document. Start with a clean slate.

Save ($\boxed{\text{F6}}$) what is already in the system, unless you're through with it for good.

F10 FC is equivalent to <Esc> CLear.

Clear (F10 FC) the worksheet.

F10 CM is equivalent of <Esc> MANual.

Turn off (F10 CM) automatic calculation.

Before entering anything on the new document, think about

- The displays you plan to create.
- The formulas that they require.
- The necessary definitions.

The Fast Fourier Transform (fft) Functions

The problem statement tells you to prepare a series of wave-forms, together with their frequency spectra as computed by means of MathCAD's fast Fourier transform (fft) function. In return for its superior speed, fft requires you to set up the waveform as a sequence of exactly 2^m evenly spaced samples of the signal over a period of time, beginning with sample number zero.

Therefore, you will set up a vector of time intervals, specifying it by m, by its length $L = 2^m$, and by its index

```
j: = 0 ..L-1.
```

With the cursor at the top left corner (0,0) enter a title for this worksheet.

```
"SIGNAL PROCESSING
```

Define the time scale of L intervals. Type

```
m:7 ⏎
L:2^m ⏎
j:0;L-1 ⏎
```

In a convenient location, label these definitions. Type

```
"Set up a vector of time intervals
```

Since you will want to vary the signal frequency, define it as a variable named a, assign it an initial value of 6, and label it.

Type

```
a:6 ⏎
```

Put the cursor in a suitable place, and insert a label. Type

```
"Frequency
```

Now we're ready to set up the signal vector, apply fft to it, and present pictures of the signal and its frequency spectrum.

Built-In Trigonometric Functions

MathCAD includes a full set of trigonometric functions.

sine, entered as	$\sin(z)$
cosine	$\cos(z)$
tangent	$\tan(z)$

together with their inverses

arcsine	$\text{asin}(z)$
arccosine	$\text{acos}(z)$
arctangent	$\text{atan}(z)$

MathCAD also provides the hyperbolic analogues of all six trigonometric functions: $\sinh(z)$, $\cosh(z)$, $\text{asinh}(z)$, $\text{acosh}(z)$, and $\text{atanh}(z)$.

Finally, the angle (x, y) function returns the angle (in radians, in the range from 0 to 2π) measured from the positive x-axis to the point (x, y) in the x-y plane.

The argument of each trigonometric or hyperbolic function, as well as the result of each inverse function, is normally expressed in radians.

If you want to express the argument in degrees instead, enter the following global definitions:

```
rad ~ 1 ⏎
deg ~ ⟨Alt-P⟩/180*rad
```

Then, append "*deg" to your argument.

We'll set up the signal as a simple sine wave s_j with unit amplitude and frequency a. Type

```
s[j:sin((2*⟨Alt-P⟩*a*j)/L) ⏎
```

Label the formula as

"Waveform

Graphic Options

To see the waveform, we'll set up a plot of s_j versus j.

With the cursor underneath what you've entered so far, type

@

Using the ⟨Tab⟩ key to move between placeholders, label the horizontal axis as j, running from 0 through $L-1$.

Label the vertical axis as s_j, running from -4 to $+4$. Move the cursor into the plot area, press

f

and adjust the format to provide a suitable size and a horizontal zero line: change subdivs=1,1 to subdivs=2,1.

These "subdivs" create the horizontal and vertical subdivisions or grid lines, that appear on the plot. Since you have labeled the vertical axis to run between $+4$ and -4, asking for two horizontal subdivisions creates a zero line across the plot.

Figure 53

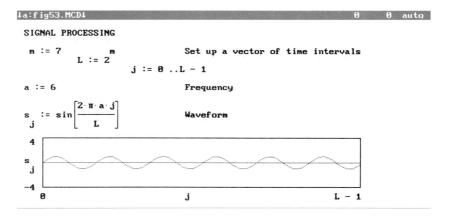

Set size= to suit yourself; Figure 53 shows a plot with size=6,60.

Press F9 to calculate.

The result should look something like Figure 53.

Now a look at the frequency spectrum. It is not very interesting thus far, since you have put only one pure frequency into the waveform. But it's useful to run a complicated function like this on a trivial case, just to make sure it's working correctly.

Start with a label. Type

```
"Analyze the waveform with ↵
the Fast Fourier Transform
```

The actual invoking of fft is very simple. Type

```
f:fft(s)   ↵
```

Note that the argument of the fft function is s, the name of the vector, not s_j, the name of its general member.

The resulting frequency spectrum is stored in the vector f, which has just one more than half as many members (that is, $2^{m-1}+1$) as has s. Let's set up its range variable, k.

Type

```
k:0;2^(m-1)   ↵
```

To display the spectrum, you need another plot.

With the cursor underneath what you've entered so far, type

```
@
```

Label the horizontal axis as k, running from 0 through 20.

It could extend farther, even all the way to $2^{m-1}=64$, but you don't need to see the whole spectrum, especially when it will show only one frequency.

Label the vertical axis by typing

```
|f[k,0
```

Set the limits as 0 through 8.

Press $\boxed{\text{F 9}}$.

The vertical bar (|) keystroke, located over the backslash($\backslash$), signals the absolute value (or, in the case of complex numbers, the magnitude) of a number.

Before proceeding with the frequency spectrum display, let's digress briefly to introduce the topic of complex numbers in MathCAD.

Complex Numbers

For each component frequency, the Fourier transform computes a **complex Fourier coefficient,** carrying both amplitude and phase information, and it stores it in the corresponding element of the vector f.

Each coefficient is a complex number of the form

    z=x+yi

where;

- i is the square root of -1
- x is the real part of the complex number
- y is the **imaginary part** of the complex number.

The MathCAD functions re(z) and im(z) return the real and imaginary parts, respectively, of their complex argument z.

MathCAD handles imaginary and complex numbers as easily as it does real numbers. It represents an imaginary number, or the imaginary part of a complex number, by appending i or j to the end of the number. It appends i by default, but if you want to show j instead, enter

    ⟨Esc⟩FORMat $\boxed{\rfloor}$

and change im=i to im=j.

The **magnitude** of the Fourier coefficient denotes the amplitude of the corresponding entry in the frequency spectrum. The size of this amplitude reflects the importance of its frequency in the waveform.

The phase, with which you are not directly concerned here, is given by $\tan^{-1}(y/x)$. MathCAD also provides a built-in function to compute phase.

The function arg(z) returns the angle (in radians) between the x-axis and the point $z=x+yi$ in the complex (x,y) plane, expressed in the range from $-\pi$ to $+\pi$. This is also called the "complex argument of z."

The magnitude $|z|$ of a complex number is given by

$$|z| = |x + yi| = x + y$$

To see this clearly, let's display the first elements of f in a table.

Set up an index. Type

    kk:1;12 ⏎

Request tables of kk, of f_{kk}, and of $|f_{kk}|$, spacing them out horizontally so that they line up conveniently. Type

    kk=⬆〈Ctrl-→ 〉f[kk=〈Ctrl-→ 〉〈Ctrl-→ 〉〈Ctrl-
    → 〉|f[kk= ⏎

Press F9 to calculate and display.

Global Output Formatting

The three tables you just created reveal a need for some global output formatting. They contain some very small numbers, on the order of 10^{-4}.

MathCAD will display such small numbers as zeros, if you tell it to. You've done **local** formatting already, to make individual numbers or tables of numbers look the way you want them to. Here, though, you need to change MathCAD's zero tolerance, and that's available only at the **global** level.

Type

    〈Esc〉FORMat ⏎

Change zt=15 to zt=10.

Press ⏎ to execute the change.

You have just changed the zero tolerance of all the numbers that MathCAD displays on this worksheet. Before the change, it treated all numbers smaller than 10^{-15} as zero; now, the threshold is 10^{-10}.

Move ($\boxed{\text{F 3}}$, $\boxed{\text{F 4}}$) the three tables to line them up with each other.

After this digression, it's time to get back to the spectrum plot you were working on.

You put a double label on the y-axis of this plot because you want to use the **error bar** format for the spectrum display. Error bars show up as vertical bars, highlighting the difference between the two y-axis variables. Listing zero as the second y-axis variable causes the bars to run between the x-axis and the f value.

Move the cursor into the plot area, press f and adjust format to provide suitable size and plot formats.

Set size= to suit yourself; Figure 54 shows a plot with size=6,58.

Change type=l to type=e to get the error bar display.

Label the plot as

        "FREQUENCY SPECTRUM

Press $\boxed{\text{F 9}}$ to calculate.

The result should resemble Figure 54, in which the single peak at frequency $k = 6$ is obvious.

Now let's proceed to a slightly more complex waveform by adding in a second sine wave. To this one, you will assign frequency b.

Near the definition a, type

        b:11 $\boxed{\lrcorner}$

With the cursor on the bracket at the right of the current waveform definition, type

        +sin((2*⟨Alt-P⟩*b*j)/L)

Press $\boxed{F9}$ to calculate. The result, reorganized somewhat into Figure 55, reveals a more interesting waveform, with exactly the double-peak spectrum that you would have expected. The only two nonzero entries in the frequency table are at 6 and 11.

Your waveform thus far oscillates just as far below zero as it does above it. Its average is zero; an electrical engineer would

Figure 54

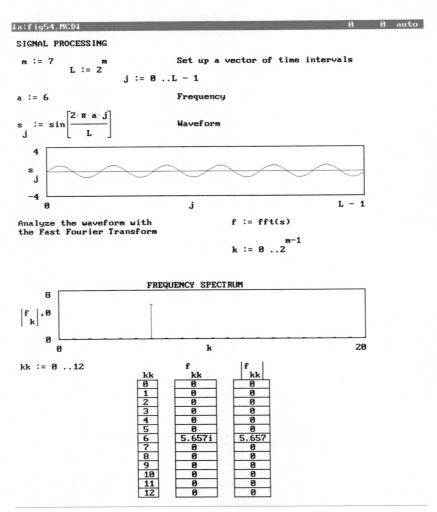

say that it shows no "DC (direct current) bias," and this is convenient for display purposes.

Now it's time to add in noise. The rnd function conveniently provides the required uniform spectrum; if we call the noise amplitude c, then rnd(c) will generate a number that is equally likely to take on any value between 0 and c.

Figure 55

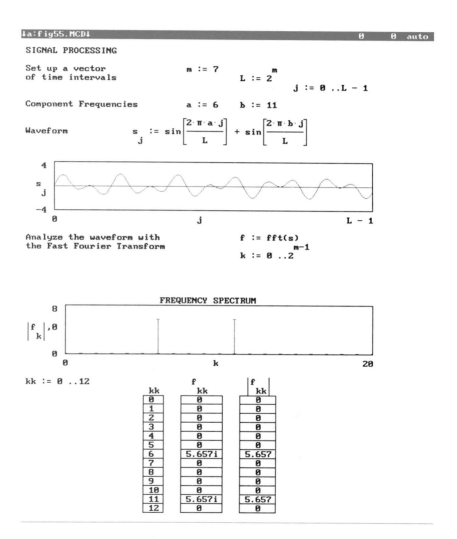

The average of rnd(c) is, of course, $\frac{c}{2}$. To avoid adding in the associated DC bias, we'll just subtract that average from the noise term.

Make room ($\boxed{\text{F 3}}$, $\boxed{\text{F 4}}$, $\langle$Ctrl–$\boxed{\text{F 9}}\rangle$) in the definitions section of your worksheet for the definition of the noise amplitude.

Type the label

```
"Noise Amplitude
```

and the definition

```
c:4 ⏎
```

With the cursor on the right bracket that ends the definition of the current waveform, type

```
+rnd(c)-c/2 ⏎
```

This time, you will want to see the full frequency spectrum, all the way out to the highest frequency (2^{m-1}) for which the Fourier transform computes a weight. So, change the upper limit of the frequency spectrum plot from 20 to 64.

Press $\boxed{\text{F 9}}$ to calculate.

This final spectrum shows the two signals sticking up above a noise level of randomly varying magnitude. Figure 56 (or your version of it) is suitable for submission to your instructor.

Save ($\boxed{\text{F 6}}$) and print ($\boxed{\text{F10}}$SP) your final worksheet, giving it a name.

Suggestions for Further Exploration

1. Try other frequencies and noise levels by varying a, b, and c.

2. Try sine waves with different amplitudes by introducing amplitude parameters d and e, multiplying the first and second sine wave terms, respectively.

Figure 56

SIGNAL PROCESSING

Set up a vector
of time intervals $m := 7$

$$L := 2^m$$

$$j := 0 \,..\, L - 1$$

Component Frequencies $a := 6$ $b := 11$

Noise Amplitude $c := 4$

Waveform $s_j := \sin\left[\dfrac{2 \cdot \pi \cdot a \cdot j}{L}\right] + \sin\left[\dfrac{2 \cdot \pi \cdot b \cdot j}{L}\right] + \mathrm{rnd}(c) - \dfrac{c}{2}$

Analyze the waveform with
the Fast Fourier Transform $f := \mathrm{fft}(s)$

$$k := 0 \,..\, 2^{m-1}$$

FREQUENCY SPECTRUM

$kk := 0 \,..\, 12$

kk	f_{kk}	$\lvert f_{kk} \rvert$
0	0.236	0.236
1	-0.768 + 0.601i	0.975
2	-0.185 + 0.2i	0.273
3	-1.022 - 1.594i	1.894
4	0.295 - 0.397i	0.494
5	0.529 - 1.072i	1.195
6	0.222 + 5.569i	5.573
7	-0.006 + 1.301i	1.301
8	-0.731 + 1.26i	1.457
9	0.385 - 0.797i	0.885
10	0.286 - 0.47i	0.55
11	0.187 + 5.492i	5.495
12	-0.744 - 0.29i	0.799

Hint: You can save in your waveform definition formula by predefining a function. Type

```
x(j):(2*⟨Alt-P⟩*j)/L ⏎
```

3. Turn the frequency and amplitude constants *a, b, c, d,* and *e* into functions of time.

4. Experiment with phase shifting by adding constant or variable terms into the arguments of the sine functions.

5. Add more terms to the waveform formula, as simple or as complex as you want.

4 Properties of e

Mathematics abounds in symmetries and surprises. There is great beauty in mathematical patterns, and some people have even found magical and religious significance in them.

At the center of many remarkable results is the number

e = 2.71828...

discovered by the great Scots mathematician John Napier in the sixteenth century. The number e is like the more familiar

π = 3.14159...

which we owe to Hippocrates, one of the Greek mathematical geniuses who flourished in the fifth century B.C. Like π, e is a **transcendental number**: its decimal fraction can be carried out to an infinite number of places without ever falling into a predictable pattern. This means, of course, that you can never write either number down exactly, and any numerical result that involves either of them is an approximation. Well, almost any numerical result, as we shall see.

In this fourth lab exercise, you will investigate and demonstrate a few of the surprising properties of e. You will also practice using several important MathCAD capabilities:

- Enabling and disabling equations
- Complex numbers
- Iteration
- Seeded iteration

- Global formatting of numerical results
- Differential and integral calculus
- Error tolerance adjustment
- Appending one document to another
- Generalizing a MathCAD document

Figure 57 sets forth the problem.

As always, start with a clean worksheet.

Save ($\boxed{F6}$) what is in the system, unless you just booted Math-CAD, or unless you're ready to throw away your previous work.

Clear ($\boxed{F10}$ FC) the worksheet.

Figure 57

```
↓a:fig57.MCD↓                                           2      1 calc F9
```

MathCAD Tutorial Lab Exercise #4:   PROPERTIES OF e

Mathematics has discovered several numbers with surprising and
useful properties.   For example:

    π = 3.1416..., the ratio between the circumference and the
      diameter of a circle;

   -1, the smallest integer that is "less than nothing";

   i, the "imaginary" square root of minus one; and

   e = 2.718..., the base of natural logarithms.

All of these turn up over and over in mathematics and in its
scientific and technological applications.   The number e, in
particular, seems to be fundamental to many kinds of
relationships.

Use a MathCAD worksheet to explore and illustrate some of e's
distinctive properties:

  A. Multiply i by π, and raise e to the resulting power.

      That is, compute $e^{i\pi}$

  B. Compute the value of e to eight decimal places.   HINT:

$$e := 1 + \frac{1}{1} + \frac{1}{1 \cdot 2} + \frac{1}{1 \cdot 2 \cdot 3} + \dots$$

  C. Using plots and tables, demonstrate that $f(x) := e^x$ is
      numerically equal both to its own derivative and to its own
      integral.

  D. Generalize the worksheet of Part C, and use it to show that
      other common functions are not equal to their own derivatives
      and integrals.

Turn off ((F10) CM) automatic calculation.

Move the cursor to the top left corner of the worksheet, if necessary, and type in as a text region (" ...) any header material you want.

Evaluating $e^{i\pi}$

Part A asks you to evaluate an odd-looking expression, combining three strange and unwieldy numbers. The task is very simple for MathCAD, although proving the result algebraically is certainly not. It is included here only because it is too beautiful and too improbable to leave out. It puts together four of the "magic numbers" of mathematics and asserts a relationship among them that nobody would guess in advance.

Type

```
e^(1i*〈Alt-P〉)= (↵) (F9)
```

Note that you enter the number i as 1i, to distinguish the imaginary unit from an ordinary variable that might be named "i." When you move the cursor out of the affected region, Math-CAD gets rid of the superfluous "1."

Despite the presence of two transcendental numbers and one imaginary number, Euler's identity

$$e^{i\pi} + 1 = 0$$

is *not* an approximation.

If the result in Figure 58 doesn't surprise you, then (1) you knew it already, (2) you peeked, or (3) you should apply immediately for membership in the American Academy of Mathematics.

Figure 58

```
↓a:fig58.MCD↓                                    0     0   auto

  PROPERTIES OF e

                     i ·π
  A.  EVALUATE   e

                   i ·π
             e         = -1
```

Since Part A took up so little space, you can put Part B on the same worksheet.

Move the cursor down two or three lines (⏎ will do the trick), and type in any header information you want.

Enter the infinite-series formula for *e*. Type

```
e:1+1/1+1/(1*2)+1/(1*2*3)+...
```

This last entry is only a label: "..." is not standard MathCAD notation. The actual formula setup requires a few steps.

You would get an error message if you were to order calculation now (with ⌐F9⌐ — or if you entered the formula with automatic calculation turned on). You don't want MathCAD to use this formula as such, so **disable calculation**.

Move the cursor into the region containing the formula. Press 〈Esc〉and type

```
EQuation ⏎
```

A small square will appear to the right of the formula to remind you that this expression is not participating in the mathematical structure of the worksheet. If you wish to reenable a disabled entry, repeat the same procedure.

Part B illustrates **seeded iteration**, a common and powerful mathematical process that MathCAD handles very conveniently. Most of the exercises thus far have required **iteration**, that is, the repetition of a calculation over a range of values of some participating variable.

Seeded iteration means that each successive computation depends on the result of the preceeding one, so that you have to supply the first result (the "seed") as part of the setup.

The formula implies an infinity of terms, and you can extend your evaluation as far as you wish in that direction. If the formula is well-behaved, you'll get more precision from each additional step. But the more terms you evaluate, the longer you'll have to wait for MathCAD to complete its calculations.

Since you do not know in advance how many terms of the series it will take to reach the required accuracy of eight decimal places, set up a variable number, N, of terms to be evaluated.

Type

```
N:20 ↵
```

Next, you will need an index that runs to $N-1$.

Type

```
k:0;N-1 ↵
```

Now you can tell MathCAD to fill up a vector named $term_k$ with the values of $N + 1$ terms of the series, from $term_0$ through $term_N$. First, we supply $term_0$.

Type

```
term[0:1 ↵
```

Next, we set up the rule that relates each term to the preceding one.

$term_1$ is $term_0$ divided by 1
$term_2$ is $term_1$ divided by 2
$term_3$ is $term_2$ divided by 3

.

.

.

$term_{k+1}$: is $term_k$ divided by $(k + 1)$

In MathCAD language, type

```
term[(k+1):term[k/(k+1) ↵
```

Figure 59 shows your progress to this point.

Now set up a vector est_k of successive estimates of the value of e, so that you can plot a graph to see how rapidly your estimates converge. At each step in the series, the cumulative sum of the terms is such an estimate. Type

```
est[0:term[0 ↵
est[(k+1):est[k+term[(k+1) ↵
```

Now you can plot a graph that shows the convergence of the series estimate.

With the cursor below the definitions and formulas, press @.

Label the vertical axis by typing

    est[k,e

over the place holder at its center.

This procedure will cause two curves to be plotted on the same axis: est_k, the successive estimates, and, for comparison, e itself, as MathCAD stores it internally.

Give the y-axis limits of 0 and 2.8.

Label the horizontal axis as k, with limits of 0 and N.

Adjust the size of the plot to suit yourself.

The result you seek is the value of est_k that gives you the required accuracy to eight decimal places. Here, a couple of tables will help.

Figure 59

↓a:fig59.MCD↓   0   0   auto

PROPERTIES OF e

A.   EVALUATE $e^{i \cdot \pi}$

$$e^{i \cdot \pi} = -1$$

B.   ESTIMATE e FROM AN INFINITE SERIES

The number e, the base of natural logarithms, may be estimated to any desired degree of precision by means of the following infinite series:

$$e := 1 + \frac{1}{1} + \frac{1}{1 \cdot 2} + \frac{1}{1 \cdot 2 \cdot 3} + \ldots \; \square$$

Range of terms: $N := 20$ $k := 0 \, .. N - 1$

Provide first term (the seed): $term_0 := 1$ $term_k$

Compute succeeding terms: $term_{k+1} := \dfrac{term_k}{k + 1}$

First, set up two partial ranges so that you can display a table with 20 entries in two segments. Type

```
k1:0;9  ↵
k2:10;20  ↵
```

Now, order the tables. Type

```
k1=  ↵
```

Then, a little to the right, type

```
est[k1=  ↵
```

Farther to the right, type

```
k2=  ↵
```

And farther yet, type

```
est[k2=  ↵
```

And finally, type F9 .

These tables don't show enough decimal places for our purpose. Therefore, to see more precision in the display, type

```
⟨Esc⟩FORMat  ↵
```

and change the global precision to pr=8.

Press F9 again.

Cut (F3) and paste (F4) as necessary to arrange the tables conveniently.

Press F9 yet again.

Figure 60 shows the results.

It appears that twelve terms (0 through 11) are enough to provide the accuracy you want:

```
= 2.71828183...
```

Summation notation gives you another way to display the final result. Type

```
e.N:k$term[k  ↵
e.N=  ↵
```

Figure 60

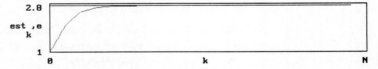

PROPERTIES OF e

A.   EVALUATE $e^{i \cdot \pi}$

$$e^{i \cdot \pi} = -1$$

B.   ESTIMATE e FROM AN INFINITE SERIES

The number e, the base of natural logarithms, may be estimated to any desired degree of precision by means of the following infinite series:

$$e := 1 + \frac{1}{1} + \frac{1}{1 \cdot 2} + \frac{1}{1 \cdot 2 \cdot 3} + \ldots \square$$

Range of terms: $N := 20$ $k := 0 .. N - 1$

Provide first term (the seed): $\text{term}_0 := 1$ term_k

Compute succeeding terms: $\text{term}_{k+1} := \dfrac{\text{term}_k}{k + 1}$

Successive estimates: $\text{est}_0 := \text{term}_0$ $\text{est}_{k+1} := \text{est}_k + \text{term}_{k+1}$

```
2.8 ┌──────────────────────────────────────┐
    │                                      │
est ,e
   k
  1 └──────────────────────────────────────┘
    0                   k                   N
```

$k1 := 0 .. 9$ $k2 := 10 .. 20$

$k1$	est_{k1}		$k2$	est_{k2}
0	1		10	2.7182818
1	2		11	2.71828183
2	2.5		12	2.71828183
3	2.66666667		13	2.71828183
4	2.70833333		14	2.71828183
5	2.71666667		15	2.71828183
6	2.71805556		16	2.71828183
7	2.71825397		17	2.71828183
8	2.71827877		18	2.71828183
9	2.71828153		19	2.71828183
			20	2.71828183

With the factorial operator (!), you can express the series even more elegantly. Type

```
e.N:k$1/k! ⏎
e.N= ⏎ F9
```

Clean up the worksheet, save it, and print it.

The result will look something like Figure 61.

Figure 61

PROPERTIES OF e

A. EVALUATE $e^{i \cdot \pi}$

$$e^{i \cdot \pi} = -1$$

B. ESTIMATE e FROM AN INFINITE SERIES

The number e, the base of natural logarithms, may be estimated to any desired degree of precision by means of the following infinite series:

$$e := 1 + \frac{1}{1} + \frac{1}{1 \cdot 2} + \frac{1}{1 \cdot 2 \cdot 3} + \ldots \square$$

Range of terms: $\qquad N := 20 \qquad k := 0 .. N - 1$

Provide first term (the seed): $\qquad term_0 := 1$

Compute succeeding terms: $\qquad term_{k+1} := \dfrac{term_k}{k + 1}$

Successive estimates: $\qquad est_0 := term_0 \qquad est_{k+1} := est_k + term_{k+1}$

$$
\begin{array}{c}
2.8 \\
est_k, e \\
1 \\
0 \qquad\qquad\qquad k \qquad\qquad\qquad N - 1
\end{array}
$$

$k1 := 0 .. 9 \qquad k2 := 10 .. 20$

k1	est$_{k1}$
0	1
1	2
2	2.5
3	2.66666667
4	2.70833333
5	2.71666667
6	2.71805556
7	2.71825397
8	2.71827877
9	2.71828153

k2	est$_{k2}$
10	2.7182818
11	2.71828183
12	2.71828183
13	2.71828183
14	2.71828183
15	2.71828183
16	2.71828183
17	2.71828183
18	2.71828183
19	2.71828183
20	2.71828183

$$e_N := \sum_k term_k$$

$$e_N = 2.71828183$$

$$e_N := \sum_k \frac{1}{k!}$$

$$e_N = 2.71828183$$

Calculus in MathCAD

Parts C and D will give you a feel for one of the most useful properties of *e*. As it turns out, the exponential function

$$f(x) = e^x$$

is both its own derivative (in differential calculus) and its own indefinite integral (in integral calculus).

What is more, it is the only function for which this statement is true except for two trivial exceptions: $f(x) = ke^x$, which differs from $f(x) = e^x$ only by a constant factor, and $f(x) = 0$. This property of e comes in exceedingly handy in the study of calculus.

Now use MathCAD to verify this claim (and to clarify its meaning, in case you are not very familiar with derivatives and integrals).

First of all, let's clear the screen once again.

Save (F6) what's in the system, unless you have already done so.

Clear (F10 FC) the worksheet.

Turn off (F10 CM) automatic calculation.

Head your worksheet with any text you choose.

The Derivative

The derivative of a function $f(t)$ with respect to t, written as

$$\frac{\mathrm{df}(t)}{\mathrm{d}t}$$

is the rate at which the function changes when t changes. On a plot of $f(t)$ versus t, the derivative is the slope of the graph. If the graph is a straight line, the derivative is a constant; if the graph is a curve, the derivative changes from point to point along the curve.

For $f(t) = e^t$, the derivative at each point is equal to e^t.

The plot of de^t/dt versus t should therefore look just like the plot of e itself.

Test it out now for a few values of t. Set up a range variable t, and let it range between 0 and 5.

Type

t:0;5 ⏎

Now order up plots of e^t and de^t/dt versus t.

Type

@

Label the horizontal axis as t, the vertical axis as e^t, and press F9 to have MathCAD choose axis limits as it draws the graph.

With the cursor inside the plot area, type f and adjust the plot's size to your liking.

That takes care of e^t vs. t. Now, rather than starting from scratch for the plot of the derivative, just copy and then edit the one you just made.

With the cursor still in the plot region, type F2 to make a copy of the region.

Move the cursor below the plot region, and type F4.

Change the middle label of the vertical axis to invoke the derivative, as follows.

Place the cursor at the immediate right of the t in e^t, and backspace until the label has vanished and is replaced by a square placeholder.

With the cursor on the placeholder, type

t?e^t

Press F9.

The result should resemble Figure 62, in which the two curves certainly do look very much alike.

The Integral

Now check the integral in the same fashion. In a plot of $f(t)$ versus t, the integral is the area between the curve and the x-axis. For $f(t) = e^t$, once again, you expect the integral plot to look like the derivative plot, which resembles the plot of the function e^t itself.

Figure 62

PROPERTIES OF e

C. Demonstrate that $f(x) := e^x$ is numerically equal both to its own derivative and to its own integral.

$t := 0 ..5$

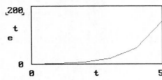

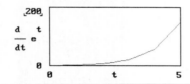

Appending Previously Saved Documents

MathCAD's append feature lets you add to a current document another document that you have previously saved to disk. In this context, appending doesn't save any time and may even cost a little, but it's a handy feature that you should learn to use.

For safety's sake, save the current document as DERIV.MCD.

Type

    F6 deriv ↵

F7 is equivalent to <Esc> SPlit.

Put the cursor on a line that lies a little above the middle of the screen, and press F7 to open a window ("split" the screen).

F8 is equivalent to <Esc> SWitch.

Press F8 to switch the cursor back to the top window.

Put the cursor in the region of the plot you most recently created, and press F2 to copy it.

Press $\boxed{\text{F8}}$ to switch the cursor back to the bottom window, and type $\boxed{\text{F4}}$ again.

This window hasn't heard of the variable *t*; so you will have to provide the definition.

Press $\langle$Ctrl–$\boxed{\text{F9}}\rangle$ twice to insert two blank lines, and type

$$t:0;5$$

This time, change the middle label of the vertical axis to invoke the integral.

Place the cursor at the immediate right of the *t* in e^t, and backspace until the label has vanished and is replaced by a square placeholder.

With the cursor on the placeholder, type &.

Replace the resulting four place holders, as follows:

- Put zero at the bottom of the integral sign and put *t* at the top.
- Put e^x (keystrokes: e^x) to the left of the *d*, and *x* to its right.

Press $\boxed{\text{F9}}$.

Now, you will save the contents of the bottom window to a temporary file and then append it to the contents of the top window.

Type

$$\boxed{\text{F6}}\ \text{temp}\ \boxed{\downarrow}$$

$\langle$Ctrl–$\boxed{\text{F7}}\rangle$ is equivalent to $\langle$Esc$\rangle$ Unsplit.

Press $\langle$Ctrl–$\boxed{\text{F7}}\rangle$ to close the lower window ("unsplit" the screen).

Type

$$\langle\text{Esc}\rangle\text{APpend temp}\ \boxed{\downarrow}$$

Except for the redundant definition of *t* just above the third plot, this is the result you were looking for.

Ctrl–$\boxed{\text{F10}}$ is equivalent to $\langle$Esc$\rangle$ DEleteline.

Delete ($\boxed{\text{F3}}$) the region containing the extra definition of *t*, and close up any unwanted blank space with $\langle$Ctrl–$\boxed{\text{F10}}\rangle$.

The result should look like Figure 63. The third curve, which you just added, plots the definite integral (area under the curve) of $f(x) = e^x$ from zero to t, for t from zero to 5.

As predicted, the integral curve looks very much like the other two. If you examine it closely, however, you'll notice that it is very slightly lower.

It is lower because the integral of e^x that is exactly equal to e^t is the integral from minus infinity to t. You have evaluated the integral from zero to t, thus neglecting the small piece of the area under the curve that lies between minus infinity and zero. The lower limit was set to zero instead of minus infinity

Figure 63

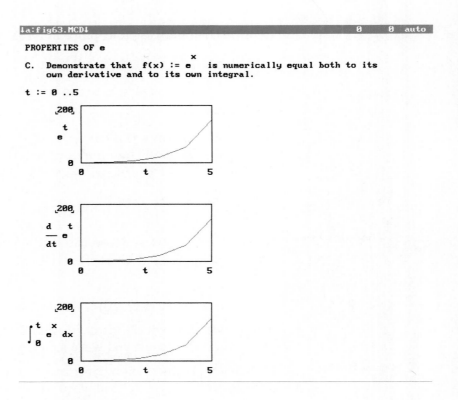

because MathCAD's numerical approximation routines don't deal well with infinities.

How small is the area from minus infinity to zero? Well, as demonstrated in this exercise, the integral of e^t from minus infinity to x is equal to e^x. For $x = 0$, therefore, it is $e^0 = 1$. So you can expect the integral curve, as defined here, to lie just one unit lower than the curves of the derivative and function.

The plots are too crude to show such small differences. You can create tables, so that you can compare the numbers directly.

With the cursor to the right of the top of the first plot, type

    t= ⏎

To the right of that, type

    e^t= ⏎

Similarly, put tables of t and of de^t/dt at the side of the second plot. For the derivative, once again, the keystroke sequence is

    t?e^t= ⏎

And finally, put tables of t and of the integral beside the third plot. For the integral, type

    t&f(t)

Replace the two limit placeholders by zero and t as before. Type

    = ⏎

Press F9 .

Figure 64 shows the result.

Error Tolerance

The numbers in the first table seem to correspond exactly to those in the second, as expected. And each number in the third table is about one smaller than its counterpart in the other tables. But compare the values for $t=5$.

Though they correspond quite closely, they're not exactly the same. In fact, if we change the precision to eight decimal places by using ⟨Esc⟩FORMat, none of the numbers match.

What accounts for the difference? Have we disproved the theory? Or is MathCAD just sloppy with its numbers?

The fact of the matter is that MathCAD uses numerical approximation routines to evaluate derivatives and integrals, and it's just as precise or as sloppy as you tell it to be.

As with the infinite series that you evaluated in Part B, Math-CAD *could* keep those approximations going forever, getting more and more precise. But then it would never finish, and you would never get the answer. Just as you stopped evaluating the series when it had given you the eight decimal places you wanted, MathCAD has to know when enough is enough,

Figure 64

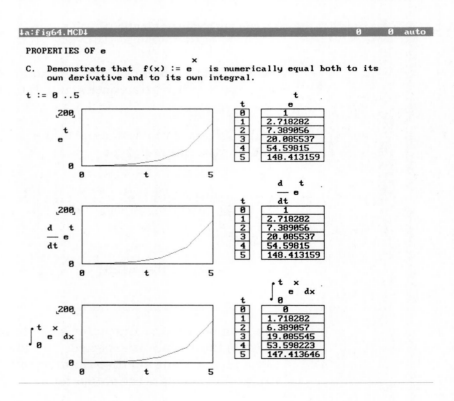

somewhere between an unacceptably inaccurate answer now and a perfect one many years hence.

MathCAD finds out when to stop from a built-in constant called **TOL**. Unless you change it, TOL defaults to 10^{-3}. That is, it stops the approximation process as soon as the results of successive iterations, rounded off, differ only in the third decimal place.

You can change TOL with a simple definition, local or global. You can change TOL as many times as you like within a document. Try it now.

With the cursor at some convenient spot above the plots, type

$\qquad$ TOL:10^-5 ⏎

Press F9.

Be patient. Figure 65 shows the result. Now the tables match perfectly to the three decimal places displayed. In fact, they also correspond exactly to four decimal places. To check, type

$\qquad$ 〈Esc〉FORMat

and set pr=4.

TOL is one of a small class of MathCAD system variables that you can choose to reset for all your work, rather than for one document at a time. If you type

$\qquad$ 〈Esc〉SET

you will see a menu of system variables from which to choose. Put the cursor on TOL and press

$\qquad$ ⏎

The message line displays the current value of TOL for you to edit and accept. Any value you assign there will last until the end of your current MathCAD session.

You can also save this value of TOL for subsequent MathCAD sessions, along with other useful settings, such as a printer selection with the command CONfigsave. See the Reference Section for more information.

Figure 65

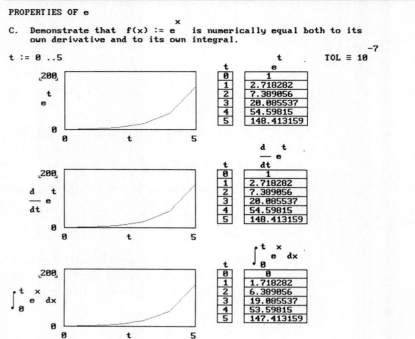

PROPERTIES OF e

C. Demonstrate that $f(x) := e^x$ is numerically equal both to its
    own derivative and to its own integral.

$t := 0 \,..5$ t $TOL \equiv 10^{-7}$
                                                       e

t	e^t
0	1
1	2.718282
2	7.389056
3	20.085537
4	54.59815
5	148.413159

$\dfrac{d}{dt} e^t$

t	$\dfrac{d}{dt} e^t$
0	1
1	2.718282
2	7.389056
3	20.085537
4	54.59815
5	148.413159

$\displaystyle\int_0^t e^x \, dx$

t	$\displaystyle\int_0^t e^x \, dx$
0	0
1	1.718282
2	6.389056
3	19.085537
4	53.59815
5	147.413159

Generalizing a MathCAD Document

Part D of the lab asks that we generalize the worksheet of
Figure 65 to test functions other than $f(x) = e^x$ to see if any of
them might also be equal to their own derivatives or integrals.

First, generalize the limits of the test, so that MathCAD can
investigate ranges other than $t = 0...5$.

Delete (F3) the range definition "t := 0 ..5" at the top of the
worksheet. Replace it with

> t1:0 ⏎
> T:5 ⏎
> t:t1;T ⏎

Move ($\boxed{\text{F 3}}$ $\boxed{\text{F 4}}$) these three entries onto the same line to save space. Label them, if you like; "Limits of the test" would be a good label.

Now that t is defined, we can define the function to be tested. For the moment, let's stick with e^t.

Insert two lines (⟨Ctrl–$\boxed{\text{F 9}}$⟩ twice) below the range definition.

Enter a label at the left of the new open space. Type

```
"The function: ⏎
```

Enter the function to the right of the label. Type

```
f(t):e^t ⏎
```

Change the limits on the horizontal axis of each of the three plots: they should now run from $t1$ to T, instead of from 0 to 5.

Also, change e^t to $f(t)$ in the vertical-axis labels of the first two plots, and at the tops of the associated tables.

Similarly, change e^x to $f(x)$ in the label and table of the third plot. Also change the lower limit of the integration: replace 0 with $t1$ at the bottom of the integral sign.

Press $\boxed{\text{F 9}}$. Figure 66 shows the result.

Now you can use the worksheet to compare a couple of common functions to their derivatives and integrals, to verify that they, unlike e^t, are not self-differentiating and self-integrating. Start with $f(x) = t^2$.

Edit the definition of $f(t)$, changing it from e^t to t^2.

Order document-wide calculation with the PROcess command. Type

```
⟨Esc⟩PROcess ⏎
```

Figure 67 shows the result. You clearly don't need the precision of the tables to see that the three plots represent different curves. A glance at the three different scales on the vertical axes confirms this impression.

Now try another function.

Figure 66

PROPERTIES OF e

**D.   This display compares a function with its derivative
and with its definite integral.**

$$TOL \equiv 10^{-2}$$

Limits of the test: t1 := 0   T := 5   t := t1 ..T

The function: $f(t) := e^t$

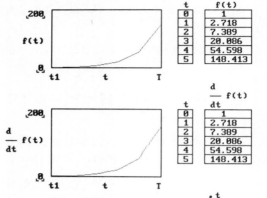

t	f(t)
0	1
1	2.718
2	7.389
3	20.086
4	54.598
5	148.413

t	$\frac{d}{dt} f(t)$
0	1
1	2.718
2	7.389
3	20.086
4	54.598
5	148.413

t	$\int_{t1}^{t} f(x)\,dx$
0	0
1	1.718
2	6.389
3	19.086
4	53.598
5	147.414

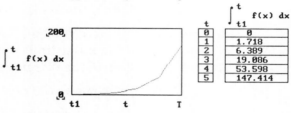

Edit $f(t)$ again, this time changing it to 10^t.

As Figure 68 shows, the three plots look alike, just as they did in the case of e^t. The similarity of curve shape seems to be associated with exponential functions. But the scales of the three curves are very different. Self-differentiation and self-integration appear indeed to be properties of only one very specific exponential function.

The quest for further self-differentiating and self-integrating functions seems hopeless, but make one more try.

Figure 67

PROPERTIES OF e

D. This display compares a function with its derivative
and with its definite integral.

$$TOL \equiv 10^{-2}$$

Limits of the test: t1 := 0   T := 5   t := t1 ..T

The function: $f(t) := t^2$

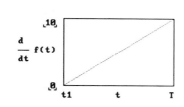

t	f(t)
0	0
1	1
2	4
3	9
4	16
5	25

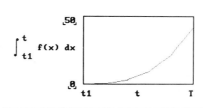

$\dfrac{d}{dt} f(t)$

t	$\dfrac{d}{dt} f(t)$
0	0
1	2
2	4
3	6
4	8
5	10

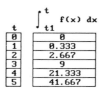

$\displaystyle\int_{t1}^{t} f(x)\, dx$

t	$\displaystyle\int_{t1}^{t} f(x)\, dx$
0	0
1	0.333
2	2.667
3	9
4	21.333
5	41.667

Edit the function definition, changing it to a sine function.

Delete (F3) the current definition. In its place, type

```
f(t):sin(<Alt-P>*t/T) ⏎
```

Press F9 .

As Figure 69 indicates, you are only getting further and further from similarity. Q.E.D.

Figure 68

PROPERTIES OF e

D. This display compares a function with its derivative
and with its definite integral.

$$TOL \equiv 10^{-2}$$

Limits of the test: t1 := 0   T := 5   t := t1 ..T

The function: $f(t) := 10^t$

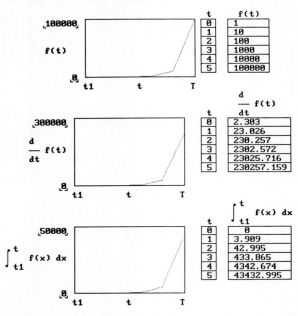

t	f(t)
0	1
1	10
2	100
3	1000
4	10000
5	100000

$$\frac{d}{dt} f(t)$$

t	$\frac{d}{dt}f(t)$
0	2.303
1	23.026
2	230.257
3	2302.572
4	23025.716
5	230257.159

$$\int_{t1}^{t} f(x)\,dx$$

t	$\int_{t1}^{t} f(x)\,dx$
0	0
1	3.909
2	42.995
3	433.865
4	4342.674
5	43432.995

Suggestions for Further Exploration

1. Compare selected numerical values of

    $$f(x) = \cos(x)$$

    with corresponding values of

    $$g(x) = \frac{1}{2}\left(e^{ix} + e^{-ix}\right)$$

2. Replicate the bell curve in Figure 37 by plotting the derivative of the cumulative normal function, cnorm(x) for x from

−4 to +4. The normal is a particularly interesting and important exponential function of e.

3. Modify the worksheet of Figure 61 to compute π to eight decimal places. Hint:

$$\frac{\pi}{4} = 1 - \frac{1}{3} + \frac{1}{5} - \frac{1}{7} + \cdots$$

4. Contrast the efficiency of this series with that of the series with which you computed e.

Figure 69

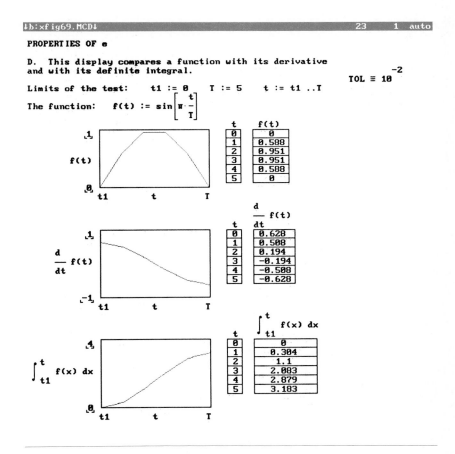

5. Modify the worksheet of Figure 66 to compare a longer segment of a sine curve with its derivative and integral. Use the function

$$f(t) = \sin(4\pi t/T)$$

To get smooth curves, you'll need to set T a lot higher than 5 (and you'll need to have patience while MathCAD completes the calculation). You'll also find that the tables get in the way; feel free to delete them.

Comment on the curious form of self-differentiation and self-integration that the sine curve exhibits. It's fundamental to the mathematical description of a lot of important phenomena (the propagation of light, for example).

5 Matrices

The shorthand of matrix algebra has become central to mathematically based science, engineering, and pure mathematics. Release 2.0 of The Student Edition of MathCAD includes a full range of matrix operations, extending MathCAD's capacities and convenience to a significant degree.

In this tutorial, we shall run quickly through several applications of matrix notation and related features:

- solving simultaneous equations
- simultaneous parallel calculations with the vec operator
- correlational and regression analyses with matrices

These applications will give you practice in manipulating matrices in MathCAD. When you have finished the tutorial, you will be able

- to enter matrices of various sizes, by hand and from disk storage
- to transpose a matrix
- to partition a matrix
- to multiply matrices
- to compute the determinant of a matrix
- to invert a matrix
- to define several constants and variables simultaneously in vector format
- to vectorize parallel calculations for simultaneous computation

- to solve a system of simultaneous equations and inequalities with a MathCAD solve block
- to save a matrix to a disk file

MathCAD offers a lot of other matrix operations; the Reference Section discusses them exhaustively. This tutorial will give you enough practice to be comfortable with MathCAD's distinctive way of handling matrices.

This tutorial assumes that you are already familiar with matrix algebra; if you need an introduction or a review, we recommend Appendixes A.7 and A.8 in Thomas and Finney, *Calculus and Analytic Geometry*, 7th Edition (Addison-Wesley, 1988) as a clear, compact summary of the subject.

Solving Simultaneous Equations with Matrices

Our first example, in fact, is borrowed from Thomas and Finney (pp. A-32 through A-36). The authors compute the determinant and inverse of the matrix through elementary row operations; you'll accomplish the same purpose by telling MathCAD what you want. You may enjoy the contrast that you'll observe if you follow the example in both books at once.

The problem is to solve a simple system of three simultaneous equations in three unknowns:

$$2x+3y-4z=-3$$
$$x+2y+3z=3$$
$$3x-y-z=6$$

Unless these relationships are redundant, there should be one and only one set of values of x, y, and z for which all three equations hold true.

The specified system of equations is equivalent, by definition, to the single matrix equation.

$$AX = B$$

where $A = \begin{vmatrix} 2 & 3 & -4 \\ 1 & 2 & 3 \\ 3 & -1 & -1 \end{vmatrix}$, $X = \begin{vmatrix} x \\ y \\ z \end{vmatrix}$, and $B = \begin{vmatrix} -3 \\ 3 \\ 6 \end{vmatrix}$

Premultiplying each side of this equation by A^{-1} (the inverse of A), we obtain

$$A^{-1}AX = X = A^{-1}B$$

So, if we can invert A, the solution matrix X will be ours by simple matrix multiplication. MathCAD makes the task easy. Let's approach it step by step.

Enter matrices A and B by typing:

```
A:⟨Alt-M⟩3 3 ⏎
2⟨Tab⟩1⟨Tab⟩3⟨Tab⟩3⟨Tab⟩2⟨Tab⟩−1⟨Tab⟩⟨Tab⟩
−4⟨Tab⟩⟨Tab⟩3⟨Tab⟩−1 ⏎
B:⟨Alt-M⟩⟨Bksp⟩⟨Bksp⟩⟨Bksp⟩3 1 ⏎
−3⟨Tab⟩⟨Tab⟩3⟨Tab⟩6 ⏎
```

Now let's check the determinant of A, to make sure that the three equations are really independent. If they're redundant, the determinant will be zero. Without MathCAD, this is a very tedious computation; with MathCAD it is a very simple task. In a matrix context, the usual symbol for absolute value calls for a determinant. Type

```
¦A=
```

The determinant is 60 — definitely not zero. So, we may proceed to compute the inverse of A. Like the inverse or reciprocal of a number, the inverse of a matrix is its negative first power. Again, MathCAD does all the work. Type

```
A^−1=
```

To check MathCAD's work, premultiply A by its inverse:

```
A^−1*A=
```

The result, as expected, is the 3×3 unit matrix. Now we only need to perform one other simple multiplication to obtain the solution matrix X. Type

```
X:A^−1*B ⏎
X=
```

To check MathCAD's work once again, substitute the values of x, y, and z into the original equations.

Identify the elements of X with the individual variables x, y, and z:

```
⟨Alt-M⟩⟨Bksp⟩⟨Bksp⟩⟨Bksp⟩3 1 ⏎
x⟨Tab⟩y⟨Tab⟩z:⟨Alt-M⟩ ⏎
2⟨Tab⟩-1⟨Tab⟩⟨Tab⟩1 ⏎
```

The vector format provides a convenient, compact way to define or evaluate several constants or variables at once. You saw this approach in Tutorial #2 used as an alternative way to tabulate empirical and theoretical statistics for easy comparison.

Finally, enter the left-hand sides of the original equations as MathCAD expressions. Type

```
2*x+3*y-4*z= ⏎
x+2*y+3*z= ⏎
3*x-y-z= ⏎
```

The result, after some cleaning up and labeling, appears as Figure 70.

Solving Simultaneous Equations with a Solve Block

Not only does MathCAD simplify the labor of solving a system of simultaneous equations with matrices, it also offers the **solve block**, an even easier way to do the same thing. To show how it works, set up the system we just solved in a solve block.

Provide an initial "guess value" for each unknown.

```
x:2 ⏎
y:2 ⏎
z:2 ⏎
```

As in the case of the root function (Tutorial #1), these guesses don't have to be particularly close to the actual solutions. If you don't provide them, though, MathCAD will indicate that x, y, and z are undefined.

The solve block always begins with the keyword Given, followed by the **constraints** that the solution must obey. In this case, the constraints are the three simultaneous equations. In other cases, they might include both equations and inequalities. You enter the squiggly equals sign in a constraint

Figure 70

```
↓a:fig70.MCD↓                                          0    0   auto
```

Solve the following system of simultaneous linear equations (Thomas, pp. A32-37) by means of matrix operations:

$$2x + 3y - 4z = -3$$
$$x + 2y + 3z = 3$$
$$3x - y - z = 6$$

Set up matrices of coefficients:

$$A := \begin{bmatrix} 2 & 3 & -4 \\ 1 & 2 & 3 \\ 3 & -1 & -1 \end{bmatrix} \qquad B := \begin{bmatrix} -3 \\ 3 \\ 6 \end{bmatrix}$$

Compute the determinant of A:

$$|A| = 60$$

...and its inverse:

$$A^{-1} = \begin{bmatrix} 0.017 & 0.117 & 0.283 \\ 0.167 & 0.167 & -0.167 \\ -0.117 & 0.183 & 0.017 \end{bmatrix}$$

Check the inverse by multiplication:

$$A^{-1} \cdot A = \begin{bmatrix} 1 & 0 & 0 \\ 0 & 1 & 0 \\ 0 & 0 & 1 \end{bmatrix}$$

Compute the solution matrix X:

$$X := A^{-1} \cdot B \qquad X = \begin{bmatrix} 2 \\ -1 \\ 1 \end{bmatrix} \qquad \text{That is,} \quad \begin{bmatrix} x \\ y \\ z \end{bmatrix} := \begin{bmatrix} 2 \\ -1 \\ 1 \end{bmatrix} \quad \text{is the solution of the system of equations.}$$

Check by substitution in the original equations:

$$2 \cdot x + 3 \cdot y - 4 \cdot z = -3$$
$$x + 2 \cdot y + 3 \cdot z = 3$$
$$3 \cdot x - y - z = 6$$

equation by pressing ⟨Alt=⟩. (For the keystrokes ⟨Alt=⟩ and ⟨Alt−⟩ — vectorize — we have omitted the dash used in other such combination keystrokes, like ⟨Alt–M⟩. ⟨Alt=⟩ should be typed ⟨Alt–equals⟩, and ⟨Alt−⟩ should be typed ⟨Alt–minus⟩.) Type

```
Given ↵
2*x+3*y−4*z⟨Alt=⟩−3 ↵
x+2*y+3*z⟨Alt=⟩3 ↵
3*x−y−z⟨Alt=⟩6 ↵
```

The Find function tells MathCAD that you are through entering constraints and want the solution.

Specify the elements of the solution (x, y, and z) as arguments of the Find function:

```
X:Find(x,y,z) ↵
```

Finally, display the solution vector X:

```
X=
```

Figure 71 shows the results.

Figure 71

MathCAD Tutorial Lab Exercise #5:   MATRIX ALGEBRA

Now solve the same system with a MathCAD solve block:

Start by providing a guess value for each of the three unknowns.   If
you don't, MathCAD will tell you that they are undefined.

Guess values: x := 2   ▪ y := 2   z := 2

The block begins with the keyword "Given", followed by the specified
constraints:

Given

$$2 \cdot x + 3 \cdot y - 4 \cdot z \approx -3$$
$$x + 2 \cdot y + 3 \cdot z \approx 3$$
$$3 \cdot x - y - z \approx 6$$

$$X := Find(x,y,z)$$

$$X = \begin{bmatrix} 2 \\ -1 \\ 1 \end{bmatrix}$$

...just as before.

Simultaneous Calculation with the Vectorization (vec) Operator

While we're on a digression from the subject of matrices, let's introduce the related topic of **vectorization**.

We saw in Tutorial #4, Properties of *e*, that we could compute the number *e* to any desired degree of precision by adding a sufficient number of terms from the infinite series defined in Figure 72.

With only a slight elaboration of the series formula, as illustrated in Figure 73, we can compute not only *e* itself but any desired power of *e*. At the same time, we can illustrate Math-CAD's ability to perform many related calculations simultaneously.

In Tutorial #1, you learned that this kind of MathCAD formula makes it easy to calculate one value of *y* at a time. All you have to do is to change the value of *x*, let MathCAD do the calculation, and record the result.

Figure 72

```
↓a:fig72.MCD↓                                        11     1   auto
```

Simultaneous Calculation with the VEC Operator

Compute the number e, to any desired degree of precision, from an
infinite series:

N := 15   k := 0 ..N - 1

$$e := \sum_{k} \frac{1}{k!}$$ e = 2.718

Range variables further automate the process of multiple calculations, one at a time: we could

- define a range variable j,
- set up a vector x_j,
- replace x with x_j in the formula, and
- tell MathCAD to iterate through each value of j in turn, evaluating the formula for each value.

This works fine, but it's slow, and the subscript on x detracts somewhat from the elegance of the series formula.

Suppose that x in the summation formula shown in Figure 73 is not a single number, but the name of a vector.

Try predefining x as a three-element vector with the values 2, 2.5, and 4, as shown in Figure 74.

Figure 73

```
↓a:fig73.MCD↓                                         0     0   auto
```

Compute e to the power x, to any desired degree of precision, from an
infinite series:

N := 15   k := 0 ..N - 1   x := 2

$y := e^{x}$

$$y := \sum_{k} \frac{x^{k}}{k!}$$ y = 7.389

Suddenly, MathCAD no longer knows how to interpret the formula and flags it as an "illegal vector operation."

Now vectorize the formula by moving the cursor onto the summation sign and pressing ⟨Alt−⟩.

The arrow that now appears over the formula in Figure 74 indicates that MathCAD will carry out the summation for each of the three values in the x vector independently and simultaneously, generating the result, y, in the form of a similar three-element vector.

What is more, it will perform the calculation much more rapidly than if you had set up the equivalent range variable x_i, with

$$i := 1 \ ..3$$

The ⟨Alt−⟩ keystroke (the vec operator) for vectorization acts on expressions or parts of expressions by the same rules as the ⟨Ctrl−F3⟩ keystroke cuts parts of regions. The main difference is that ⟨Ctrl−F3⟩ will nearly always cut something, whereas vec makes sense in only certain situations. MathCAD will let you know when you try to vectorize something nonsensical. The Reference Section discusses the rules for applying the vec operator correctly.

Figure 74

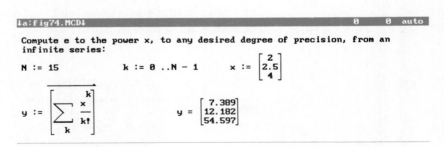

A typical research study collects a number (J) of pieces of information on each of its N subjects. It then organizes the resulting data into a rectangular **raw-data matrix** of J columns and N rows. Statistical computer programs begin with raw data and massage them into matrices of correlations, vectors of regression coefficients, and other numbers that help the researcher see the patterns in the data and decide whether they are likely to have arisen by chance.

MathCAD has a built-in function (corr (v_1, v_2)) that computes the correlation between two vectors containing paired data. Formulated in matrix algebra, the process turns out to be rather simple. An example will help you understand it.

We borrow a small raw-data matrix from Schaefer and Anderson, *The Student Edition of Minitab* (Addison-Wesley, 1989). It is saved as BLOOD.PRN on your Auxiliary Disk. For each of nine cases (people), it contains data on four variables:

> $V1$: Blood pressure (points above normal)
> $V2$: Overweight (kilograms)
> $V3$: Saturated fat consumed (grams per day)
> $V4$: Exercise (minutes per day)

We are predisposed to expect $V2$ and $V3$ to correlate positively with $V1$ (fatter people and fatter diets go with higher blood pressure), while $V1$ and $V4$ should show a negative correlation (more exercise lowers blood pressure). Do the calculation and see if it bears out these expectations.

Read the raw data matrix in from BLOOD.PRN and display it:

```
Y:READPRN(blood)  ⏎
Y=
```

Define the dimensions of the matrix:

```
⟨Alt-M⟩⟨Bksp⟩⟨Bksp⟩⟨Bksp⟩2 1  ⏎
N⟨Tab⟩J: ⟨Alt-M⟩  ⏎
9⟨Tab⟩4  ⏎
```

Or, alternatively, read the dimensions directly off the matrix:

```
N:rows(Y) ⏎
J:cols(Y) ⏎
```

Now set up two index variables to map it:

```
i:0;N-1 ⏎
j:0;J-1 ⏎
```

Your screen should show approximately the content of Figure 75.

Now let's turn the raw-data matrix into a corresponding **standardized data matrix**, in which each of the 36 raw values is replaced by its standardized value. First, we need the mean and standard deviation of each of the four variables (columns):

```
M[j:mean(Y⟨Alt-^⟩j) ⏎
M=
S[j:stdev(Y⟨Alt-^⟩j) ⏎
S=
```

$Y^{(j)}$ is a vector formed out of the jth column of the matrix Y. The ⟨Alt-^⟩ keystroke defines the superscript that indexes the column.

A standard score is simply the deviation of the raw score from its mean, expressed in standard deviations. We have to define

Figure 75

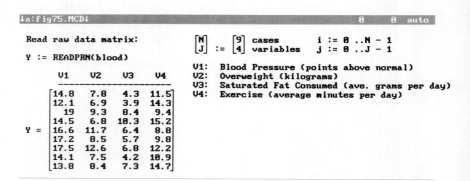

each member of the standardized data matrix individually, with a doubly subscripted variable:

```
y['i,j:(Y['i,j →  - M[j)/S[j ↵
y=
```

The standardized value (-1) of $V2$ for the second case, for example, means simply that the raw score (6.9 kilograms overweight) for this person is one standard deviation (1.933) lower than the mean (8.833) of all nine cases.

The standard deviation of each column of the standardized data matrix is 1.00, as you may wish to verify.

Since we'll want it again soon, save the standardized data matrix y to SDM.PRN:

```
WRITEPRN(sdm):y ↵
```

Figure 76 shows your progress thus far.

Now compute and save the correlation matrix r. Its matrix formula is quite simple: Premultiply the standardized data

Figure 76

Read raw data matrix:

$\begin{bmatrix} N \\ J \end{bmatrix} := \begin{bmatrix} 9 \\ 4 \end{bmatrix}$ cases $i := 0 .. N - 1$
                        variables $j := 0 .. J - 1$

Y := READPRN(blood)

V1: Blood Pressure (points above normal)
V2: Overweight (kilograms)
V3: Saturated Fat Consumed (ave. grams per day)
V4: Exercise (average minutes per day)

	V1	V2	V3	V4
	14.8	7.8	4.3	11.5
	12.1	6.9	3.9	14.3
	19	9.3	8.4	9.4
	14.5	6.8	10.3	15.2
Y =	16.6	11.7	6.4	8.8
	17.2	8.5	5.7	9.8
	17.5	12.6	6.8	12.2
	14.1	7.5	4.2	10.9
	13.8	8.4	7.3	14.7

$M_j := \text{mean}\left[Y^{<j>} \right]$ $S_j := \text{stdev}\left[Y^{<j>} \right]$

$M = \begin{bmatrix} 15.511 \\ 8.833 \\ 6.367 \\ 11.867 \end{bmatrix}$ $S = \begin{bmatrix} 2.062 \\ 1.933 \\ 2.004 \\ 2.261 \end{bmatrix}$

Standardized data matrix:

$y_{i,j} := \dfrac{Y_{i,j} - M_j}{S_j}$

WRITEPRN(SDM) := y

$y = \begin{bmatrix} -0.345 & -0.534 & -1.031 & -0.162 \\ -1.655 & -1 & -1.231 & 1.076 \\ 1.692 & 0.241 & 1.014 & -1.091 \\ -0.49 & -1.052 & 1.962 & 1.474 \\ 0.528 & 1.483 & 0.017 & -1.356 \\ 0.819 & -0.172 & -0.333 & -0.914 \\ 0.965 & 1.948 & 0.216 & 0.147 \\ -0.684 & -0.69 & -1.081 & -0.428 \\ -0.83 & -0.224 & 0.466 & 1.253 \end{bmatrix}$

matrix by its transpose, and divide the result by N, the number of cases:

```
r:(y⟨Alt-!⟩*y)/N ⏎
r=
WRITEPRN(corr):r ⏎
```

Just as we expected, $V2$ and $V3$ correlate positively as shown by the positive number in row 2, column 3 of the matrix r, and $V4$ and $V1$ correlate negatively as shown by the number in row 4, column 1.

Furthermore, in this sample

- $V2$ and $V3$ correlate positively with each other (not surprising: fat consumption ought to go with overweight)
- $V2$ and $V4$ (overweight and exercise) correlate negatively
- $V3$ and $V4$ (fat consumption and exercise) correlate positively

Does this mean that the more you weigh the less you exercise or that the more you exercise the less you weigh? The data don't say, although either interpretation is consistent with common sense.

Finally, check MathCAD's work by applying the corr function to each pair of columns in the raw data matrix.

First, define a second four-member range variable to go with j in defining pairs of columns:

```
k:0;3 ⏎
```

Now set up rr, the new version of the correlation matrix:

```
rr['j,k:corr(Y⟨Alt-^⟩j,Y⟨Alt-^⟩k) ⏎
rr=
```

Figure 77 shows the final result of the correlation analysis.

Figure 77

```
Read raw data matrix:            ⎡N⎤   ⎡9⎤  cases      i := 0 ..N − 1
                                 ⎣J⎦ := ⎣4⎦  variables   j := 0 ..J − 1
Y := READPRN(blood)
                                 V1:  Blood Pressure (points above normal)
      V1    V2    V3    V4        V2:  Overweight (kilograms)
    ─────────────────────        V3:  Saturated Fat Consumed (ave. grams per day)
    ⎡14.8   7.8   4.3   11.5⎤     V4:  Exercise (average minutes per day)
    ⎢12.1   6.9   3.9   14.3⎥
    ⎢ 19    9.3   8.4    9.4⎥                  ⎡  <j>⎤                  ⎡  <j>⎤
    ⎢14.5   6.8  10.3   15.2⎥     M   := mean⎢Y    ⎥    S   := stdev⎢Y    ⎥
Y = ⎢16.6  11.7   6.4    8.8⎥      j          ⎣     ⎦     j          ⎣     ⎦
    ⎢17.2   8.5   5.7    9.8⎥
    ⎢17.5  12.6   6.8   12.2⎥              ⎡15.511⎤             ⎡2.062⎤
    ⎢14.1   7.5   4.2   10.9⎥              ⎢ 8.833⎥             ⎢1.933⎥
    ⎣13.8   8.4   7.3   14.7⎦      M =     ⎢ 6.367⎥     S =     ⎢2.004⎥
                                           ⎣11.867⎦             ⎣2.261⎦
```

Standardized data matrix:

$$y_{i,j} := \frac{Y_{i,j} - M_j}{S_j}$$

```
                                    ⎡−0.345  −0.534  −1.031  −0.162⎤
                                    ⎢−1.655     −1   −1.231   1.076⎥
                                    ⎢ 1.692   0.241   1.014  −1.091⎥
                                    ⎢ −0.49  −1.052   1.962   1.474⎥
                                y = ⎢ 0.528   1.483   0.017  −1.356⎥
                                    ⎢ 0.819  −0.172  −0.333  −0.914⎥
WRITEPRN(SDM) := y                  ⎢ 0.965   1.948   0.216   0.147⎥
                                    ⎢−0.684   −0.69  −1.081  −0.428⎥
Correlation Matrix:                 ⎣ −0.83  −0.224   0.466   1.253⎦
```

$$r := \frac{y^T \cdot y}{N}$$

```
                                    ⎡    1     0.66   0.383  −0.707⎤
                                    ⎢ 0.66       1    0.123  −0.484⎥
                                r = ⎢0.383   0.123      1    0.221⎥
                                    ⎣−0.707  −0.484   0.221      1 ⎦

WRITEPRN(corr) := r        k := 0 ..3

                ⎡ <j>   <k>⎤         ⎡    1     0.66   0.383  −0.707⎤
rr    := corr⎢Y    ,Y    ⎥           ⎢ 0.66       1    0.123  −0.484⎥
  j,k          ⎣          ⎦    rr =  ⎢0.383   0.123      1    0.221⎥
                                     ⎣−0.707  −0.484   0.221      1 ⎦
```

Regression Analysis with Matrices

If we know a person's weight, fat consumption, and exercise habits, we feel that we also know something about the likelihood that he has high blood pressure. The correlations computed in the last section seem to confirm the conventional wisdom on which we base our assumption.

Multiple regression summarizes data like our blood-pressure raw data matrix into prediction equations, and it provides ways to estimate the confidence that can be placed in the resulting predictions.

Just as the raw-data matrix is the starting point for correlational analysis, the correlation matrix is the starting point for multiple regression. We saved a 4 × 4 correlation matrix from the blood-pressure example; let's get it back and see how well the observed values of overweight, fat consumption, and exercise enable us to predict elevated blood pressure.*

First, save the current worksheet to CORREL.MCD, if you wish:

⟨F6⟩correl ⏎

Next, clear the worksheet:

⟨Esc⟩CLear ⏎

Now retrieve the correlation matrix from CORR.PRN:

r:READPRN(corr) ⏎

We're aiming to predict $V1$ (the **dependent** or **criterion variable**) from knowledge of $V2$, $V3$, and $V4$ (the **predictors**). The next step is to partition the 4 × 4 correlation matrix into two smaller matrices:

1. *Rx*, the 3 × 3 matrix of correlations among the predictors
2. *ry*, the column vector of correlations between the criterion and the three predictors

Set up three range variables:

i:0;8 ⏎
j:1;3 ⏎
k:1;3 ⏎

*This won't be real prediction because we're applying the prediction equation to the same data that generated it — not a very demanding test. A real prediction would require you to apply the prediction rule to fresh data.

Pick out the elements of *r* that you need for *ry* and *Rx*:

```
ry['j-1:r['j,0 ⏎
ry=
Rx['j-1,k-1:r['j,k ⏎
Rx=
```

The result of a regression calculation is a vector of **standardized regression weights**. In this example, we'll have three:

1. *Beta*$_0$, for the first predictor (overweight)
2. *Beta*$_1$, for the second (fat consumed)
3. *Beta*$_2$, for the third (exercise)

We compute the *Beta* vector by premultiplying *ry* by the inverse of *Rx*:

```
Beta:Rx^-1*ry ⏎
Beta=
```

Save the *Beta* vector as BETA.PRN for use in the next worksheet:

```
WRITEPRN(beta):Beta ⏎
```

Figure 78 shows the result.

Now we want to apply the prediction equation and see how close the results come to the actual blood-pressure data. We're going to need worksheet space; so, once again save the current worksheet and clear your screen for a new one:

```
⟨F6⟩weights ⏎
⟨Esc⟩CLear ⏎
```

Read in the data that we still want to work with:

```
sdm:READPRN(sdm)
Beta:READPRN(beta)
```

To predict the standardized blood pressure of any one of the nine cases (say, the *i*th one), simply multiply each of the three standardized predictor scores by its corresponding *Beta* weight, and add the three products:

$$\text{ypred}_i = Beta_0 * y_{i0} \text{ (overweight)}$$
$$+ Beta_1 * y_{i1} \text{ (fat consumption)}$$
$$+ Beta_2 * y_{i2} \text{ (exercise)}$$

In matrix terminology, this calculation is called the **scalar product** or the dot-product of the *Beta* vector with the individual predictor vector y_i. We could take the *y*-matrix apart into predictor vectors and compute the dot-product of each with *Beta*; MathCAD handles dot-products with ease. Fortunately, matrix multiplication does the whole job in a single operation.

We want to postmultiply the standardized data matrix *sdm* by the *Beta* vector to get the *ypred* vector. But *sdm* is too big: you can't premultiply a three-element vector by a four-column matrix. In addition to the predictor scores (columns 1–3), *sdm* also contains the criterion scores (column zero). We could repair the situation in at least three ways:

- We could cut sdm down to size by picking out the elements we want, one by one, as before:

$$Newsdm_{i,j-1} = sdm_{i,j}$$

Figure 78

‌a:fig78.MCD‌   0 0 auto

REGRESSION ANALYSIS OF MEDICAL RESEARCH DATA

Retrieve the correlation matrix   r := READPRN(corr)
from CORR.PRN:

Partition it: i := 0 ..8   j := 1 ..3   k := 1 ..3

Vector ry contains the correlation of the blood pressure
variable (V1) with each of the three predictors:

$$ry_{j-1} := r_{j,0}$$

Matrix Rx contains the correlations among the predictors:

$$Rx_{j-1,k-1} := r_{j,k}$$

The results:

$$ry = \begin{bmatrix} 0.66 \\ 0.383 \\ -0.707 \end{bmatrix} \qquad Rx = \begin{bmatrix} 1 & 0.123 & -0.484 \\ 0.123 & 1 & 0.221 \\ -0.484 & 0.221 & 1 \end{bmatrix}$$

Compute and save the vector of standardized regression weights:

$$Beta := Rx^{-1} \cdot ry \qquad Beta = \begin{bmatrix} 0.264 \\ 0.503 \\ -0.69 \end{bmatrix}$$

WRITEPRN(beta) := Beta

- Or we could isolate columns 1–3 as three vectors with MathCAD's **superscript** notation, and then reassemble them into a three-column matrix with the **augment** function; the keystroke sequence would be as follows:

```
j:1;3 ⏎
V1:sdm⟨Alt-^⟩1 ⏎
V2:sdm⟨Alt-^⟩2 ⏎
V3:sdm⟨Alt-^⟩3 ⏎
Newsdm:augment(v1,V2) ⏎
Newsdm:augment(Newsdm,V3) ⏎
```

- Or we could leave *sdm* alone and turn *Beta* into a four-element vector named *beta*, tacking on a zero in position zero. That would make the matrix multiplication legal, and it would tell it simply to ignore *sdm*'s zero column. We'll take this approach here; feel free to try out the others for practice.

```
j:1;3 ⏎
beta[j:Beta['j−1 ⏎
sdm= ⏎
beta= ⏎
```

The prediction equation, in matrix form, is then simply:

```
ypred:sdm*beta
```

Let's display these eight predictions alongside *yobs*, the vector of eight observed standardized blood-pressure values (column zero of the standardized data matrix, and the vector of **residuals** (the difference between each observed value and the value predicted by regression):

```
i:0;8 ⏎
yobs[i:sdm['i,0 ⏎
residual:yobs-ypred ⏎
```

Some of these predictions come closer than others; let's make a picture to see how well the prediction tracks the observed values:

```
@i⟨Tab⟩⟨Tab⟩⟨Tab⟩ypred[i,yobs[i ⏎
```

Actually, the correspondence doesn't look bad at all. Let's repeat the picture with error bars, to emphasize the residuals. Make a copy ($\boxed{\text{F2}}$) of the plot region, move the cursor into adjacent empty space, and paste it in ($\boxed{\text{F4}}$).

Put the cursor in the new plot area, type

f

and change Type=1 in the message line to Type=e.

Figure 79 shows the result.

For real prediction, the next step would be to apply the regression weights in the *Beta* vector to independently gathered data on other individuals' weight, diet, and exercise habits. If the resulting predictions conformed to observation as well, then we could believe that the regression equation reflects something about relationships in the real world.

Suggestions for Further Exploration

1. Solve the following system of simultaneous linear equations (Thomas and Finney, p. A–40) by means of matrix operations:

$$2x-3y+4z = -19$$
$$6x+4y-2z = 8$$
$$x+5y + 4z = 23$$

2. Solve the same system with a solve block.

3. Read in (with READPRN) the data set saved on your Auxiliary Disk as REALEST.PRN. Its five columns contain data on the scale of 51 homes:

Column 0: *Selling Price* (in $1000)
Column 1: *Asking Price* (in $1000)
Column 2: *Number of Baths*
Column 3: *Number of Bedrooms*
Column 4: *Number of Cars* (garage)

Figure 79

REGRESSION ANALYSIS OF MEDICAL RESEARCH DATA

Retrieve the standardized data matrix   sdm := READPRN(SDM)
and the beta-weight vector: Beta := READPRN(BETA)

Create an augmented beta vector, with a zero in position zero:

$$j := 1 .. 3 \qquad beta_j := Beta_{j-1}$$

To compute ypred, the vector of predicted values, weight each row (case)
of the standardized data matrix by the beta weights:

$$sdm = \begin{bmatrix} -0.345 & -0.535 & -1.031 & -0.162 \\ -1.655 & -1 & -1.231 & 1.076 \\ 1.692 & 0.241 & 1.014 & -1.091 \\ -0.491 & -1.052 & 1.962 & 1.474 \\ 0.528 & 1.483 & 0.017 & -1.357 \\ 0.819 & -0.172 & -0.333 & -0.914 \\ 0.965 & 1.948 & 0.216 & 0.147 \\ -0.685 & -0.69 & -1.081 & -0.428 \\ -0.83 & -0.224 & 0.466 & 1.253 \end{bmatrix} \qquad beta = \begin{bmatrix} 0 \\ 0.264 \\ 0.503 \\ -0.69 \end{bmatrix}$$

ypred := sdm·beta

The actual standardized values of V1, the blood pressure variable,
are found in the first column (column zero) of sdm:

$$i := 0 .. 8 \qquad yobs_i := sdm_{i,0} \qquad residual := yobs - ypred$$

Compare predicted with observed values:

$$yobs = \begin{bmatrix} -0.345 \\ -1.655 \\ 1.692 \\ -0.491 \\ 0.528 \\ 0.819 \\ 0.965 \\ -0.685 \\ -0.83 \end{bmatrix} \qquad ypred = \begin{bmatrix} -0.548 \\ -1.626 \\ 1.327 \\ -0.309 \\ 1.337 \\ 0.418 \\ 0.522 \\ -0.43 \\ -0.69 \end{bmatrix} \qquad residual = \begin{bmatrix} 0.203 \\ -0.029 \\ 0.365 \\ -0.181 \\ -0.809 \\ 0.401 \\ 0.443 \\ -0.254 \\ -0.14 \end{bmatrix}$$

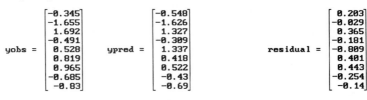

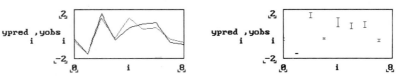

a. Carry out a regression analysis, predicting *Selling Price* from the other four variables.

b. Repeat the analysis, leaving out the best predictor. Compare the fit of the predicted selling price to the realized price in each case.

Reference

Part Three

⬆ ⬇ ➡ ⬅	Moves the cursor one character in the direction of the arrow.
⟨**Tab**⟩	Moves the cursor forward one word in text regions. Moves the cursor to the next operator or placeholder in equation or plot regions. Moves right to next 10-character tab stop between regions.
⟨**Shift–Tab**⟩	Moves the cursor back one word in text regions. Moves the cursor to the previous operator or placeholder in equation or plot regions. Moves the cursor left to the next 10-character tab stop between regions.
⟨**PgUp**⟩	Moves the cursor up five lines.
⟨**PgDn**⟩	Moves the cursor down five lines.
⟨**Ctrl–⬅**⟩	Moves the cursor left to next 10-character tab stop.
⟨**Ctrl–➡**⟩	Moves the cursor right to next 10-character tab stop.
⟨**Ctrl–PgUp**⟩	Moves the screen up 80% of the page.
⟨**Ctrl–PgDn**⟩	Moves the screen down 80% of the page.
⟨**Home**⟩	Moves the cursor to the previous region.
⟨**End**⟩	Moves the cursor to the end of the region you are in, or to the beginning of the next region.
⟨**Ctrl–Home**⟩	Moves the cursor to the beginning of the document (the cursor will be in the first region).
⟨**Ctrl–End**⟩	Moves the cursor to the end of the document (the cursor will be in the last region).
⟨**Ins**⟩	Toggles the insert/append mode in equation and plot regions.
⟨**BackSpace**⟩	Erases the current character in equation and plot regions. Erases the previous character in text regions.
⟨**Del**⟩	Erases the current character.
⟨↵⟩	Moves the cursor even with the left edge of the region, two lines down in equation regions and plot regions. Produces a line break in text regions. Moves the cursor to the beginning of the next line between regions.
⟨**Ctrl–↵**⟩	Resets the text width to that of the current column in a text region. Inserts three dots, a line break, and a plus sign in an equation region, so your equation can be more than one line long.

@	Creates a plot region.	
"	Creates a text region.	
(F10)	Displays command menus.	
(F1)	Displays help screens.	
⟨**Esc**⟩	Allows you to enter any command on the message line. When the message line is not blank, it erases the message line.	
⟨**Alt–M**⟩	Creates a matrix.	
f	Specifies local (for that region only) format for an equation, table, or plot. The cursor must be on the calculated result in the table or in the rectangle for the plot.	
d	Restores to global format. The cursor must be on the calculated result.	

Special Characters

To See This		Type This	Use For
α	(alpha)	⟨Alt–A⟩	
β	(beta)	⟨Alt–B⟩	
δ	(delta)	⟨Alt–D⟩	Kronecker's delta function
ϵ	(epsilon)	⟨Alt–E⟩	
ϕ	(phi)	⟨Alt–F⟩	
Γ	(capital gamma)	⟨Alt–G⟩	gamma function
Φ	(capital phi)	⟨Alt–H⟩	step function
∞	(infinity)	⟨Alt–I⟩	a predefined variable
λ	(lambda)	⟨Alt–L⟩	
η	(eta)	⟨Alt–N⟩	
Ω	(capital omega)	⟨Alt–O⟩	
π	(pi)	⟨Alt–P⟩	a predefined variable
θ	(theta)	⟨Alt–Q⟩	
ρ	(rho)	⟨Alt–R⟩)	
σ	(sigma)	⟨Alt–S⟩	
τ	(tau)	⟨Alt–T⟩	
μ	(mu)	⟨Alt–U⟩	
ω	(omega)	⟨Alt–W⟩	

Predefined Variables

	These predefined variables have the following values when you start MathCAD:
$e = 2.71828...$	Base of natural logarithms. MathCAD uses the value of e to 15 decimal places.
$\pi = 3.14159...$	Pi appears as the Greek letter π. To type π, press ⟨Alt–P⟩. MathCAD uses the value of π to 15 decimal places.
$\infty = 10^{307}$	Infinity. The largest integer in MathCAD, approximately 10^{308}. This appears as an infinity symbol. To type infinity, press ⟨Alt–I⟩.
$\% = 0.01$	Percent. To enter 5%, type

> 5*%

Can also be used as a scaling unit after a value has been computed and displayed.

$TOL = 10^{-3}$	Tolerance for derivatives, integrals, and equation solving.
$ORIGIN = 0$	Array origin. The index of the first element in a vector and of the first row or column in a matrix.
PRNPRECISION =4	Number of decimal places used when writing files with the WRITEPRN function.
PRNCOLWIDTH =8	Column width used when writing files with the WRITEPRN function.

Numbers and Variables

Numbers	MathCAD uses the following types of numbers:
Floating point numbers	Such as 6 or -3.14159.
Exponential notation	To enter very large or very small numbers, such as $3 \cdot 10^8$ or $2.16 \cdot 10^{-5}$.
Imaginary numbers	To enter an imaginary number, follow it with i or j. For example, 1i or $-2.5j$. You can't use i or j alone to enter the imaginary

unit; you must always type 1i or 1j. The unnecessary 1 will disappear when you move the cursor out of the region.

Octal integers

To enter a whole number in octal, follow it with the letter o or O. For example, −705o. Octal numbers are limited to 32-bit integers.

Hexadecimal integers

To enter a whole number in hexadecimal, follow it with h or H. To represent digits above 9, use the uppercase or lowercase letters A through F. For example, 10AE9h. Hexadecimal numbers are limited to 32-bit integers.

Dimensional values

Numbers that are associated with one of the MathCAD dimensions:

- length (1L=1 unit of length)
- mass (1M=1 unit of mass)
- time (1T=1 unit of time)
- charge (1Q=1 unit of charge)

MathCAD uses these dimensions to keep track of units for dimensional analysis and unit conversions. To enter a dimensional value, type a number followed by an uppercase or lowercase L, M, T, or Q. For example, 4.5m represents 4.5 mass units.

If you want to work with specific units of length, such as feet and yards, you can make global definitions like ft ≡ 1L and yd ≡ 3·ft. Type

```
ft ~ 1L  ⏎
yd ~ 3*ft  ⏎
```

The dimension suffixes L, M, T, and Q are associated by default with the names length, mass, time, and charge when displaying computed results. You can choose other names using the DImension command if you prefer. For example, if you want to use Q to represent a temperature dimension instead of charge, type

```
⟨Esc⟩ DImension  ⏎
```

MathCAD will show the dimension names on the message line:

```
M=mass L=length T=time Q=charge
```

Edit the last entry to read Q=temp, and press ⏎. Then you could let one degree Kelvin be the basic unit of temperature with the definition Kelvin $\equiv 1Q$.

<table>
<tr><td>Numeric format</td><td>MathCAD numbers can be displayed according to the following specifications, which have no effect on the internal value stored:</td></tr>
<tr><td>rd</td><td>Radix, or base, used to display a number: d for decimal, o for octal, or h for hexadecimal. The default is decimal. MathCAD rounds all hexadecimal and octal numbers to the nearest integer.</td></tr>
<tr><td>ct</td><td>Complex tolerance: an integer between 0 and 308. If the ratio between the two parts of a complex number is less than 10^{-ct}, then the smaller part is not shown. The default is 10; this means that numbers like $1 + 1i \cdot 10^{-12}$ will appear simply as 1.</td></tr>
<tr><td>im</td><td>Imaginary unit symbol: either i or j. The default is i.</td></tr>
<tr><td>et</td><td>Exponential notation threshold: an integer between 0 and 15. Numbers of magnitude greater than or equal to 10^{et} or less than or equal to 10^{-et} are shown in exponential notation instead of floating point notation. The default value is 3.</td></tr>
<tr><td>zt</td><td>Zero tolerance: an integer between 0 and 308. Numbers less than 10^{-zt} are shown as zero. The default is 15.</td></tr>
<tr><td>pr</td><td>Precision: an integer between 0 and 15. Indicates the number of decimal places shown. The default is 3. MathCAD always omits trailing zeros as well.</td></tr>
</table>

To change the global format for all calculated results in a document, use the FORMat command, and edit any of the specifications listed above. To change the local format for a single number or table of values (of a vector or matrix), move the cursor to the result you wish to reformat and type

f

You can edit the values of rd, ct, et, and pr on the message line as before and press ⏎. To remove the local format for a result, move the cursor back to the result and type

d

MathCAD **variable names** must start with a letter, followed by any combination of letters, numbers, underscores, periods, or percentage signs. You can also use certain Greek letters and the infinity sign. (See the Reference Card for instructions on how to enter these characters in a document.) Variable names cannot include spaces or special characters. MathCAD distinguishes uppercase from lowercase letters in variable names: *diam*, for example, is a different variable from *Diam*.

Operators — Listed in Order of Precedence

To See This	Type This	Operator
$(\mathbf{x})$	`'x` or `(x)`	Parenthesis
$\mathbf{x}^{\langle i \rangle}$	`x⟨Alt-^⟩i`	Superscript (*i*th column of matrix *x*)
$\vec{\mathbf{x}}$	`⟨Alt-⟩`	Vectorize (treat operations elementwise)
$\mathbf{x}_i$	`x[i`	Subscript
$\mathbf{x}!$	`x!`	Factorial
$\bar{\mathbf{x}}$	`x"`	Complex conjugate
$\mathbf{x}^T$	`x⟨Alt-!⟩`	Transpose
$\mathbf{x}^y$	`x^y`	Power; matrix power (for matrix inverse, $y=-1$)
$-\mathbf{x}$	`-x`	Negation
$\sum\mathbf{x}$	`⟨Alt-$⟩x`	Sum of vector elements
$\sqrt{\mathbf{x}}$	`\x`	Square root
$|\mathbf{x}|$	`|x`	Absolute value; determinant; norm
$\dfrac{\mathbf{x}}{\mathbf{y}}$	`x/y`	Division

To See This	Type This	Operator
$x \cdot y$	x*y	Multiplication; dot product; matrix product
$x \times y$	x⟨Alt-*⟩y	Cross product
$\displaystyle\sum_i x$	i$x	Summation over range
$\displaystyle\prod_i x$	i#x	Product over range
$\dfrac{d}{dx}f(x)$	x?f(x)	Derivative
$\displaystyle\int_a^b f(x)dx$	x&f(x)	Integral
$x-y$	x-y	Subtraction
$x+y$	x+y	Addition
$x...$ $+y$	x⟨Ctrl-⏎⟩y	Addition with line break
$x>y$	x>y	Greater than
$x<y$	x<y	Less than
$x \geq y$	x⟨Alt-)⟩y	Greater than or equal to
$x \leq y$	x⟨Alt-(⟩y	Less than or equal to
$x \neq y$	x⟨Alt-#⟩y	Not equal to
$x \approx y$	x⟨Alt=⟩y	Relational equals
$x,y..z$	x,y;z	Range

Calculus Operators

Integrals and Derivatives

MathCAD uses two calculus operators: the definite integral and the derivative. These two operators are numerical, not symbolic: they use numerical methods to approximate an exact answer. By setting the MathCAD tolerance variable, TOL, you can determine the accuracy of these answers.

Tolerances

MathCAD includes three types of calculations — integrals, derivatives, and equation solving — that use internal iterative algorithms to converge to an answer. To change the accuracy MathCAD requires in its internal iteration, set the value of the built-in variable TOL, MathCAD's internal tolerance.

TOL starts with the value 10^{-3}. To change the tolerance, enter an equation to redefine TOL (for example, TOL := 10^{-6}). To change the tolerance everywhere in a document, define TOL globally; to change the tolerance for a specific equation, enter a local definition for TOL above that equation. As with other variables, the definition you enter for TOL applies to all equations below it. You can also use the SET command, especially in a configuration file, to change the default value of TOL on all subsequent documents.

When you change the tolerance in a document, keep in mind the tradeoff between accuracy and computation time. If you decrease (tighten) the tolerance, MathCAD will compute more accurate answers for derivatives, integrals, and solutions to equations, but it will take longer. If you increase (loosen) the tolerance, MathCAD will compute more quickly, but the answers will be less accurate.

Integration

MathCAD can show and calculate definite integrals. To create an integral sign, press the ampersand key (&). MathCAD will show an integral with placeholders. MathCAD uses a numeric algorithm to approximate the integral of an expression over an interval of real numbers. You must enter the expression to be integrated, the limits of integration and the variable of integration as follows.

Enter expressions for the limits of integration (the ends of the interval) at the top and bottom of the integral sign.

Enter an expression to be integrated (the integrand) before the d but after the integral sign.

Enter a single variable name after the d (the integrating variable). MathCAD will integrate with respect to the variable.

The limits of integration must be real. The expression to be integrated can be either real or complex.

Except for the integrating variable, all variables in the integrand must be defined.

MathCAD approximates integrals by using numerical methods. Internally, MathCAD makes successive approximations to the value of the integral, stopping when the approximations differ by less than the value of the built-in variable TOL. If MathCAD's approximations to an integral fail to converge to an answer, MathCAD marks the integral with the message

```
not converging
```

Like all numerical methods, MathCAD's integration algorithm can be "fooled" by an ill-behaved integrand. If the expression to be integrated has singularities, discontinuities, or large and rapid fluctuations, MathCAD's solution may be inaccurate.

Contour Integrals and Double Integrals

You can use MathCAD to do complex contour integrals. You must first parameterize the contour, then integrate over the parameter. If the parameter is not arc length, you must also include the derivative of the parameterization as a correction factor.

You can also use MathCAD to compute double or multiple integrals. To set up a double integral, type two ampersands in a row (&&). Fill in the integrand, the limits, and the integrating variable for each integral.

Numerical Methods Used for Integration

When you compute an integral, MathCAD makes all the computations internally and shows the answer. You need not know the details of this internal computation to use MathCAD integration. The steps MathCAD follows when it integrates $f(x)$ from a to b are outlined below so that advanced users can get a better understanding of the integral operator.

First, MathCAD uses the trapezoid rule to estimate the integral, dividing the interval from a to b into four subintervals. This process is repeated with eight subintervals.

If the two estimates agree within relative tolerance, MathCAD returns the most recently computed estimate. The relative tolerance is the smaller of TOL and TOL $\cdot$ |ans|, where *ans* is the most recently computed estimate.

If the two answers do not agree within the relative tolerance, MathCAD continues. At each step MathCAD divides the subintervals in half, estimates the integral, and returns the estimate if it is within the relative tolerance of the previous estimate.

Differentiation

To create a derivative in MathCAD, press the question mark key (?). MathCAD shows a derivative, with placeholders for the expression to be differentiated, and the differentiation variable.

MathCAD differentiates numerically, returning an approximation to the derivative at a particular point. You must enter a variable name (the differentiation variable) in the denominator of the derivative and an expression to be differentiated to the right of the derivative symbol. The differentiation variable must be defined. MathCAD evaluates the derivative of the expression at the defined value of the differentiation variable.

Keep in mind that the result of differentiating is not a function, but a single number — the computed derivative at the indicated value of the differentiation variable.

The expression to be differentiated can be either real or complex.

The differentiation variable must be a single variable name.

MathCAD approximates derivatives by using numerical methods. Internally, MathCAD makes successive approximations to the value of the derivative, stopping when the approximations differ by less than the value of the built-in variable TOL. You can change the accuracy with which integrals are calculated by changing the value of TOL. If MathCAD's approximations to a derivative fail to converge to an answer, MathCAD marks the derivative with the message

```
not converging
```

If you try to compute the derivative at a point where it does not exist, you will also see this message.

Although differentiation returns just one number, you can set up one function as the derivative of another. For example:

$$f(x) \; := \; \frac{d}{dx} \; g(x)$$

Then evaluating $f(x)$ will return the numerically computed derivative of $g(x)$ at x.

Numerical Methods Used for Differentiation

When you compute a derivative, MathCAD makes all the computations internally and shows the answer. You need not know the details of this internal computation to use MathCAD differentiation. The steps MathCAD follows when it takes the derivative of $f(x)$ at x are outlined below so that advanced users can get a better understanding of MathCAD's derivative operator.

First, MathCAD defines the initial value of h as either $\sqrt{\text{TOL}}$, or $\sqrt{\text{TOL}} \cdot x$ if $|x| > 10^5$. Next, MathCAD finds the slope between the points for x and $x \pm h$ on the curve and averages these to get a two-point estimate. MathCAD also finds the slope between the two points for x and $x \pm h/z$, and takes the weighted average of these four slopes (a four-point estimate).

If the two estimates agree within the relative tolerance, MathCAD returns the most recently computed slope. The relative tolerance is the smaller of TOL and TOL $\cdot$ |ans|, where *ans* is the most recently computed slope.

If the two slopes do not agree within the relative tolerance, MathCAD continues. At each step MathCAD computes a new four-point estimate from the slopes of the lines through $f(x)$ and the four points half as far from x as the previous four points. MathCAD returns the new estimate if it is within the relative tolerance of the previous estimate.

Commands

System Commands

Help (F1) Enters the Help system. Press ⟨Esc⟩ to leave Help. (See "Getting Started.")

Quit (⟨Ctrl–Q⟩) Quits MathCAD and returns you to DOS. Warns you if you have made changes since the document was last saved.

DOs Interrupts MathCAD to execute a single DOS command. Prompts on the message line for a DOS command to execute.

MEmory Shows memory use (bytes used and total bytes available) on the message line.

REDraw (⟨Ctrl–R⟩) Redraws the screen.

PRInt (⟨Ctrl–O⟩) Prints the current document. Prompts on the message line for printer type, print area, and printer device. When specifying a device for printing, give a device name like PRN or a filename.

SELectprinter Displays a menu of possible printer types so you can select one.

CONfigsave Saves the current configuration as a command file: includes current printer type, plot and number formats, dimension names, etc.

EXecute Executes a previously saved text file containing MathCAD commands.

File Commands

LOad (F5) Loads a document file from disk. Prompts on the message line for a filename. Also warns you if your current file has been changed since it was last saved.

SAve (F6) Saves the current document in a disk file. Prompts you for a filename. Uses current filename by default.

APpend Appends a file to the current document. Prompts on the message line for the name of the file to append.

FIlename Associates a variable with a filename for file-access functions. Prompts on the message line for the filename to associate with the variable given as the argument. If the variable is already associated with a filename, you see that filename on the message line.

CLear	Clears the current document and reloads the configuration file. Warns you if you have made changes since the document was last saved.
RESet	Clears the current document. Uses built-in system defaults instead of reloading the configuration file.

Compute Commands

CAlculate ($\boxed{\text{F 9}}$)	Processes and calculates all equations from the start of the document through those currently visible. Use this command to calculate equations when

```
calc  F 9
```

appears at the right of the message line when you edit or enter an equation, indicating that MathCAD is in the manual calculation mode.

PROcess	Processes and calculates all equations in the document.
MANual	Enters manual computation mode; equations are processed and calculated only on explicit command. When you use this command, the right side of the message line shows nothing until you enter or edit an equation; then it shows

```
calc  F 9
```

to remind you that there are pending calculations. Use the **calculate** command or the **process** command or press $\boxed{\text{F 9}}$ to carry out these pending calculations.

AUtomatic	Enters automatic computation mode; processes and calculates each equation as it is entered or viewed. When you use this command, MathCAD shows

```
auto
```

at the right of the message line.

FORMat	Sets global format for all calculated results and output tables. Shows format specification on the message line; edit this specification and press $\boxed{\text{⏎}}$ to change the global format. (For local formatting, move the cursor to a calculated result and press f.)

RAndomize
number

Resets MathCAD's random-number generator. If you use this command with no *number*, the rnd function will return the same random values that you see when you start MathCAD. If you use a different *number*, you get a new set of random values. Each time you use the RAndomize command with the same *number*, you regenerate the same set of random values. (See "Random numbers" in the "Built-In Functions" section below.)

DImension

Changes dimension names. Shows the current dimension names on the message line; edit them and press ⏎ to execute the command, or ⟨Esc⟩ to abort it.

EQuation (on/off)

Disables the current equation or plot, or reenables it. A disabled equation or plot is marked with a small rectangle and is not calculated.

MATrix

Generates a new matrix with the indicated dimensions or changes the size of an existing matrix.

Edit/Move Commands

COPy (F2)

Makes a copy of the current region.

CUt (F3)

Deletes the current region from the document.

PASte (F4)

Inserts the region most recently copied or cut. You can paste the same region any number of times.

SEParate

Separates any overlapping regions on your document.

INSertline
(⟨**Ctrl–** F9 ⟩)

Inserts a blank line at the current cursor position.

DEleteline
(⟨**Ctrl–** F10 ⟩)

Deletes one line of space from a document.

Goto *line column*

Prompts for a screen position for the cursor. Enter two numbers separated by a space to indicate the line and column positions. If the column is omitted, MathCAD assumes column 0.

MOve *lines and*
columns

Scrolls the document up or down by the number of lines you specify, leaving the cursor in the same relative position on the screen. When you issue the MOve command, MathCAD gives you 2 zeros to edit in the message line. If you replace the first zero by n, MathCAD will scroll n lines (positive = the document scrolls up; negative = the document scrolls down). Don't

	try to edit the second number (the columns): If you try to scroll to the right, MathCAD will ignore the *columns* argument in the command. If you try to scroll to the left, nothing will happen.
SEArch *text* **or** −*text* (⟨**Ctrl**–F5⟩)	Searches forward (*text*) or backward (−*text*) through text and equation regions for the next string of characters matching *text*. You can continue the search forward or backward by responding + or −, respectively, to the prompt.
REPlace *text1* *text2* (⟨**Ctrl**–F6⟩)	Searches forward from the current cursor position for the next string of characters matching *text1* and replaces it with *text2* according to your response (yes, no, quit, all) to the prompt.

In-Region Commands

INCOpy (⟨**Ctrl**–F2⟩)	Copies marked text or part of an equation from within a region. To select an expression from an equation, you should put the cursor on the highest level operator of the expression.
INCUt (⟨**Ctrl**–F3⟩)	Deletes marked text from a text region or an expression from the equation indicated by the cursor.
INPaste (⟨**Ctrl**–F4⟩)	Inserts at the cursor the text or expression previously cut or copied. You can paste the same text or expression any number of times.

Text Commands

Width *chars*	Sets the width and rewraps the text region. Shows the current width and prompts for the new width.
MARK (⟨**Ctrl**–X⟩)	Marks one end of a text region. Once you mark both ends of a text region, you can use INCOpy, INCUt or INPaste on the text between them. To unmark, move the cursor out of the text region, or press ⟨Ctrl–X⟩ again. You can paste text even after you have unmarked it.
CEnter	Moves the current line of text to the center of the text region.
BAckward (⟨**Ctrl**–B⟩)	Causes the text motion commands ⟨Ctrl–W⟩, ⟨Ctrl–L⟩, ⟨Ctrl–S⟩, and ⟨Ctrl–P⟩ to move the cursor backward one word, line, sentence, or paragraph.

FORWard (⟨**Ctrl–F**⟩)	Causes the text motion commands ⟨Ctrl–W⟩, ⟨Ctrl–L⟩, ⟨Ctrl–S⟩, and ⟨Ctrl–P⟩ to move the cursor forward one word, line, sentence, or paragraph.
Justify (⟨**Ctrl–N**⟩)	Rewraps the text in the current region to make the lines more even after editing.

Window/Page Commands

SPlit (F7)	Splits the screen into two windows at the current cursor position. If there are already two windows, moves the window divider to the current cursor position.
Unsplit ⟨**Ctrl–** F7 ⟩	Unsplits the screen and discards the document in the current window. Warns you if you changed the document in the current window since it was last saved.
SWitch F8	Toggles from one window to the other; also referred to as jump.
PAGelength	Prompts for page length in lines. Shows page breaks on screen. Use 0 for no page breaks.
BReakpage	Shifts equation and plot regions so they do not cross page boundaries. Also, moves other regions down to maintain the arrangement of equations in the document.

Other Commands

PLotformat	Displays the global plot format for you to modify.
SET *var value*	Sets values for the system variables: TOL, ORIGIN, PRNPRECISION, and PRNCOLWIDTH.
SKIPWord (⟨**Ctrl–W**⟩)	Skips one word in text region.
SKIPLine (⟨**Ctrl–L**⟩)	Skips one line in text region.
SKIPSentence (⟨**Ctrl–S**⟩)	Skips one sentence in text region.
SKIPParagraph (⟨**Ctrl–P**⟩)	Skips one paragraph in text region.

For the arguments shown here

- x indicates a real argument.
- z indicates a real or complex argument.
- n indicates an integer argument.
- v indicates a vector argument.
- M indicates a matrix argument.
- X represents a variable associated with a filename.
- $:=$ indicates a form that must be followed exactly to use the function.

Except where otherwise noted, functions take one argument. For complex numbers, functions return principal value.

MathCAD includes the most essential mathematical functions, including the trigonometric and hyperbolic functions, logarithmic and exponential functions, complex coordinate functions, the Bessel functions and Fourier transforms.

Trigonometric Functions

All trigonometric functions use or return arguments in radians.

sin(z)   Sine.

cos(z)   Cosine.

tan(z)   Tangent.

asin(z)   Inverse sine.

acos(z)   Inverse cosine.

atan(z)   Inverse tangent.

angle(x,y)   Angle (in radians) from x-axis to the point (x,y) in the x-y plane. Arguments must be real. Result is between zero and 2π.

If you wish to convert degrees to radians or radians to degrees, define the dimensionless units **rad** and **deg** as follows:

```
rad ~ 1
deg ~ 〈Alt-P〉/180 * rad
```

Now the unit deg, for example, can be substituted in the final placeholder of any result computed in radians, and the conversion will be automatic. For example, to compute the arccosine of 1/2, type

```
acos(1/2)=
```

This shows the result as 1.047 (radians are understood). Move the cursor into the region and type deg in the placeholder of the result to see the more recognizable answer

```
acos(1/2)=60·deg
```

Replacing deg by rad would convert the answer explicitly to radians again. You could also express this value as a multiple of π simply by replacing deg with π to get

```
acos(1/2)=.333·π
```

Hyperbolic Functions

sinh(*z*)   Hyperbolic sine.

cosh(*z*)   Hyperbolic cosine.

tanh(*z*)   Hyperbolic tangent.

asinh(*z*)   Inverse hyperbolic sine.

acosh(*z*)   Inverse hyperbolic cosine.

atanh(*z*)   Inverse hyperbolic tangent.

Logs and Exponential Functions

exp(*z*)   *e* raised to the power *z*.

log(*z*)   Base 10 logarithm.

ln(*x*)   Natural logarithm.

Bessel Functions

J0(*x*)   Bessel function $J_0(x)$; x real.

J1(*x*)   Bessel function $J_{1}(x)$; x real.

Jn(*n,x*)   Bessel function $J_n(x)$; x real, n positive integer. For example, the MathCAD expression

```
Jn(3,x)
```

represents the mathematical Bessel function $J_3(x)$.

Y0(x)	Bessel function $Y_0(x)$; x positive.
Y1(x)	Bessel function $Y_1(x)$; x positive.
Yn(n,x)	Bessel function $Y_n(x)$; x positive; n positive integer. For example, the MathCAD expression `Yn(2,x)` represents the mathematical quantity $Y_2(x)$.

Complex Functions

Re(z)	Real part of z.
Im(z)	Imaginary part of z.
arg(z)	Angle to z in complex plane.

Vector Functions

length(v)	The number of elements in v including v_0.
last(v)	The last subscript i for which v_i is defined. In general, last (v)=length$(v)-1$.
min(v)	Returns the minimum element in (v). For complex values, it returns the minimum real part of the vector elements plus i times the minimum imaginary part.
max(v)	Returns the maximum element in (v). For complex values, it returns the maximum real part of the vector elements plus i times the maximum imaginary part.

Matrix Functions

rows(M)	Number of rows in the matrix.
cols(M)	Number of columns in the matrix.
tr(M)	Trace of the matrix: the sum of the diagonal elements.
identity(n)	Identity matrix of size n.
$\delta(x1,x2)$	Kronecker's delta function. To type the δ, hold down ⟨Alt⟩ and press d.
$\epsilon(n1,n2,n3)$	Completely antisymmetric tensor of rank 3. To type the ϵ, hold down ⟨Alt⟩ and press e.
augment($M1,M2$)	New matrix made by combining arguments.

Fast Fourier Transforms

MathCAD contains four functions to perform fast Fourier transforms: for real data fft and its inverse ifft, and for complex data cfft and its inverse icfft. These functions are discrete; they apply to and return vectors.

Note that these functions take vector names as arguments. If you use a vector as an argument to a function, make sure you follow these conventions:

- Use the vector name by itself; do not include a subscript. v is a valid argument for fft; v_1 is not.
- All vectors used with fft functions should start with v_0 not v_1.

fft(*vector*)

Use this function to take the fast Fourier transform of a real vector. The fft function can appear only in an equation of this form:

$$c := \texttt{fft}(v)$$

The argument, v, is the name of a vector of real data. This definition creates a vector c containing the values of the complex coefficients of the discrete Fourier transform of v. If v contains n elements, the coefficients are generated to satisfy this formula:

$$c_j = (1/\sqrt{n}) \cdot \sum_k v_k \, e^{2\pi i j k/n}$$

There should be 2^m values in v, where m is a whole number. If the number of values is not an even power of two, MathCAD will ignore some values. For example, you could perform the Fourier transform of v with values from v_0 through v_{63} ($2^6 = 64$ values.) On the other hand, given an argument v with values from v_0 through v_{100}, MathCAD would ignore all values beyond v_{63}.

If there are 2^m values of v, MathCAD computes $2^{m-1} + 1$ values for the c vector. For example, if v had values for v_0 through v_{63}, MathCAD would compute values for c_0 through c_{32}. This function does not generate values for the remaining $2^{m-1} + 1$ elements of the transform, since they would just be the conjugates of the values it does generate.

ifft(*vector*)

The inverse Fourier transform function (ifft) can appear only in an equation of the following form:

$$z := \text{ifft}(v)$$

The argument v is the name of a vector containing complex Fourier coefficients like those generated by the fft function. This equation creates and fills a vector z with values of the inverse Fourier transform. The results of the inverse transform obey a similar formula to the one shown above under fft, including the $1/\sqrt{n}$ form that precedes the formula. When using this function, keep in mind that

- There should be $2^m + 1$ values in v, where m is a whole number. If the number of values is not one more than an even power of two, MathCAD will ignore some values. For example, you could perform the inverse Fourier transform of v with values from v_0 through v_{32} ($2^5 + 1 = 33$ values). On the other hand, given an argument v with values from v_0 through v_{50}, MathCAD would ignore all values beyond v_{32}.
- If there are $2^m + 1$ values in v, MathCAD computes $2^m + 1$ values for the resulting z vector. For example, if v had values for v_0 through v_{32}, MathCAD would compute values for z_0 through z_{32}.
- The fft and ifft functions are exact inverses. That is, if

$$c := \text{fft}(x) \text{ and } z := \text{ifft}(c)$$

then the x and z vectors are identical.

cfft(*v*)

Use this function to take the fast Fourier transform of a complex vector. The cfft function can appear only in an equation of this form:

$$c := \text{cfft}(v)$$

The cfft function is identical to the fft function described above, except that

- The argument v can contain complex values.
- There should be 2^m values in v, where m is a whole number. This function returns 2^m values, the same number of values

in the argument vector. (Compare this to fft, which returns one more than half this many values.)

icfft(*v*)

The inverse complex Fourier transform function (icfft) can appear only in equations of the form

$$z := \text{icfft}(v)$$

This function is the inverse of the cfft function. It takes a vector with 2^m values and returns a vector with the same number of values.

Like fft and ifft, cfft and icfft are exact inverses. That is, if

$$c := \text{cfft}(x)$$

and

$$z := \text{icfft}(c)$$

then the x and z vectors are identical.

Miscellaneous

floor(*x*)   Greatest integer $\leq x$ (x real).

ceil(*x*)   Least integer $\geq x$ (x real).

Φ(*x*)   Heaviside step function. Returns 0 if x is negative, 1 if x is 0 or positive. The argument must be real. (To type the Greek letter Φ, press ⟨Alt–H⟩.)

mod(*x,modulus*)   Remainder on dividing x by *modulus*. The arguments must be real. The result has the same sign as x.

Iteration and Conditionals

MathCAD has two functions that deal with iterated processes and conditional branching: **until** and **if**.

The Until Function

until

MathCAD's until function allows you to halt an iterative process based on a condition.

The syntax for the until function is an expression

until(*Expr1,Expr2*)

Here, *Expr1* is the test expression; MathCAD halts any iteration in the equation when it becomes negative. *Expr2* is the value returned for each iteration until *Expr1* causes it to halt the iteration.

The until function has no effect on a scalar equation. On an equation with a range variable, MathCAD will iterate the equation as usual until the first time *Expr1* returns a negative value. At that point, all iteration is halted for the equation in question.

The until function is useful in iterative processes with a specified convergence condition.

The If Function

if

By using MathCAD's **if** function and relational operators, you can test a condition and change the behavior of an expression based on that condition. The if function has the following syntax:

if(*condition, x1,x2*)

An expression of this form returns the value *x1* or *x2*, depending on the value of *condition*.

The arguments *x1* and *x2* can be any expressions. The *condition* argument can be any expression, but most often it involves a relational operator that returns either 1 (for true) or 0 (for false). If *condition* is zero (false), the if expression returns the value of *x2*. If *condition* is one (true), the if expression returns the value of *x1*.

Here is a list of the relational operators used in MathCAD:

Condition	What to type	Description
$e1 \approx e2$	$e1 < \text{Alt} = > e2$	Relational equals (true if $e1 = e2$, otherwise false).
$e1 > e2$	$e1 > e2$	Greater than.
$e1 < e2$	$e1 < e2$	Less than.
$e1 \geq e2$	$e1 < \text{Alt}-) > e2$	Greater than or equal to. (To type the operator, hold down $<\text{Alt}>$ key and press the 0 key at the top of the keyboard.
$e1 \leq e2$	$e1 < \text{Alt}-(> e2$	Less than or equal to. (To type the operator, hold down $<\text{Alt}>$ key and press the 9 key at the top of the keyboard.)
$e1 \neq e2$	$e1 < \text{Alt}-\# > e2$	Not equal to. (To type the operator, hold down $<\text{Alt}>$ key and press the 3 key at the top of the keyboard.)

When the *condition* argument of an if function is false, Math-CAD does not evaluate x_1. When the *condition* argument is true, MathCAD does not evaluate x_2.

For example, suppose the function $f(x)$ is to be defined by the rule

$$f(x) = \begin{cases} x-3, & \text{if } x \leq 5 \\ 2, & \text{if } x > 5 \end{cases}$$

We can assign this value $f(x)$ in MathCAD by typing

```
f(x):if(x>5,2,x-3)
```

Statistical Functions

MathCAD includes three functions for population statistics, two functions for statistical distributions, three functions for correlation and regression, a histogram function, and a random-number generator.

Many of these functions take vectors as arguments — for example, mean(v). If you use an vector as an argument to a function, make sure you follow these conventions:

- Use the vector name by itself; do not include a subscript. For example, compute mean(v), not mean(v_i).
- The vector should start with v_0 not v_1.

Population Statistics

In the descriptions below, N represents the number of elements in the vector.

mean(v)

Returns the mean of the values of the vector v, including v_0.

$$\text{mean}(v) := (1/N) \cdot \sum_i v_i$$

var(v)

Returns the variance of the values of the array v, including v_0.

$$\text{var}(v) := (1/N) \cdot \sum_i [v_i - \text{mean}(v)]^2$$

stdev(v)

Returns the standard deviation (square root of the variance) of the values of the vector v, including v_0.

$$\text{stdev}(v) := \sqrt{\text{var}(v)}$$

Common Statistical Functions

erf(x)

Returns the value of the error function at x. x must be real.

$$\text{erf}(x) := \int_0^x 2/\sqrt{\pi} \cdot e^{-t^2} dt$$

$\Gamma(z)$

Returns the value of the Euler gamma function at z, for z real.

$$\Gamma(z) := \int_0^\infty t^{z-1} e^{-t} dt$$

MathCAD returns values for all real z except nonnegative integers and 0. MathCAD also returns values for all complex z with Im(z) $\langle 3$, but accuracy degrades for Im(z) near 3 or -3.

cnorm(*x*)   Returns the cumulative normal distribution: the integral from $-\infty$ to x of the standard normal distribution. x must be real.

$$\text{cnorm}(x) := \int_{-\infty}^{x} \frac{1}{\sqrt{2\pi}} \cdot \exp\left(\frac{-t^2}{2}\right) dt$$

Correlation Functions

corr(*vx*,*vy*)   The following functions compute correlations and linear regression by the least-squares method for complex numbers as well as real numbers. The arguments of each function are two vectors of data, *vx* and *vy*, which must contain the same number of elements.

Returns a single number: the correlation (Pearson's *r*) of the vectors *vx* and *vy* including vx_0 and vy_0.

slope(*vx*,*vy*)   Returns the slope of the least-squares line for the data points with *x* and *y* coordinates in *vx* and *vy*.

intercept(*vx*,*vy*)   Returns the *y*-intercept of the least-squares line for the data points with *x* and *y* coordinates in *vx* and *vy*.

Histogram Function

hist(*intervals*,*data*)   The histogram function computes frequency distributions needed to plot histograms. It must be used in an equation of this form:

```
freqs := hist(intervals,data)
```

In this equation *intervals* and *data* are one-dimensional vectors of real numbers, starting with $intervals_0$ and $data_0$. MathCAD creates and fills a vector *freqs* with the frequencies for a histogram defined by *intervals* (the interval limits) and *data* (the data). MathCAD interprets intervals as a set of points defining a sequence of intervals in a histogram; the values in *intervals* must be in ascending order. The *data* vector contains the data values to be tabulated. The vector *freqs* that this function computes is one element shorter than the *intervals* vector.

Each of its elements, *freqs*$_i$ holds a count of the number of values in the *data* vector such that

$$intervals_i \leq data \text{ value} < intervals_{i+1}$$

MathCAD ignores data points less than the first value of *intervals* or greater than the last value of *intervals*.

Random Numbers

MathCAD's random numbers are controlled by the rnd function and the RAndomize command discussed earlier. This section describes how to use them.

The function rnd(x) calculates a random number between 0 and x. Each time you recalculate an equation with the rnd function, MathCAD generates new random numbers. To force MathCAD to generate new random numbers, move the cursor into the equation with the rnd function, and press the calc key (F9). The RAndomize command restarts MathCAD's random number generator and controls the numbers it creates. To reset MathCAD's random numbers, type

⟨ESC⟩RAndomize ↵

Then put the cursor in the equation with the rnd function and press F9. Since the randomizer has been reset, MathCAD generates the same random numbers it generated when you first started MathCAD.

To see a new set of random numbers, use the RAndomize command with a numeric argument. For example,

⟨ESC⟩RAndomize 10 ↵

This resets the random number function, but starts it with a different "seed." This causes MathCAD to generate a different set of random numbers from what you saw when you started MathCAD. Each time you want to reset MathCAD to generate this new set of random numbers again, use the RAndomize 10 command. To see a different set of random numbers, use the RAndomize command with a different numeric argument.

MathCAD includes a linear interpolation function and four functions for cubic spline interpolation.

For all interpolation functions, be sure your data vectors start with element zero. If you use a vector v and don't define v_o, MathCAD will automatically set $v_0 = 0$. This spurious data point can distort your results. If all your data vectors start with element one, you can change the predefined variable ORIGIN to one with a global definition or the SET command.

Linear Interpolation

linterp(vx,vy,x)

MathCAD's **linterp** function performs linear interpolation on a set of data points with coordinates given in vectors of vx and vy to estimate the y value at a new point x.

The vectors vx and vy must have the same length, and vx must contain real values in ascending order. The number x must also be a real value.

Linear interpolation corresponds to drawing straight lines between data points. To find the estimated y value associated with an x value, MathCAD finds the two points that the x value falls between and returns the y value found on the straight line between the two points. For x values before the first point in vx, MathCAD extrapolates the straight line between the first two points in vx; for x values after the last point in vx, MathCAD extrapolates the straight line between the last two points in vx.

Cubic Spline Interpolation

Cubic spline interpolation fits a curve to a set of points in such a way that the first and second derivatives of the fitted curve are continuous. The curve is constructed from a series of cubic equations, each connecting one point and the next.

For efficiency, MathCAD implements spline interpolation as a two-step process. The two steps are as follows.

1. Use the lspline, pspline or cspline function on the data in vectors vx and vy to generate a vector vs. The vector vs contains the second derivatives of the fitted curve at the points

in question. The three spline functions correspond to three different end conditions: the ends of the curve can approach a straight line (lspline), a parabola (pspline) or a cubic curve (cspline.)

2. Use the interp function, together with the vector vs from step 1, to interpolate values of the fitted curve.

lspline(*vx,vy*)
pspline(*vx,vy*)
cspline(*vx,vy*)

All arguments to the cubic spline functions must be real.

For reference, here are details of how spline functions work and what arguments they use:

```
lspline(vx, vy)
pspline(vx, vy)
cspline(vx, vy)
```

These functions can be used only in equations of the form

```
vs:= lspline(vx, vy)
```

Here, vx and vy are vectors that contain the x and y coordinates of the points to be fitted. This equation automatically defines and fills a vector vs with the values of the second derivatives, one for each point. (You can use lspline, pspline, or cspline in this format, depending on the desired end condition.) When using these functions, keep in mind that

- The vectors vx and vy must be the same size. The fitted points should start with vx_0 and vy_0, not vx_1 and vy_1.
- MathCAD takes the real part of the vectors vx and vy before proceeding; imaginary parts are ignored.
- The values in vx must be in ascending order.

Use the lspline function to generate a spline curve that approaches a straight line at the endpoints. The lspline function constrains the spline curve so that $vs_0 = 0$ and $vs_N = 0$.

Use the pspline function to generate a spline curve that approaches a parabola at the endpoints. The pspline function constrains the spline curve so that $vs_0 = vs_1$ and $vs_N = vs_{N-1}$.

Use the cspline function to generate a spline curve that can be fully cubic at the endpoints. The cspline function constrains the spline curve by extrapolating the vs values; vs_0 is extrapolated linearly from vs_1 and vs_2, and vs_N is extrapolated linearly from vs_{N-1} and vs_{N-2}.

interp(vs,vx,vy,x)   This function returns the interpolated value of the spline curve at x. The spline curve is determined from the vectors vx and vy, together with the second derivatives vs determined by one of the spline functions. When using the interp function, keep in mind that

- The vs argument to interp must be computed by applying lspline, pspline, or cspline to the same vectors used in the interp function. If you use vs values generated in any other way, the results will probably be meaningless.

As with the spline functions, the interp function uses only the real parts of the vectors vx, vy, and vs, and all three vectors must have the same number of values. MathCAD uses values starting with vx_0, vy_0 and vs_0.

If x falls within the range of values in vx, MathCAD uses the cubic spline curve determined by the given points. For x beyond the range of values in vx, MathCAD extrapolates using either the cubic that applies between the first two points or the cubic that applies between the last two points.

Equation Solving

MathCAD includes two special features for solving equations numerically: the root function and solve blocks.

The root function finds the zeros of an arbitrary expression. This is equivalent to solving a single equation for one unknown.

Solve blocks are used to solve simultaneous equations and inequalities. By entering these equations and inequalities as constraints, you can ask MathCAD to compute the variables that solve them and then use those variable values in other equations in your documents.

The root function solves for the roots of expressions. To solve for the point x at which an expression *expr* is zero, you need two equations: one to define a "first guess" for x and a second to find the root. Typically, these two expressions look like this:

```
variable := guess value
root value := root(expr, variable)
```

To determine a good guess value for the root function, plot the expression and estimate where it crosses the zero line.

When you enter two equations like these, MathCAD uses the given value of *variable* as a starting point for its approximations. If the approximations converge to an answer, then that answer is the value of the root function at a point at which *expr* is zero. Such a value is called a "zero" or root of *expr*.

MathCAD computes the root function using a numerical method called the "secant method." Internally, MathCAD uses the defined value of *variable* as a starting point for successive approximations to the root value, stopping when the magnitude of *expr*, evaluated at the proposed root, is less than the predefined variable TOL.

MathCAD's root function does not always yield a solution. If MathCAD cannot find a root, it marks the root function with the error

```
not converging
```

This error can be caused by any of the following:

- The expression has no zeros.
- The zeros of the expression are far from the initial guess.
- There are local maxima or minima in the curve between the initial guess and the zeros.
- There are discontinuities in the curve between the initial guess and the zeros.

To find the cause of the error, plot the expression. This will help determine whether there are any points where the expression crosses the zero axis and, if so, approximately where they are. If you use an initial guess value close to where the expression crosses the zero axis, the root function is more likely to converge quickly.

If an expression has multiple roots, vary the initial guess to find them. Plotting the function is a good way to determine how many roots there are, where they are, and what initial guesses are likely to find them. If two roots are close together, you may have difficulty finding both.

For an expression $f(x)$ and known root a, solving for additional roots of $f(x)$ is equivalent to solving for roots of

$$g(x) = f(x) \, / \, (x \, - \, a)$$

This procedure is known as "dividing out" known roots. Dividing out known roots is useful for resolving two roots that may be close together. It is often easier to solve for roots of $g(x)$ as defined above than to find other roots for $f(x)$ with different guesses.

Usage Note: If $f(x)$ has a low slope near its root, then root $(f(x),x)$ may converge to a value r that is relatively far from the actual root. In such cases, even though $f(r) \langle$ TOL, r may be far from the point where $f(r) = 0$. To find a more accurate root, decrease the value of TOL. Or try finding root $(g(x),x)$, where

$$g(x) = f(x) \, / \, f'(x)$$

and $f'(x)$ represents the derivative of $f(x)$.

Numerical Methods Used to Find Roots   When MathCAD tries to find a root of $f(x)$ using the initial guess x, it uses the secant method and follows these steps internally:

If $f(x)$ is within TOL of zero, then x is already a root, so MathCAD returns it as an answer.

If not, MathCAD sets a variable h either to the value of TOL, if $x=0$, or to TOL$\cdot x$ if $x \neq 0$. It also sets x_0 to the original x value, letting $x_1 = x + h$ be the next point chosen. Then MathCAD constructs the straight line connecting the two points corresponding to x_0 and x_1 on the curve and locates the point x_2 where the line crosses the zero axis.

If $f(x_2)$ is within TOL of zero, MathCAD returns x_2 as the answer.

Otherwise, MathCAD continues to find a new x as before by locating the point x_n (with $n=3$ next) where the line through the last two points crosses the zero axis. MathCAD stops and returns the value x_n when $f(x_n)$ is within TOL of zero.

Solve Blocks

To solve several equations and inequalities simultaneously, use MathCAD's **solve blocks**. A solve block holds a group of equations or inequalities and ends with a **Find** or **Minerr** function that solves for the unknown variables in those equations and inequalities.

The solve block consists of the following parts:

- A block begins with the keyword **Given** in an equation region by itself.
- The body of the block is made up of ordinary definition equations and **constraints**. The constraints are the equations or inequalities that MathCAD will try to solve simultaneously. Any equation that starts on a line below Given and above the bottom of the block is considered to be in the block.
- The block ends with the first equation involving either of the functions

      Find(*variable1*,*variable2*,...)

  or

      Minerr(*variable1*, *variable2*,...)

The arguments of Find or Minerr are the variables to be solved for. These variables must be assigned guess values above the top of the solve block. Find and Minerr return values as follows:

- If Find has only one argument variable, it returns the value of that variable that solves the constraints.
- If Find has more than one argument, it returns a vector of answers: one value for each variable to be solved. These values together solve the constraints.

Minerr is similar, but it returns values that minimize the errors in the constraints without necessarily solving them.

Constraints   Equation and inequality constraints appearing in the body of a solve block consist of any two scalar MathCAD expressions (represented by *e1* and *e2* below) connected either by the constraint-equals sign ($\approx$) or by one of the inequality signs ($\langle$, $\rangle$, $\leq$, $\geq$). More precisely, you may use constraints having any of the following forms:

Constraint	What you type	Description
$e1 \approx e2$	e1⟨Alt=⟩e2	Constrained to be equal. (To type this sign, hold down the ⟨Alt⟩ key and press =.)
$e1 \langle e2$	e1⟨e2	Less than.
$e1 \rangle e2$	e1⟩e2	Greater than.
$e1 \leq e2$	e1⟨Alt-(⟩e2	Less than or equal to. (To type this operator, hold down the ⟨Alt⟩ key and press the 9.)
$e1 \geq e2$	e1⟨Alt-)⟩e2	Greater than or equal to. (To type this operator, hold down the ⟨Alt⟩ key and press the 0.)
expression	expression	Single expression constraint. (MathCAD tries to find a solution where this expression is zero.)

Note that MathCAD does not allow constraints using $\neq$ in solve blocks. Furthermore, it does not accept constraints containing range variables, vectors, or matrices.

Examples   Figure 80 shows a document containing a solve block with one constraint and one unknown variable x. After a solve block has been calculated, you can check the value of the system variable ERR, which MathCAD sets equal to the magnitude of the error vector each time it calculates a solve block.

You can check it the same way you check the value of any variable. Type

ERR=

This gives you a measure of how close the solution comes to satisfying all the constraints. In this example we have also tested the solution by substituting it in the original equation.

When entering a solve block, it is best to put MathCAD into manual calculation mode with the MANual command. This prevents MathCAD from trying to calculate with an incomplete solve block. Once the solve block is complete, you can change back into automatic calculation mode with the AUtomatic command or press $\boxed{F9}$ to calculate.

Figure 81 shows a solve block with two constraints and two unknown variables. In order for MathCAD to be able to work on the solve block, you must provide at least as many constraints as there are variables.

Observe that you can choose either to display the results of the Find or Minerr function right in the solve block or to assign

Figure 80

```
↓a:fig80.MCD↓                                          0    1   auto

SOLVE BLOCK EXAMPLE

Solve equation   x^2 + 10 = e^x

        Guess value:     x := 2

           Given
                                    HERE IS
           2       x
          x  + 10 ≈ e              THE SOLVE

           a := Find(x)            BLOCK


        Display result:    a = 2.9188269823

                          2
Verify result:           a  + 10 = 18.5195509526

                          a
                         e  = 18.5195509526

Check error:             ERR = 0
```

these values to variable names and use them elsewhere in your document.

The following problems may cause MathCAD to return the message

```
did not reach solution
```

You should check ERR to see how close it came.

- There may be no solution which satisfies all the constraints. MathCAD will still try to find the variable values that give the smallest possible error.
- If the solution for a variable is a complex number, the MathCAD will not find it unless the starting value for that variable is also complex.
- It is possible for MathCAD to get trapped in a local minimum for the error values. To find the actual solution, you may need to change the additional guesses or add an inequality.

Figure 81

```
↓a:fig81.MCD↓                                          0    1   auto

Find the intersection of a circle and a line

Guess values . . .   x := 0      y := 0

Given
      2   2
     x + y ≈ 6  . . . Circle              THIS VERSION OF THE

     x + y ≈ 2   . . . Line               SOLVE BLOCK DISPLAYS

                                          THE ANSWERS DIRECTLY
             ⎡ 2.414⎤   ERR = 0
Find(x,y) = ⎣-0.414⎦

--------------------------------------------------------------

Given                                     THIS VERSION ASSIGNS
      2   2
     x + y ≈ 6  . . . Circle              NAMES TO THE RESULT

     x + y ≈ 2   . . . Line               VALUES FOR X AND Y

  ⎡xval⎤                                  FOR FURTHER USE
  ⎣yval⎦ := Find(x,y)

Display answers:  xval = 2.414       yval = -0.414

                     2     2
Check answer:    xval + yval = 6       x + y = 0
```

- It may not be possible to solve the constraints to within the given tolerance of TOL. If the value of ERR is small, Math-CAD may have reached a near solution. Try changing the error tolerance by increasing the value of TOL.

If you are interested in the values calculated in the solution even if they are not accurate, change Find to Minerr in the last equation of your solve block. Minerr returns the values found even when they do not reduce the errors to within TOL of zero.

Numerical Methods Used in Solve Blocks   MathCAD's solve areas use the iterative Levenberg-Marquardt method to solve for several constraints simultaneously. The public-domain MINPACK algorithms, developed and published by the Argonne National Laboratory in Argonne, Illinois, are used with a few modifications. For more information, see the "User's Guide to MINPACK I," by J. More, B. Garbow, and K. Hillstrom (Argonne National Laboratory publication ANL-80-74, 1980). The following is a brief summary of this method for advanced users.

MathCAD applies the MINPACK algorithm to the problem of finding the zeros of an error vector built out of the set of constraints in the solve block as follows:

- for equality constraints (using $\approx$):

    error = left side − right side

- for inequality constraints (using $\langle, \rangle, \leq, \geq$)

    error = 0 if the inequality is true
    error = left side − right side if the inequality is
         not true

The algorithm tries at least to minimize the sums of squares of the elements of this error vector relative to the values of the variables specified.

The Levenberg-Marquardt method is a quasi-Newtonian method (a variation on the gradient method). At each step, MathCAD estimates the first partial derivatives of the error function $f(x)$ with respect to the variables to be solved, creating a Jacobian matrix J. The MathCAD tries to solve the matrix function

$$J \cdot s = -f(x)$$

for the step vector s, where x is the vector of current estimates for the unknown variables. If s can be found, then $x + s$ becomes the new value of x. If this calculation fails because the matrix J cannot be inverted, then an additional condition is added: to minimize the quantity

$$\sum_j D_j{}^2 \cdot s_j{}^2$$

where D is a vector of weight factors computed from the norms of the columns of the matrix J.

This method ends when either of the following conditions is satisfied:

- When it is no longer possible to reduce the norm of the error vector significantly, relative to the value of TOL
- When s becomes relatively close to zero, i.e., closer than the larger of TOL and $\mathrm{TOL} \cdot |x|$

There is also a limit on the number of calculations that Math-CAD will perform in search of an answer for a solve block. If it exceeds this limit without returning an answer, the Find or Minerr function is marked with the error

```
not converging
```

Data Files

MathCAD can read and write data files — ASCII text files containing numerical data. By reading data files, you can pull in data from other sources and analyze it in MathCAD. By writing data files, you can export MathCAD's results to word processors, spreadsheets, and other programs on your computer.

MathCAD includes two sets of functions for reading and writing data: READ, WRITE, and APPEND, which read or write a single value at a time, and READPRN, WRITEPRN and APPENDPRN, which read a whole matrix from a file with rows and columns of data or write such a file from a matrix in MathCAD.

The following information concerns features common to all MathCAD's file functions.

A MathCAD data file must be a text file in ASCII format. MathCAD reads data files that consist of numbers separated by commas, spaces, brackets, carriage returns, or any other nonnumeric delimiters. The numbers in the data files can be integers, floating point numbers, or numbers in exponential notation (E-format). MathCAD does not read complex numbers from data files (see instructions below under "Reading and Writing Complex Data"). For example, this list of numbers could be one line in a MathCAD data file:

```
200, 50, 25.1256, 16E-2, -16.125E15
```

MathCAD writes data files with numbers separated by spaces and carriage returns. Numbers of very large or very small magnitude are written to the file in E-format.

File-Access Functions	MathCAD has six file-access functions. The argument of these functions, shown below as *filevar*, can be any single variable name and is commonly the name of an existing file.
READ(*filevar*)	Read a value from a data file. Returns a scalar.
WRITE(*filevar*)	Write a value to a data file. If the file already exists, replace it with a new file. Must be used in a definition form:

```
WRITE(filevar) := expr
```

APPEND(*filevar*) — Add a value to an existing data file. Must be used in a definition of the form:

```
APPEND(filevar) := expr
```

READPRN(*filevar*) — Read a structured data file. Returns a matrix. Each line in the data file becomes a row in the matrix.

WRITEPRN (*filevar*) — Write a matrix into a data file. If the file already exists, replace it with a new file. Each row in the matrix becomes a line in the data file. Must be used in a definition of the form:

```
WRITE(filevar) := matrix expr
```

APPENDPRN
(*filevar*)

Add a matrix to an existing data file. Each row in the matrix becomes a new line in the data file. Must be used in a definition of the form:

```
APPEND(filevar) := matrixexpr
```

These functions share the following properties:

- You must type the function name in all caps.
- MathCAD looks for a data file with the same name as *filevar*. For example, if the argument is expermnt.dat, then MathCAD will read or write to the file EXPERMNT.DAT.
- If the *filevar* name does not contain a period, MathCAD chooses the file extension for you. For READ, WRITE, and APPEND, the default file extension is .DAT. For READPRN, WRITEPRN, and APPENDPRN, the default extension is .PRN.
- If MathCAD cannot find or open a data file, it marks the file-access function with an error. If MathCAD tries to read a file and the format is incorrect, it also marks the function with an error.
- Each new equation reopens the data file. The READ and WRITE functions start reading or writing at the beginning of the file. If you have already written an equation to a particular file, you must use APPEND or APPENDPRN after the first equation to avoid overwriting the earlier data.

Changing File Associations   You can also use the FIle-name command to let a file-access function read or write from a file without using the filename as its argument. For example, suppose you want to read data from a file called EXPER-MNT.DAT. To associate the file with the variable *edata*, use the FIlename command as follows:

```
⟨Esc⟩FIlename edata ⏎
```

MathCAD prompts you for a filename on the message line. Type the filename and press ⏎:

```
EXPERMNT.DAT ⏎
```

If you want, you can specify a full pathname, including directories.

If you use the FIlename command and specify a variable that is already associated with a filename, MathCAD shows the existing filename on the message line. Press ⏎ to keep the same filename, or edit the message line to associate the variable with a new filename.

Now you can use the file variable *edata* as the argument of any file-access function in your document.

Reading and Writing Unstructured Files

The functions READ, WRITE, and APPEND read and write data in unstructured files. An unstructured data file is one that contains numbers, but not necessarily in rows and columns.

Reading Data with the READ Function   Each equation using READ is treated separately, causing MathCAD to open a file and read one or more values starting from the beginning.

The simplest use of the READ function is to read one value from the beginning of a file (possibly containing no other numbers). An equation such as

    N:= READ(sizefile)

defines N as the first value in the data file SIZEFILE.DAT (unless the FIlename command has associated the name "sizefile" with some other data file).

It is also possible to have a single equation read more than one value from a data file with READ. For example, define a range variable, say i, ranging from 1 to the number of data points in the file. Then enter an equation like this one:

    x[i: READ(edata)

When MathCAD processes this equation, it retrieves numbers from the data file one by one. This equation fills the array x with values from the data file. These values can be used in other equations in MathCAD.

In an equation with a range variable and a single READ function, MathCAD reads one data point from the file for each value of the range variable.

If an equation includes two READ functions with a common argument, MathCAD reads two values from the data file each time it evaluates the equation. For example, if j ranges from one to ten, then this equation will read 20 data values and sum them in pairs:

```
x[j:READ(edata)+READ(edata)
```

MathCAD behaves similarly with three or more READ functions in the same equation.

Writing Data with the WRITE and APPEND Functions

To write to a data file, use an expression such as:

```
WRITE(sizefile) : N
```

or

```
WRITE(experment) : yi
```

If you enter a definition with a WRITE function preceding the colon, MathCAD sends each value of the expression to the file. If the expression includes a range variable, then Math-CAD will write one data value for each value of the range variable. Successive data values are separated by spaces; Math-CAD also inserts line breaks to keep the lines shorter than 80 characters.

When you use WRITE or APPEND, all values are saved to the file with maximum precision, regardless of the global format of the document. Units, however, are ignored when writing data with these functions.

Like the READ function, the WRITE function reopens the file and starts at the beginning for each new equation. If you want to write data to a file from several different equations, use the APPEND function instead of the WRITE function in the second and subsequent equations.

Caution: If you use the WRITE function with two separate equations in the same file, the data from the second equation will overwrite the data from the first equation.

The functions READPRN, WRITEPRN, and APPENDPRN read and write data in structured files. A structured data file is a data file with a fixed number of values per line, such as a rectangular array of numbers from a spreadsheet or a MathCAD matrix.

Reading a Matrix with the READPRN Function　The READPRN function reads an entire data file, determines the number of rows and columns, and creates a matrix from those data. For example, the MathCAD equation

    M := READPRN(spread)

will open and read all the data in a structured file called **SPREAD.PRN** (or from another file whose name was associated with "spread" by the filename command), filling a matrix M with the data. No subscript should be used when defining M with READPRN.

MathCAD will ignore blank lines and anything other than numbers in the file, but it will return an error message if any line has fewer or more values than the preceding lines. Spaces, commas, or other text must separate consecutive numbers on a line.

If each column of the file represents a different variable, you can use superscripts to rename them selectively. For example,

    $v0 := M^{\langle 0 \rangle}$

assigns the name $v0$ to the first (zero) column of the matrix M.

Writing Data with the WRITEPRN and APPENDPRN Functions　If M is a MathCAD matrix having n rows and m columns, the equation

    WRITEPRN(expermnt) := M

creates a structured file called EXPERMNT.PRN (unless another filename has been associated with expermnt) with n rows of m numbers each from the matrix M. No range variables or subscripts should be used in an equation containing WRITEPRN.

Each WRITEPRN equation writes a new file. Use APPEND-PRN in the equations if you want to append more rows of values to the same file.

The built-in variables PRNCOLWIDTH and PRNPRECISION determine the format of the data file that MathCAD creates. The current value of PRNCOLWIDTH specifies the width of the column in characters. The current value of PRNPRECISION specifies the number of decimal places shown.

By default, PRNCOLWIDTH is set at 8 and PRNPRECISION is set at 4. WRITEPRN and APPENDPRN can create files with more than 80 columns per line, depending on the number of columns and their widths.

Suppose you have three MathCAD vectors x, y, and z of the same length n. You can use the matrix function augment to juxtapose the three columns in an $n \times 3$ array to be recorded in a structured data file as follows:

WRITEPRN(data):augment(augment(x,y),z)

Reading and Writing Complex Data

MathCAD will read and write only real numbers to data files. If you use WRITE to write a complex number to a data file, MathCAD writes two numbers — the real part and the imaginary part.

You can use two READ statements in a single equation to read the real and imaginary parts of data in a data file.

If you use WRITEPRN to write a complex matrix, $n \times m$, to a file, each column in the matrix becomes two columns in the data file: one representing the real part and one the imaginary part of each number.

To read the data file back as a matrix of complex numbers, first use READPRN to read in the whole array as an $n \times 2m$ real matrix. Then use superscripts to combine pairs of columns into complex vectors as shown by the following equations:

```
k := 0 ..m
A⟨k⟩ := B⟨2·k⟩+i·B⟨2·k+1⟩
```

Plotting

You can create a MathCAD plot just by typing the symbol @. Then fill in the placeholders for what to plot and optional axis limits. Once you've created a plot, you can modify its format in a wide variety of ways, setting the size, grid lines, scaling, and plot symbols. This section describes how to create, use, and format MathCAD plots.

Creating a Plot

The simplest way to start is to press the at-sign key (@). Math-CAD shows an empty plot with placeholders along each axis. To create a plot, you must fill in the placeholders.

- The placeholder at the middle of the horizontal or x-axis holds the variable to plot against. Enter an expression containing a range variable (perhaps as a subscript).
- The placeholder at the middle of the vertical or y-axis holds an expression to plot. Enter an expression containing a range variable (perhaps as a subscript) or a constant.
- The other four placeholders are for the axis limits. For example, the horizontal axis could include values from -10 to 10, and the vertical scale could include values from 0 to 100. If you leave some or all of the limits blank, MathCAD will scale those limits automatically.

Use the ⟨Tab⟩ key or the arrow keys to move around between placeholders. When you have filled them in, move the cursor out of the region and, if you are not in automatic mode, press F9 to have MathCAD draw the plot. One point will be drawn for each value of each range variable in the x- and y-axis expressions, and the points will be connected with straight lines by default. Figure 82 shows an example of a simple plot.

Use this short cut for drawing a plot quickly: instead of pressing @ and filling in the blanks, type

y-axis expression @ x-axis expression

In the case of Figure 82, you could have typed

`f(x)@x`

Note also that only the real parts of complex numbers will be graphed.

What to Plot

In most MathCAD plots, the x- and y-axis expressions involve a single range variable. For example, you could define x as a range variable and then plot a function of x, or define a range variable t, together with functions $x(t)$ and $y(t)$. It is important to remember that the range variable must appear explicitly in both x- and y-axis expressions unless one of them happens to be a constant.

Another common way to generate a plot is to use a range variable as a subscript. If x and y are two vectors of the same length, and i is a range variable running through the possible subscripts for x and y, then you can plot the corresponding pairs of x and y values by labeling your axes as y_i and x_i. Note that subscripts are always integers greater than or equal to 0 (more generally, greater than or equal to the value of ORIGIN,

Figure 82

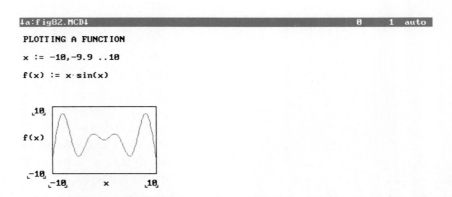

if you have changed this predefined variable). Figure 83 is an example of this type of plot.

The examples above involved only one set of connected points, called a trace, on each plot. You can create a plot with multiple traces in two different ways:

1. Enter several y-axis expressions versus one x-axis expression. MathCAD plots one trace for each of the y-axis expressions. All expressions should share the same range variable (or be constant).

2. Enter several y-axis expressions, and the same number of corresponding x-axis expressions. Each matching pair of expressions must share the same range variable. Math-CAD plots one trace for each pair.

Multiple x- or y-axis expressions should be separated by commas, as shown in Figure 84.

Note that you can draw a horizontal line by plotting a constant value on the y-axis versus a range variable on the x-axis. Similarly, you can create a vertical line by plotting a range variable on the y-axis versus a constant value on the x-axis.

Figure 83

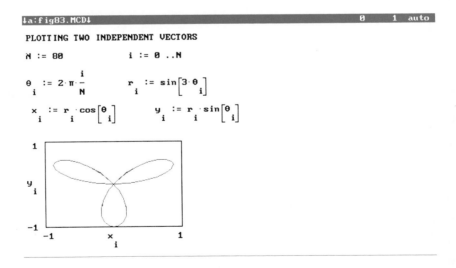

A plot can be disabled with the EQuation (on/off) command just as an equation can be. If you do this, the graph is frozen and will not reflect later changes in the document until it is reenabled with the same command. A small hollow rectangle next to a plot indicates that it has been disabled.

Axis Limits and Autoscaling

The *x*- and *y*-axis limits determine the scale of the plot. You can enter any valid scalar expression as an axis limit. Only points that have *x* and *y* coordinates lying within the limits will be plotted.

When you leave an axis limit blank, MathCAD computes and shows an appropriate limit for that axis automatically. This is called **autoscaling**. Relatively round numbers are chosen for the limits so that no points will be missing from the plot.

Autoscaled axis limits are indicated on the screen with half brackets under the numbers. (These half brackets are not shown in printouts.) You can replace any of these autoscaled values simply by moving the cursor to one and typing a new number.

Autoscaled plots can take up to twice as long to compute. For faster plots, especially when revising an old plot, set the axis

Figure 84

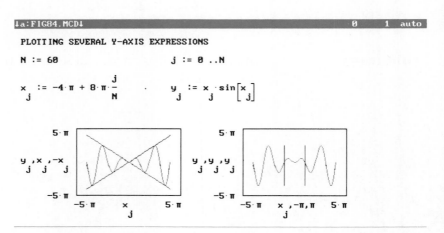

limits directly. Also, if you want the units of measurement or dimensions to appear on the axes, you must enter the limits yourself.

Formatting Plots

When you create a plot, you can change the size, show grid lines, set logarithmic scaling, or change the plot symbol by **formatting** the plot. The format may be changed either locally, for only that plot, or globally, affecting all subsequent plots created in the document.

To format a plot locally, put the cursor on the plot and type

f

To change the plot format globally, type

⟨Esc⟩PLotformat

In each case, MathCAD shows a plot specification on the message line that displays the parameters that you can change.

logs=y,x

Log cycles. The first number is for the *y*-axis, and the second is for the *x*-axis as follows:

- 0 means an ordinary linear axis.
- l means a logarithmic axis.
- n⟩1 means a logarithmic axis divided into n cycles, shown as grid lines. Each cycle is a constant multiple of the previous cycle.
- A logarithmic axis ($n \geq 1$) must have positive limits.

subdivs=y,x

Subdivisions. The first number is for the *y*-axis, and the second is for the *x*-axis as follows:

For a linear axis, the number represents the number of evenly spaced subdivisions.

- 1, the default, means no grid lines for subdivisions.
- n⟩1 means that evenly spaced grid lines divide the axis into n subdivisions.

For a log axis, the number represents the number of subdivisions *per cycle.* On a log axis, this setting must be either 1, 2, or 9.

- 1, the default, means no grid lines.
- 2 means one grid line per cycle halfway up (measured logarithmically).
- 9 means nine logarithmically spaced subdivisions per cycle. Figure 85 shows a plot with logarithmic subdivisions on each axis.

size=y,x Plot size. The first number determines the *y*-axis height, in lines; the second number determines the *x*-axis width, in columns.

type=... Plot type. This can be one letter or more. Each letter corresponds to one trace on the plot. Generally, uppercase letters represent symbols connected by lines; lowercase letters represent distinct symbols for each point. The following plot types are available:

l or L	Line. The points are connected with straight lines.
d	Dot. One dot for each point.
s	Step. Each pair of points is connected with a vertical and a horizontal line segment, forming a step.
e	Error bar. If there are two or more *y*-axis expressions and one *x*-axis expression, vertical error bars are drawn from the first trace to the second.
b	Bar chart. One bar is drawn from the bottom of the plot for each point.
x	One X is shown for each point.
X	The X's are connected with lines.
p	One plus sign (+) is shown for each point.
P	The plus signs are connected with lines.
o	One rectangle is shown for each point.
O	The rectangles are connected with lines.
v	One small diamond is shown for each point.
V	The diamonds are connected with lines.

Figure 85

FORMAT: logs=2,2 subdivs=9,9 size=12,30 type=b

x := 0.1,0.2 ..10

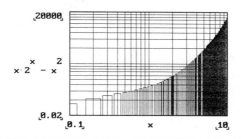

Error Messages

array size mismatch
You tried to perform a vector or matrix operation on arrays whose sizes don't match. Many operations, such as vector addition and subtraction, dot product, linterp and corr, require vectors that are the same size. Matrix multiplication requires that the number of columns in the first matrix match the number of rows in the second matrix.

cannot be defined
You put something other than a legally definable expression on the left side of a definition symbol (:=). The only items that can appear here are

- A variable name: x
- A variable name with a subscript: x_i.
- A variable name with a superscript: $x^{\langle i \rangle}$
- An explicit vector or matrix generated by typing ⟨Alt–M⟩. The vector or matrix can hold variable names or subscripted variable names only.
- A function name with arguments $f(x,y)$.

Any other expression is illegal. If you want to compute a result instead of defining a variable, use an equals sign (=) instead of a colon.

cannot take subscript	You used a subscript on something other than a vector or a matrix.
cannot take superscript	You used a superscript on something other than a matrix.
definition stack overflow	You used too many nested function definitions.
did not find solution	In a solve block, MathCAD was unable to find a solution to the constraints. To see the results of the solve block anyway, replace Find by Minerr.
dimension to nonreal power	The indicated expression uses units but is raised to a complex or imaginary power. If an expression is defined with units, you can raise it only to a real scalar power; otherwise, MathCAD cannot determine units for the result. This rule applies whether the expression raised to a power involves units directly or is defined in terms of units in earlier equations.
domain error	You evaluated a function at an illegal argument value. For example, you see this error if you try to compute $\ln(0)$.
duplicate	You tried to define the same variable twice in the same definition. You see this error if you create a vector on the left side of a definition and use the same name twice in that vector.
equation too large	You entered an equation too complicated for MathCAD to evaluate. Break the equation down into two or more subequations.
error in constant	MathCAD has interpreted the indicated expression as an invalid constant. MathCAD tries to interpret anything beginning with a digit as a constant; if you enter a number immediately followed by a few letters, MathCAD will interpret it as an invalid constant. For a complete list of valid forms for constants, see "Numbers."
error in list	The indicated function definition contains an invalid list of arguments. A valid function definition must begin like this:

$$functionname(\textit{argument list}) :$$

The argument list must be a name or a list of names separated by commas. Any other expression is illegal.

You also see this error message if you create an invalid list in another context, for example, in the list of *y*-axis expressions for a plot.

file error
MathCAD encountered an error trying to read values from a data file associated with a variable. Use the FIlename command to see the filename associated with the indicated variable.

file not found
MathCAD was unable to find the data file associated with a variable. Use the FIlename command to see the filename associated with the indicated variable.

illegal array operation
You applied a function or an operation that requires a scalar to a vector or matrix. For example, you see this message if you try to take the sine or square root of a matrix. If you want to apply the operation to each element in turn, use the vec operator (⟨Alt−⟩).

illegal context
You used an operator or function in a context that MathCAD does not allow. For example, you see this error message if

- You entered a semicolon somewhere other than in a legal range definition. (The semicolon appears as two dots, called an "ellipsis." You can use a semicolon only in the definition of a range for a range variable. See "illegal range" below.)
- You used a WRITE or APPEND function somewhere other than on the left side of a definition. These functions cannot appear in expressions or on the right side of a definition.
- You used an existing function name as a variable name or an existing variable name as a function name.
- You used a constraint with ≠ in a solve block. See "Solving Equations."

illegal factor
You entered an illegal expression for the placeholder at the end of an equation. If you enter an expression for this placeholder, it must be a real, scalar value. MathCAD will show this error if you enter an expression with a complex or imaginary value or an expression that involves a range variable.

illegal function name
You used an expression that MathCAD interprets as a function, but the function name is invalid. You will see this error, for example, if you use a number as a function name, like

this: 6(x). You may also see this error if you omit an operator, like +, causing MathCAD to interpret the parentheses in your equation as defining a function instead of as a way to group operations.

illegal ORIGIN

You defined ORIGIN with a noninteger value or a value of magnitude greater than 16000. This error marks the first use of a subscript after the illegal definition of ORIGIN.

illegal range

You created an illegal range-variable definition. The range that defines a range variable is not well formed. These are the only two valid forms for ranges that define range variables:

        Rvar: n1;n2

appears as Rvar := n1 ..n2.

        Rvar: n1,n2;n3

appears as Rvar := n1,n2 ..n3.

You cannot use more than one comma and one semicolon in the definition of a range variable. If you use the second form, the value of *n2* must lie between the values of *n1* and *n3*.

illegal TOLERANCE

This message marks an integral, derivative, or instance of the root function for which the value of TOL is greater than one or less than zero. To fix this error, you must find the definition of TOL and either delete it or change it to have a value between 0 and 1.

incompatible units

You entered an expression that adds or subtracts two expressions with different dimensions. For example, you see this message if you try to add 1L (one length unit) and 1M (one mass unit). This error appears whether the two expressions involve units directly or are defined in terms of units in earlier equations.

You also see this error if you use units on the scale limits for a plot and those units either do not match each other or do not match the expression you are plotting on that axis.

indeterminate dimension

The indicated expression uses units and is raised to a power that involves a range variable or vector. You must use a real, scalar exponent. This rule applies whether the expression raised to a power involves units directly or is defined in terms of units in earlier equations.

index out of bounds
This message marks a subscript or superscript that refers to a nonexistent array value. You see this message if you use a subscript or superscript less than 0 (or less than ORIGIN, if ORIGIN $\neq$ 0), or if you use a subscript or superscript to refer to an array value beyond those defined earlier in the document.

index too large
You tried to use a subscript or superscript that exceeds MathCAD's limit of 8000.

interrupted
You interrupted MathCAD by pressing ⟨Ctrl–A⟩ or ⟨Ctrl–Break⟩ while it was calculating. To recalculate the marked equation, put the cursor in the equation and press ⟨F9⟩.

list too long
You entered too many elements in a list separated by commas. This can occur if you try to plot more expressions than MathCAD's capacity.

misplaced comma
You used a comma in an illegal place. You can use a comma in any of the following ways:

- To separate function arguments
- To separate the x-axis range variables in a plot.
- To separate the first two elements of a range in the definition of a range variable
- To separate the y-axis expressions in a plot
- To separate elements in an input table
- To separate subscripts for a matrix variable

Any other use of commas is illegal in MathCAD expressions.

missing operand
An operand is missing from an expression. For example, you see this message if you enter a plus sign without entering two expressions to add. MathCAD shows a placeholder (a small rectangle) in place of the missing operand.

missing operator
An operator is missing from an equation or expression.

must be 3-vector
You used a cross product on expressions that are not three-element vectors. The cross product works only on three-element vectors.

must be array
You attempted to use a scalar variable in an operation that requires an array. For example, you see this error if you define a

superscripted variable as a scalar. Since a superscripted variable represents a column of a matrix, you must define it as a vector.

must be dimensionless The indicated expression uses units but appears in a place where units are not permitted. Units are not permitted in the arguments for certain functions (for example, cos and ln) or in exponents. For example, the expressions $\cos(1L)$ and 10^{1M} are invalid. This message appears whether the indicated expression involves units directly or is defined in terms of units in earlier equations.

must be increasing You used a vector whose elements are not in increasing order as the argument to a function that requires a strictly increasing argument. The first argument of lspline, pspline, cspline, interp, linterp, and hist must be a vector whose elements are strictly increasing. (Remember that the first element of a MathCAD vector v is normally v_0. If you do not explicitly define it, MathCAD sets $v_0 = 0$.)

must be integer You used a noninteger expression where an integer is required: for example, as an argument to the identity function, or as a subscript or superscript. (Although you can define range variables with fractional values — for example, x:= 1,1.1 ..10 — you cannot use such ranges as subscripts.)

must be nonzero You evaluated a built-in function at zero, and the function is undefined at zero. For example, J0 and ln are undefined at zero.

must be positive This error message marks a plot in which the limits or values for a logarithmic axis are zero or negative. MathCAD can plot only positive values on a logarithmic axis.

must be range You used something other than a range variable in a place that requires a range variable, for example, as the index for a summation. The index for a summation appears below the summation symbol. The index must be a variable that is defined earlier as a range variable.

must be real You used an expression that has an imaginary or complex value where MathCAD requires a real-valued expression. For example, MathCAD requires real-valued subscripts and real-valued arguments for some built-in functions, including J0, mod, and Φ.

must be scalar	You used a vector or matrix expression where a scalar is required: for example, as the argument to the identity function.
must be square	You used a nonsquare matrix in an operation that requires a square matrix, such as finding the determinant or inverse, or raising a matrix to a power.
must be vector	This error message marks a matrix or scalar where there is an operation that requires a vector: for example, with the Σ operator.
nested solve block	You used two Givens in a row with no intervening Find or Minerr. MathCAD does not allow nested solve blocks, although you can define functions with solve blocks and use those functions in other solve blocks.
no matching Given	This message marks a Find or Minerr function with no matching Given. Each solve block must begin with a region containing only the name Given and end with an expression containing Find or Minerr.
non-scalar value	You tried to use a vector or range expression in a place where only a scalar value is permitted. For example, you see this message if i is a range variable and you try to enter an equation like $x := i$. You cannot define one range variable in terms of another. To define x in terms of the range variable i, enter an equation like $x_i := i$.
not a name	You used a number or other combination of symbols where MathCAD requires a name: for example, as the second argument of the root function.
not converging	MathCAD was unable to compute an answer for an integral, a derivative, a root, Find or Minerr function within the required tolerance. MathCAD starts with TOL $= 10^{-3}$. You can loosen the tolerance by entering a new definition for TOL above the expression that is not converging, for example, TOL:=.05. In the case of Find or Minerr, you may need to try a different starting value for the variable you are solving for.
overflow	You evaluated an expression that exceeds the largest number that MathCAD can represent (about 10^{307}).
significance lost and **significance reduced**	These error messages indicate that you tried to evaluate a function for a value beyond the accurate range for the function. For example, you see this message if you try to evaluate

$\sin(10^{100})$. Since the value of $\sin(10^{100})$ depends on the units digit of 10^{100}, any value that MathCAD could return would have no significant digits. Instead of returning a value of dubious accuracy, MathCAD shows one of these error messages.

singularity You evaluated a function or performed an operation at an illegal value. For example, you see this error message if you divide by zero, or if you try to invert a matrix with a determinant of 0.

stack overflow You evaluated an expression that overflows MathCAD's internal stack. Simplify the expression or divide it into two subexpressions.

too few arguments The indicated expression contains a function with fewer than the required number of arguments. You see this error message, for example, if you enter an expression like $\mod(x)$. For functions you define, the function definition determines the required number of arguments. Check the list of built-in functions earlier in this section to determine the number of arguments required for a built-in function.

too few constraints This error marks a Find or Given with fewer constraints than variables to be solved. Add dummy constraints or decrease the number of variables to be solved.

too few elements You have applied a Fourier transform, cubic spline, or linear interpolation function to a vector with too few elements. Splines and linear interpolation require vectors with at least two elements. Fourier transform functions and their inverses require at least four elements.

too few subscripts You used one subscript on a matrix. You must use two subscripts separated by a comma to specify a matrix element.

too large to display You tried to display a vector or matrix bigger than MathCAD can display.

too many arguments The indicated expression contains a function with more than the required number of arguments. Check the list of built-in functions to determine the number of arguments required.

too many constraints You included more than fifty constraints in a solve block.

too many subscripts You used two or more subscripts on a vector.

too many points	You tried to plot more points than MathCAD can handle in one plot.
undefined	The indicated variable is undefined. To define it, enter the variable name followed by a colon (:) and an expression or number for its definition. This error often means you have typed an equals sign (=) instead of a colon to define a variable. To define a variable, you must use a colon. If you use an equals sign, MathCAD assumes you want to calculate the value of the variable.

You also see this message if you use a variable incorrectly in a global definition. If you use a variable on the right side of a global definition, the variable must be globally defined *above* the definition in which it is used. If you use a locally defined variable or a variable whose global definition is *below* the place where it is used, MathCAD marks the variable as undefined. |
underflow	You evaluated an expression smaller in magnitude than the smallest positive number that MathCAD can represent (about 10^{-308}).
unmatched parenthesis	You entered or calculated an equation that contains a left parenthesis without a matching right parenthesis. Edit the equation by removing the left parenthesis or adding a matching right parenthesis.
wrong size vector	The argument to a Fourier transform function has the wrong number of elements. The functions fft, cfft, and icfft require as arguments vectors with 2^n elements, where n is a whole number greater than 1. The function ifft requires an argument vector with 2^n+1 elements, where n is a whole number greater than 0. Remember that MathCAD starts each vector v with an element v_0 (unless you change ORIGIN).

Problem
Sets

Part
Four

This part contains four sets of problems. Each problem set comes from a different field of study:

1. Physics
2. Electrical Engineering
3. Microeconomics
4. Operations Management

The problems were written and produced in MathCAD, and they show how you can use MathCAD to print out word processed and mathematical text together.

Once you have understood MathCAD's power and logic, you'll find it easy and exciting to create you own applications in the areas that interest you most.

1 Physics

Physics problems prepared by Richard B. Anderson.

Problem 1: Projectile Motion
================================

A projectile is fired with muzzle velocity V, at an angle θ to the
horizon. Neglecting friction:

(a)   Horizontal range: How far does the projectile go before
      returning to earth? What muzzle angle leads to the greatest
      range?

(b)   Flight time: How long does it stay in the air?

(c)   Altitude: How high does it go?

Problem 2: Mechanical Equivalent of Heat (the Joule equivalent)
==

When it goes over a waterfall, water gets warmer. Gravity imparts
kinetic energy, which is dissipated as heat at the bottom of the
cascade.

Neglecting such competing phenomena as conduction and evaporative
cooling, which depend heavily on ambient temperature and humidity,
use Joule's mechanical equivalent of heat to predict the
temperature change δT that water should experience in falling from
height H.

Plot δT vs. H for waterfall heights up to 2000 feet.

Definitions:

$$J := 2.389 \cdot 10^{-4} \cdot \frac{kcal}{joule} \qquad \text{(the Joule equivalent)}$$

$$c := 1 \cdot \frac{kcal}{kg \cdot degC} \qquad \text{(specific heat capacity of water)}$$

Problem 3: Blackbody Radiation (Planck's Law)
==

Perfect energy absorbers, also called black bodies, radiate energy
in a way that classical physics cannot explain. In 1900, Max
Planck proposed a revolutionary theory of blackbody radiation
based on a new quantum view of energy, and twentieth century
physics was born.

Planck's Law, the first fruit of the quantum theory, describes the
energy spectrum of blackbody radiation. It expresses the rate at
which radiation of wavelength L is emitted from a unit area of an
ideal black surface of temperature T:

$$F(L,T) := \frac{2 \cdot \pi \cdot h \cdot c^2}{L^5 \cdot \left[e^{\frac{h \cdot c}{k \cdot L \cdot T}} - 1 \right]}$$

where

$$\text{Planck's Constant } h \equiv 6.625 \cdot 10^{-34} \cdot \text{joule} \cdot \text{sec}$$

$$\text{Speed of Light } \quad c \equiv 2.9979 \cdot 10^{8} \cdot \frac{m}{\text{sec}}$$

$$\text{Boltzmann's Constant } k \equiv 1.380 \cdot 10^{-23} \cdot \frac{\text{joule}}{\text{degK}}$$

(a) On a single set of axes, plot the Planck emission
distribution function F(L,T) for T = 2000, 2500, and 3000 degrees
Kelvin, for wavelengths L from zero to 50000 Angstrom units.

(b) Verify that Planck's Law is consistent with the Stefan-
Boltzmann law, which states that the total energy emitted per
unit time per unit area, integrated over all wavelengths, is
directly proportional to the fourth power of the absolute
temperature T.

(c) Verify, finally, that Planck's Law is consistent with Wien's
 Displacement Law, according to which the wavelength at the peak
of each Planck's Law curve should be inversely proportional to its
corresponding temperature.

Problem 4:   The Emission Spectrum of Hydrogen (Bohr's Model)
==

Niels Bohr's orbital model of the atom gave physics an important
bridge from classical to quantum mechanics. It predicted
successfully that hydrogen, when excited, would emit light of
wavelengths L given by the following formula:

$$L(i,f) := \cfrac{1}{R_H \left[\dfrac{1}{f^2} - \dfrac{1}{i^2}\right]}$$

$f = 1,\ldots,\infty$

$i = f+1,\ldots,\infty$

where i and f are integers.

(a)   For each of the first five series of spectral lines that the
Bohr hydrogen model predicts, tabulate the wavelengths (in
Angstroms) of the first ten members. Label each series with its
conventional name (after a pioneer in spectroscopy), as follows:

Series	f	i
Lyman	1	2...11
Balmer	2	3...12
Paschen	3	4...13
Brackett	4	5...14
Pfund	5	6...15

Inasmuch as the visible spectrum lies between 1600A and 7500A,
which of the predicted hydrogen lines should be visible to the
eye?

(b)   Display the Balmer series spectrum as a frequency
distribution over wavelengths ranging from 3000 to 7000 Angstroms.
Use MathCAD's histogram function, and plot in error bar format.

(c)   The Rydberg constant is central to the study of emission
spectra, and its value is very accurately known from experiment.
Bohr's model yields a theoretical expression for the constant in
terms of the mass (m) and charge (q) of the electron, the speed of
light (c), the Coulomb's Law constant (C), and Planck's constant
(h).

Compute the value of the Rydberg constant as derived from Bohr's
model, and compare it with the empirical value:

Bohr's prediction: $$R_{HB} := \frac{2 \cdot \pi^2 \cdot C^2 \cdot m_e \cdot q_e^4}{c \cdot h^3}$$

Empirical value: $$R_{HE} := 1.097 \cdot 10^7 \cdot m^{-1}$$

===

The concepts of mass and energy, with their associated conservation
laws, have occupied much of the attention of physicists for
centuries. Beginning in 1906, Albert Einstein merged the two into
a single mass-energy concept with his Special Law of Relativity.

Special Relativity predicts, in accordance with observation, that
as an object's speed v approaches that of light, its mass m
increases in such a way that no addition of energy can accelerate
it all the way to c, the speed of light.

The Einstein relativistic mass formula is

$$m(v) := \frac{m_0}{\sqrt{1 - \dfrac{v^2}{c^2}}}$$

where m_0 is the object's mass at zero speed (its "rest mass").

(a)   Plot the ratio of relativistic mass to rest mass vs. speed,
for speeds ranging from rest to (nearly) c. At what fraction of
the speed of light does mass double? triple? Increase by a
factor of ten?

It's harder to accelerate a fast-moving object than a slower one.
At a non-relativistic speed v, to increase the speed of a 1-kg
object by $\delta v = 1$ m/sec requires the transfer of $\delta E = v$ joules of
kinetic energy.

At speeds approaching c, however, acceleration takes even more
energy, as the object gets more massive. Here, the famous
Einstein mass-energy equivalence equation takes over:

$$E := mc^2$$

As a result, it takes a huge, energy-gobbling machine to
accelerate tiny particles to relativistic speeds.

===

(b)   Create a plot which compares the relativistic and
nonrelativistic cases, showing the energy increment δE necessary
to increase the speed of a 1-kg object by δv = 1 m/sec at various
speeds.

$$\delta E(v) := \frac{m_0 \cdot v \cdot \delta v}{\left[\sqrt{1 - \left[\frac{v}{c}\right]^2} \right]^3}$$

(c)   How fast does a particle have to go before its relativistic
mass increase makes it twice as hard to accelerate?   three times?
ten times?

2

Electrical Engineering

Electrical Engineering problems prepared by Professor John P. Uyemura, School of Electrical Engineering, Georgia Institute of Technology.

Problem 1: DC Resistor Networks
==================================

Resistors connected in series simply add:

$$R_{eq} := \sum_i R_i$$

For resistors connected in parallel, it is the reciprocals (inverses) of the component resistances that add:

$$\frac{1}{R_{eq}} := \sum_i \frac{1}{R_i}$$

The unit of resistance is the ohm, derived from basic MKSA units as follows

$$m := 1L \quad kg := 1M \quad sec := 1T \quad coul := 1Q$$

$$amp := \frac{coul}{sec} \quad volt := \frac{joule}{coul} \quad ohm := \frac{volt}{amp} \quad joule := kg \cdot \frac{m^2}{sec^2}$$

Eight resistors are placed in parallel. The values are

$$i := 1 ..8 \quad \text{(the range variable)}$$

$$R_1 := 6800 \cdot ohm \quad R_2 := 22000 \cdot ohm \quad R_3 := 1.5 \cdot 10^5 \cdot ohm \quad R_4 := 1500 \cdot ohm$$

$$R_5 := 2 \cdot 10^6 \cdot ohm \quad R_6 := 10^4 \cdot ohm \quad R_7 := 4.7 \cdot 10^3 \cdot ohm \quad R_8 := 8200 \cdot ohm$$

The parallel resistor network is in series with a resistor

$$R_{ser} := 7600 \cdot ohm$$

The series combination is connected to a voltage source of value

$$V_{source} := 5 \cdot volt$$

Calculate:

(a) The equivalent resistance of the parallel network.

(b) The total current supplied by the voltage source.

(c) The current through each resistor.

(d) Check your results in (b) using conductances.

Problem 2:   AC Network Analysis Using Phasors
===

AC networks are analyzed using complex phasors which give
information on the amplitude and phase of voltages and currents.
In electrical engineering, we denote imaginary numbers using

$$j := \sqrt{-1}$$

If f is the frequency in Hertz, the angular frequency is given
by $\Omega = 2\pi f$. Ω has units of radians/sec.

An AC voltage source is specified by the parameters

$$V_0 := 10 \quad f := 2 \cdot 10^3 \quad \Omega := 2 \cdot \pi \cdot f \quad t := 0, 10^{-5} \ .. \ 10^{-3} \quad \text{(time)}$$

corresponding to a voltage phasor of the form

$$V(t) := V_0 \cdot e^{j \cdot \Omega \cdot t}$$

The voltage source is in series with a resistor, an inductor and
a capacitor with circuit values of:

Resistor:	$R := 1000$	ohms;
Capacitor:	$C := 20 \cdot 10^{-6}$	farads;
Inductor:	$L := 45 \cdot 10^{-3}$	henrys.

(a)   Calculate the circuit impedance Z and admittance Y.

(b)   Plot the real part of the phasor voltage V(t) and current
      I(t).

(c)   Plot the real part of the phasor voltage across each element.

Problem 3: Transmission Line Analysis
==

Wave propagation along a transmission line is described using complex impedance transformations. For a transmission line of length L, standing waves are established. The properties of the standing waves depend upon the load.

Consider a lossless transmission line with the following parameters:

Characteristic Impedance: Z_0 := 50   ohms

Load Impedance: Z_L := 75 + 50j   ohms $j := \sqrt{-1}$

Length: L := 1.2   meters

The source voltage oscillates at a frequency of $f := 100 \cdot 10^6$ and the velocity of the wavefronts is given by

$$v := 2.2 \cdot 10^8 \quad \text{meters/sec}$$

Using transmission line theory, calculate:

(a)   The wavenumber k;

(b)   The input impedance seen looking into the line;

(c)   The reflection coefficient;

(d)   The voltage standing wave ratio (VSWR).

Problem 4: Bipolar Transistor Amplifier Analysis
===

A simple common-emitter bipolar amplifier uses one transistor and
four resistors. The load resistor R_C is on the collector, while
the emitter resistor R_E provides bias stabilization. Two base
resistors R_{B1} and R_{B2} are used to set the base bias voltage. It
is assumed that R_{B1} and R_C are connected to the power supply V_{CC},
while R_{B2} and R_E are connected to ground. An npn transistor is
used in this problem.

The amplifier circuit is biased with resistors having values

$$R_C := 4700 \qquad R_E := 3300 \qquad R_{B1} := 100 \cdot 10^3 \qquad R_{B2} := 47 \cdot 10^3$$

with a power supply of $V_{CC} := 15$ volts.   The transistor
has parameters

$$\text{Beta} := 100 \qquad V_{BEon} := 0.7$$

and the thermal voltage is assumed to be $V_T := 0.026$ volts.

Assuming forward-active mode biasing,

(a) Calculate the bias currents and voltages for the circuit.
    Use your results to verify the assumption that the transistor
    is in the forward active amplifying mode.

(b) Find the small-signal transconductance gm of the transistor.

Problem 5: MOSFET Amplifier Frequency Response
===

A common source MOSFET amplifier is characterized by the
following circuit parameters:

Mid-band voltage gain: A_v := -20

Transconductance: g_m := 0.005 A/V

Capacitances: Gate-Drain C_{gd} := $2 \cdot 10^{-12}$ farads

Gate-Source C_{gs} := $2 \cdot 10^{-12}$

Resistances: Load (AC) R_L := $2.5 \cdot 10^{3}$ ohms

Gate Bias R_G := $75 \cdot 10^{3}$

The voltage transfer function H(Ω) for the amplifier is specified
using

$$D_1 := \left[C_{gs} + C_{gd} \cdot \left[1 + g_m \cdot R_L \right] + C_{gd} \cdot \left[\frac{R_L}{R_G} \right] \right] \cdot R_G$$

$$D_2 := C_{gd} \cdot C_{gs} \cdot R_L \cdot R_G \qquad \Omega := 1, 100 \; .. 10^{7}$$

in the form
$$D(\Omega) := 1 + j \cdot \Omega \cdot D_1 - \Omega^2 \cdot D_2$$

$$H(\Omega) := -A_v \cdot \frac{1 - \left[\dfrac{\Omega \cdot C_{gd}}{g_m} \right]}{D(\Omega)}$$

(a) Calculate the location of the zero in H(Ω);

(b) Calculate the poles of H(Ω).

Problem 6: Silicon pn-Junction Diode Properties
==

A silicon pn-junction diode has a step doping profile specified by the following parameters:

$$N_a := 5 \cdot 10^{16} \quad \#/cm^3 \qquad \text{p-side acceptor doping density}$$

$$N_d := 8 \cdot 10^{17} \quad \#/cm^3 \qquad \text{n-side donor doping density.}$$

The cross-sectional area of the diode is $A := 5 \cdot 10^{-5}$ cm^2. The minority carrier diffusion coefficients and lifetimes are

Electrons: $D_n := 25.4$ cm^2/V-sec , $t_n := 0.1 \cdot 10^{-6}$ sec

Holes: $D_p := 1.3$ cm^2/V-sec , $t_p := 1.1 \cdot 10^{-6}$ sec .

(a) Calculate the built-in voltage V_{bi}

(b) Calculate the equilibrium depletion widths W, x_n and x_p

(c) Calculate the reverse saturation current I_o.

For silicon, $\epsilon_r := 11.8$ and assume room temperature values

Thermal voltage: $V_T := 0.026$ volts

Intrinsic Density: $n_i := 1.45 \cdot 10^{10}$ $\#/cm^3$

Problem 7: Diode Operating Analysis
=====================================

A silicon diode is in series with a 10 voltage battery and a
15k ohm resistor. The forward bias voltage across the diode
is measured to be V_d = 0.72 at room temperature (300 degrees K).
The diode has an ideality factor of n = 1.8.

(a) Calculate the diode current I.

(b) Calculate the diode saturation current I_s.

(c) Calculate he small-signal resistance r_d of the diode.

Problem 8:   Resonant Modes of a Rectangular Waveguide
===

A perfectly conducting rectangular waveguide has dimensions

   $a := 0.0229$ m, $b := 0.0102$ m

and is filled with air where

$$\epsilon_o := 8.854 \cdot 10^{-12} \quad \text{F/m} \quad \text{(permittivity)}$$

$$\mu_o := 4 \cdot \pi \cdot 10^{-7} \quad \text{H/m} \quad \text{(permeability)}$$

(a)   Calculate the cutoff frequencies of TM waves in the guide.

(b)   Recalculate the lowest order mode cutoff frequencies if
      a material with relative permittivity $\epsilon_r := 2.25$ is used.

3

Microeconomics

Microeconomics problem prepared by Professor John Giglia, Department of Technology and Society, State University of New York at Stony Brook.

Problem: Utility Maximization
=================================

A consumer must decide how to allocate his income, Y, between food and clothes. The price of food is P_f, and the price of clothes is P_c. Any bundle combining F units of food and C units of clothes yields utility to the consumer according to the following utility function:

$$\text{Utility}(F,C) := C \cdot F^2$$

The consumer's objective is to maximize utility within the constraint that income imposes. Income and prices are as follows:

$$Y := 30 \qquad P_f := 5 \qquad P_c := 2$$

A given level of utility, if it can be achieved at all, can result from many different combinations of levels of spending on food and clothing. On a plot of C against F, an indifference curve defines the set of (F,C) bundles that correspond to a fixed value of Utility.

(a) Display indifference curves for utility levels of 40, 80, and 120. Plot points for values of F from 1 to 6 at intervals of 0.5. Plot the budget line on the same set of axes.

All points (F,C bundles) that lie on or below the budget line are consistent with the budget constraint. The highest utility that can be attained corresponds to the indifference curve that is just tangent to the budget line. The point of tangency defines the optimal bundle (F*,C*). At that point the curve and the line have the same slope as well as the same values of F and C.

(b) For each indifference curve and for the budget line, tabulate C and slope at each plotted level of F.

(c) Use the tables to determine F* and C*, the optimal levels of spending on food and clothes.

4

Operations Management

Operations Management problems taken from Lee J. Krajewski and Larry P. Ritzman. Copyright © 1987, Addison-Wesley Publishing Company, Inc. Used with permission.

Problem 1 (Krajewski and Ritzman, p. 67)

===

Frank Jennings has just patented a new device for washing dishes and cleaning dirty kitchen sinks, which he calls the "Easystik." This device has a tough, rubber head to scrub off difficult food deposits on dishes, and the handle is filled with a detergent that releases during use of the device. The Jennings Company, which Frank owns, has been in business since 1982 and now employs 35 people. Before trying to commercialize the Easystik and add it to his existing product line, Jennings wants reasonable assurance that it will be a success. After thinking through the production process and the cost of raw materials and new equipment, Jennings estimates the variable cost of each unit produced and sold at $7, with fixed costs per year at $56,000.

(a) If the price is set at $25, how many units must be produced and sold to break even? Use both the graphic and algebraic approaches to get your answer.

(b) Jennings forecasts sales for the first year of 10,000 Easystiks, if the price is set at $15. What would be the total contribution to profits from this new product during the first year? Set up Profit(p,Q) as a MathCAD function of Price p and Sales Volume Q.

(c) If the price is set at $10 per unit, Jennings forecasts that first-year sales will double to 20,000 units. Which pricing strategy ($15 or $10) would make the greatest total contribution to profits?

Problem 2 (Krajewski and Ritzman, p. 116)
==

The monthly demand for units manufactured by the Acme Rocket
Company has been:

Month	Units
May	100
June	80
July	110
August	115
September	105
October	110
November	125
December	120

(a) Use a single exponential smoothing model to forecast the
number of units for June through December. The initial
forecast for May was 105 units; $\alpha = 0.2$.

(b) Calculate the percentage error for each month from June
through December and the MAD (Mean Absolute Deviation) of
forecast errors as of the end of December.

(c) Calculate the tracking signal

$$\text{Tracking\_signal} := \frac{\text{Cumulative\_forecast\_error}}{\text{MAD}}$$

as of the end of December. What can you say about the
performance of your forecasting model?

Problem 3   (Krajewski and Ritzman, pp. 117-8)
===

You are in charge of inventory control for your company. As part of your job, you must obtain forecasts of demand for the products stocked in inventory. Sales data for one of the products are

Week	$D \equiv u$
1	264
2	116
3	165
4	101
5	209

(a) Use a single exponential smoothing model to forecast sales for week 6. The forecast for week 1 was 170, and $\alpha = 0.3$.

(b) During lunch with the marketing manager, you found out that there was a special advertising budget for this particular product. Advertising expenditures were:

	Advertising ($000)
Week	$Ads \equiv t$
1	2.50
2	1.30
3	1.40
4	1.00
5	2.00

Use simple linear regression analysis to develop a forecasting model for this product.

The marketing manager said that next week they will spend $1750 on advertising for that product. What is your demand forecast for week 6?

(c) Which of the two approaches would you feel more comfortable with? Why? Discuss the advantages and disadvantages of your choice.

Problem 4   (Krajewski and Ritzman, pp. 316-7)
===

A supplier to the electric utility industry has a strategy of
market-area plants, since the product is heavy and transportation
costs are high.   One market area includes the lower part of the
Great Lakes region and the upper portion of the southeastern
region.   Over 600,000 tons are to be shipped to eight major
customer locations:

Customer Locations	Shipped Tons ≡ k	Coordinates	
		x ≡ k	y ≡ k
Three Rivers, MI	5	7	13
Fort Wayne, IN	92	8	12
Columbus, OH	70	11	10
Ashland, KY	35	11	7
Kingsport, TN	9	12	4
Canton, OH	227	13	11
Wheeling, WV	16	14	10
Roanoke, VA	153	15	5

(a)   Plot a map of the customer locations, and calculate their
      center of gravity (rounding to the nearest 1/10 distance unit).

(b)   Calculate the load-distance scores for the four points that
      are 0.5 unit of distance north, east, south, and west of the
      center of gravity.   Use rectilinear distances.   Is there any
      improvement?

Problem 5   (Krajewski and Ritzman, p. 751)
==

The Webster Chemical Company produces mastics and caulking for the
construction industry. The product is blended in large mixers and
then pumped into tubes and capped. The company is concerned about
the possibility of underfilling the tubes, thereby short-changing
the customer. Twenty samples of 200 tubes each had the following
record of underfilled tubes:

$j := 1 .. 20$

Sample Number j	Number of Underfilled Tubes U := j
1	12
2	16
3	8
4	24
5	20
6	4
7	16
8	12
9	28
10	8
11	20
12	20
13	4
14	8
15	16
16	8
17	24
18	8
19	16
20	12

(a)   Construct a p-chart for this situation. Use k=3 and the
      historical average proportion defective from the above data
      as the central line of the chart.

(b)   Comment on the process average proportion defective, given
      the samples shown here.

Problem 6   (Krajewski and Ritzman, p. B36)
==

The Hairy Knoll is a discount barbershop where the students from
the Kingston Barber School serve their apprenticeship. There are
only three barber chairs, each manned by an eager student. An
instructor oversees the operation and gives guidance as needed.
Patrons are served on a first-come, first-served basis and arrive
at the rate of 10 customers per hour according to a Poisson
distribution. The time required for a haircut averages 15 minutes
according to an exponential distribution.

(a)   What is the probability that there will be no customers in
       the shop?

(b)   What is the probability that there will be five or more
       customers in the shop?

(c)   What is the average number of customers waiting in the queue?

(d)   What is the average waiting time in the queue?

Glossary

⟨Alt–⟩ keystrokes	MathCAD commands that can be issued by pressing the ⟨Alt–⟩ key while pressing a second key associated with the command.
append cursor	A cursor shaped like ⌐ that is used to edit an equation. The horizontal part of the cursor tells you where it is, and the vertical part tells you where new material will be entered. To change the cursor to its append form, simply move the cursor into any region. To change it to or from its insert form, press ⟨Ins⟩.
argument	An independent variable used to define a function.
array	A one- or two-dimensional list of values assigned to a single variable, called an array variable. In MathCAD one-dimensional arrays are referred to as vectors, and two-dimensional arrays are referred to as matrices.
array variable	The variable to which a MathCAD array is assigned.
augment	An operation that combines two vectors or matrices having the same number of rows side-by-side, returning a new, wider matrix.
automatic calculation mode	The mode in which MathCAD runs through the calculations you've ordered every time you move the cursor out of a region. Unless you tell it otherwise when you start MathCAD, you are in automatic mode, as indicated by "auto" in the message line.

autoscaling	The MathCAD facility that automatically calculates values for any unspecified axis limits on plots.
built-in functions	Functions that are already part of the MathCAD program. To redefine one of MathCAD's built-in functions, enter a function definition using the same function name as the built-in functions you want to redefine.
buffer, cut	See cut.
calculation equation	An equation that computes a result, displayed with an equals sign.
calculation mode indicator	An indicator in the message line that tells you whether you are in automatic or manual mode. In automatic mode, MathCAD runs through the calculations you've ordered every time you move the cursor out of a region. In manual mode it runs through the calculations only when you tell it to by pressing F9.
command	An instruction that you give MathCAD. To issue a command, press ⟨Esc⟩, and then type in enough characters of the command name so that MathCAD can tell which one you mean. You can also use the command keys to issue the more frequently used commands. See the Reference Card for a list of commands and their functions.
command file	A text file consisting of MathCAD commands. A command file can be carried out using the command EXecute.
command menu	A screen listing of commands. In MathCAD there are seven main logical command groups, each with its own submenu. Press the F10 key to see the menu of command groups. Use the arrow keys to move the message-line cursor to the submenu containing the command you're looking for.
compute commands	A set of MathCAD commands used to process and calculate equations in MathCAD.
conditional functions	The MathCAD functions until and if, which permit iteration and assignment depending on the current value of an expression.
configuration file	A command file, usually created with the CONfigsave command, in which MathCAD stores the current values of the system variables, printer type, dimension names, page length and

	global, numeric, and plot formats. Any configuration file named MCAD.MCC will be executed by default at startup; other configuration files may by executed instead.
constant	In MathCAD, a number whose value must be changed by the user if it is to change at all.
constraints	A set of simultaneous equations (with the relational operator $\approx$) or inequalities (with the relational operators $<$, $>$, $\leq$, or $\geq$) entered in a solve block to be solved for one or more unknowns.
⟨Ctrl-⟩ keystrokes	MathCAD commands that can be issued by pressing the ⟨Ctrl-⟩ key while pressing a second key associated with the command.
cursor	The highlighted symbol on the screen that indicates where any changes will enter the worksheet.
cursor movement keys	Keys that move the cursor around without affecting the contents of the regions it occupies.
cursor position indicator	The numbers of the line and column at which the cursor now sits. These numbers appear to the right of the message line on the MathCAD screen.
cut	Delete a region or text segment from the document and put it into a temporary storage area in your computer's memory (the cut buffer).
definition equations	Equations that define each symbol in a calculation equation. They can be either local (that is, defined earlier in the worksheet, displayed with ":=") or global (that is, defined anywhere on the worksheet, displayed with "$\equiv 0$").
dimensional values	Numbers that are associated with one of the MathCAD dimensions — length (L), mass (M), time (T), or charge (Q). MathCAD builds in these dimensions to keep track of units for dimensional analysis and unit conversions. To enter a dimensional value, type a number followed by an uppercase or lowercase L, M, T, or Q. Use the DImension command to change these labels.
disable calculation	Instruct MathCAD not to carry out the calculations that an equation implies. MathCAD marks a disabled equation or plot with a small rectangle. If applied to a plot, instruct MathCAD

	not to change the plot as the numbers change on which it depends.
document	Holds text, equations, and plots. The Student Edition of MathCAD lets you compose a document up to 80 columns wide and 120 lines long.
edit/move commands	A set of MathCAD commands used to cut, copy, and paste, as well as edit, the MathCAD screen.
edit cursor	When the cursor is inside a region, you can use it to indicate where you want to make changes to equations, plots, or text. The edit cursor can be either the append cursor or the insert cursor.
equation	In MathCAD, either a definition or a calculation. MathCAD equations are made up of numbers, variables, operators, and parentheses.
equation region	A rectangular area on the MathCAD document that contains an equation. Unless you signal otherwise, MathCAD assumes that any new region you start is an equation region.
error bar	A MathCAD plot format that highlights the difference between two variables plotted on the same set of axes.
error message	A message that appears on the screen when MathCAD detects a mistake or cannot perform a task.
expression	Any meaningful combination of MathCAD numbers, variables, functions, and operators. Expressions appear on the right side of a definition equation, on the left side of a calculation equation, on either side of a constraint, as arguments to functions, etc. Expressions may be scalar, vector, or matrix; scalar expressions may be real or complex.
file-access functions	Functions that allow you to read to and write from data files. They include READ, WRITE, APPEND, READPRN, WRITEPRN and APPENDPRN.
file commands	MathCAD commands that are used to load, save, name, add on to, and clear files.
filename	The name of the file from which you read a document in from disk or the name you supply when you write a document to disk. In MathCAD the current filename appears on the left side of the message line.

format	See local format, global format, numeric format, or plot format.
formula	An equation that defines a mathematical relationship.
function	An expression describing a relationship between two or more variables. MathCAD uses three kinds of functions: built-in functions, which are already part of the MathCAD program; user-defined functions, which you define in your documents; and file-access functions, which allow you to read from and write to data files. In MathCAD, a function can be like a command, except that it is entered into the document rather than being issued directly to the computer.
function keys	A series of ten keys ($\boxed{F\,1}$ through $\boxed{F10}$) used to issue preassigned MathCAD commands. To see a quick reference to the function keys, press $\boxed{F1}$.
global definition equation	A definition equation that appears anywhere on the worksheet and applies to the entire worksheet. Global definition equations are entered with a tilde ($\sim$) in place of the colon, and result in a triple equals sign.
global format	Parameters that control the display of calculated results or plots for a whole MathCAD document.
hard line break	A manually inserted carriage return that ends a line in a text region before it reaches the right edge of the region.
help system	MathCAD's on-line reference system. To enter the on-line help system, press $\boxed{F1}$. To leave the help system, press $\langle$Esc$\rangle$. To see help on another topic, type a letter from A to L as indicated on the main help menu.
index variable	See range variable.
in-region commands	A set of MathCAD commands used to copy, cut, and paste parts of equation or text regions.
insert cursor	A cursor shaped like an L that is used to edit an equation. To change the append cursor to the insert cursor (or back again), press $\langle$Ins$\rangle$. As with the append cursor, the horizontal line tells you where you are, and the vertical where new material will be entered.
iteration	The process of evaluating the same equation many times for many different values of the variables.

load	To retrieve a file from a disk ($\boxed{F5}$).
local definition equation	A definition equation that appears earlier in the worksheet. To MathCAD, "earlier" means "above and to the left." Local definition equations are entered with a colon in place of the equals sign.
local format	Parameters that control the display of a single calculated result or plot.
manual calculation mode	The mode used when you want MathCAD to run through the calculations you've ordered only when you tell it to by pressing $\boxed{F9}$ or entering the PROcess command.
MathCAD screen	See screen.
matrix	A two-dimensional array of values assigned to a single variable name. Each element of a matrix can be accessed using a pair of subscripts.
message line	The inverse video stripe that appears near the top of the Math-CAD screen. It shows, from left to right, the current filename, messages from MathCAD, the cursor position indicator, and the calculation mode indicator.
menu, command	See command menu.
numeric format	Parameters such as the base, precision, and zero tolerance that control the display of calculated numeric results. Numeric formats may be set locally, with the f command or globally, with the FORMat command.
operator	A symbol used in a formula to indicate the relationship between two values or the operation to be performed. The Reference Card lists the 29 valid MathCAD operators. It also shows the keystrokes you have to type to enter each one. The operators appear in precedence order.
ORIGIN	The predefined system variable that determines the index of the first element in each MathCAD vector and of the first column and row of each MathCAD matrix. Its default value is 0; if it is set to 1, all of your arrays will begin with element one.
paste	Insert the contents of the cut buffer into the document at the current cursor location.

placeholder	A small rectangle that MathCAD uses to hold a space open for numbers, operators, or units you haven't yet typed. The placeholder that appears at the end of an equation is used for unit conversion.
plot format	The parameters that control the size, plot type, axis type, and axis subdivisions of a MathCAD plot. Plot formats may be set locally, with the f command or globally, with the PLotformat command.
plot region	A rectangular area on the MathCAD document for graphic displays of relationships that you have formulated in earlier equation regions. You use an at sign (@) to signify that you are starting a plot region.
precedence	The order in which MathCAD performs operations in a formula that has several operators. MathCAD assigns precedence to each operation and performs operations with higher precedence, such as multiplication, before operations with lower precedence, such as subtraction. You can use parentheses to override MathCAD's order of precedence.
prompt	Any message that MathCAD displays on the message line when you are issuing a command. Press ⟨Esc⟩ to abort the command.
PRNCOLWIDTH	A predefined system variable that determines the number of columns used to print each value in a data file with the WRITEPRN and APPENDPRN functions. Its default value is 8.
PRNPRECISION	A predefined system variable that determines the number of decimal places for each value printed in a data file with the WRITEPRN and APPENDPRN functions. Its default value is 4.
pseudorandom number	A number which is calculated from a formula but which behaves as a random number for ordinary statistical purposes.
range variable	A variable that takes on a range of variables each time you use it. Range variables behave like the index variables in a FOR-NEXT or DO-CONTINUE loop in a programming language, and are very useful as subscripts for vector and matrix variables.

region	A rectangular area on a MathCAD document that contains an equation, text, or a plot. MathCAD keeps track of each region as an imaginary rectangle within the document. When you begin a region, MathCAD fixes the upper left corner of the rectangle for that region. When you enlarge or edit the region, MathCAD keeps the upper left corner in the same place. To see the boxes for the regions in a document, hold down the ⟨Ctrl–⟩ key and press V. To hide the boxes, press ⟨Ctrl–V⟩ again.
root	A root of a function of a variable is a value of the variable for which the function equals zero.
save	To store a file on a disk. Save your work every fifteen minutes to one-half hour by pressing ⟨F6⟩ (the save key) to avoid losing data.
scalar variable	A variable with a single value. Do not use the same name for a scalar variable and a subscripted variable. MathCAD treats variables with the same name as the same variable.
screen	The currently displayed worksheet, or document. Also, the computer's monitor.
scrolling	Moving the MathCAD document screen vertically. To scroll through the document, move the cursor past the bottom of the screen. You can also use the MOve command to scroll through the display, leaving the cursor at the same spot on the screen.
seeded iteration	Iteration in which each successive computation depends on the preceding one.
slash options	Adjustments that can be made in the way that MathCAD sets itself up when it is first started.
solve block	A block of equations starting with the keyword Given, and ending with the first equation that follows it containing the function Find or Minerr. Its body consists of a set of simultaneous equations or inequalities, called constraints, to be solved for one or more unknowns.
subscripted variable	A variable with several values, one for each value of the subscript. You can use subscripted variables anywhere you can use ordinary (scalar) variables. Subscripts can be any expression with a non-negative real value. Some single-valued vari-

ables have subscripts that are merely part of their name (e.g., r_E for radius of the earth). MathCAD handles the two kinds of variables differently.

superscript　A raised index on a matrix variable that is used to select a single column of the matrix. $M^{(0)}$, for example, denotes the first column (column 0) in matrix M.

system commands　A set of MathCAD commands that refer to the whole system.

system variables　Predefined MathCAD variables, such as TOL, ORIGIN, PRNCOLWIDTH, and PRNPRECISION. These can be redefined locally or globally in a MathCAD document, or altered with the SET command for the duration of the MathCAD session.

text commands　A set of MathCAD commands used to mark and edit text. These are used in conjunction with the in-region and skip commands.

text region　A rectangular area on the MathCAD document where you can type text to clarify your document's meaning and to help it hang together. You use a double quotation mark (″) to signal MathCAD that you are making a new text region.

tilde　A special character, normally located on the same key as the backquote, and used to denote a global definition.

TOL　A MathCAD built-in constant that tells MathCAD when to stop an approximation process. You can change the value of TOL by entering an equation that redefines it. The default value of TOL is 10^{-3}.

top-level operator　The main operator in a MathCAD expression: the division bar in a fraction, for example. Many editing tasks, such as cutting and copying with the in-region commands, use the top-level operator as a "handle" for the whole expression.

unit definitions　In MathCAD, the four basic unit standards: length (L), mass (M), time (T), and charge (Q). By entering unit definitions, you can choose whatever system of measurement you wish: MKS (meter-kilogram-second), CGS (centimeter-gram-second), U.S. Customary (foot-pound-second), or any other. Use the DImension command to change the M, L, T, and Q labels.

user-defined functions	Functions that you define in your document. To define your own functions, enter a function name followed by a list of arguments separated by commas and enclosed in parentheses. Next, press the colon key and type an expression to define the function.
variable names	A letter, followed by any combination of letters, numbers, underscores, periods, and percent signs, used as a variable in an equation. You can also use certain Greek letters and the infinity sign. Variable names cannot include spaces or special characters. MathCAD *does* distinguish uppercase and lowercase letters in variable names (i.e., *diam* and *Diam* are two different variables).
vector	A one-dimensional list of values assigned to a single variable name. Individual elements can be accessed with a single subscript.
vectorization	Using the vec operator ($\langle$Alt$-\rangle$) to apply scalar expressions element by element to vectors and matrices. For example, when v is a vector, $\sin(v)$ is an illegal expression; but if the vec operator is applied to $\sin(v)$, the result is a new vector whose elements are the sines of the elements in v.
waveform	The shortest representative sample of a repetitive wave pattern.
window	The currently displayed portion of a document. You can have two windows showing on the screen simultaneously.
window/page commands	A set of MathCAD commands that allows you to manipulate the screen.
worksheet	See document.

Index

Insert (Ins) key, 34–35
Insertion
  in equation editing, 34–35
  of mathematical operators, 38–39
  of text regions, 75–76
INSertline command, 198
Installation, 7–14
  on hard-disk system, 13–14
  on one-disk system, 7–10
  on two-disk system, 10–13
Integers
  hexadecimal, 26–27, 188
  octal, 26, 188
Integrals, 149–150, 191
  contour, 193
  double, 193
Integration, 192–193
  numerical methods used for,
    193–194
Interocular indication, 103
Interpolation functions, 212–214
Iteration, 142, 206–211
  seeded, 142–147

Justify command (Ctrl–N), 200

Keys. *See also specific keys*
  alternate (Alt), 6
  arrow, 22, 24, 49, 185
  backspace (Bksp), 34, 67, 107, 185
  command, 50–54
  control (Ctrl), 6
  for creating regions, 54
  cursor movement, 22, 24, 49,
    51–53, 84, 185–186
  delete (Del), 34, 185
  enter (⏎), 185
  insert (Ins), 34–35
  PgDn, 185
  PgUp, 185
  pressing, 6
  shift, 6
  special, 185–186
  Tab, 84, 185
  typing and, 6
Keystroke sequence, editing, 33

Labels, 93
  writing on, 9
Lambda, 186
Less than, 191
Less than or equal to, 191

Levenberg-Marquardt method,
  221–222
Linear axis, subdivisions for, 233
Linear interpolation, 212–214
LOad command (F5), 196
Local definitions, 29
  in formulas, 30
Local formatting, 54, 132
Log(s), 202
Log axis, subdivisions for, 233–234
Log cycles, 233
Lowercase letters, 190
Lspline function, 213–214

M, 201
/M option, 19
Magnitude, of Fourier coefficient,
  131
MANual command (F10 CM), 25, 71,
  82, 127, 197
Manual mode, 19, 24
MARK command (Ctrl–X), 77, 199
MathCAD
  exiting, 16
  installing, 7–14
Mathematical functions, 201–206
Mathematical operators, 28, 58,
  190–191
  deleting, 38
  editing, 37
  inserting, 38–39
  precedence rules for, 26, 28
Matrices, 163–174
  correlational analysis with,
    171–175
  raw-data, 171
  regression analysis with, 175–180
  solving simultaneous equations
    with, 164–168
  standardized data, 172
  vectorization and, 168–170
MATrix command, 198
Matrix definition, 106
Matrix functions, 203
Matrix product, 191
MCAD /options, 17
MCAD.MCC, 18
.MCD file extension, 19
Measurement systems, 40
Memory command, 196

Menus (F10), 48, 186
  command, 48–49
Message(s), 23
Message line, 23–25
Minerr function, 217
MINPACK algorithms, 221–222
Monitor
  setting colors on, 18, 50
MOve command (F10 EM), 52, 53,
  198–199
Moving, of regions, 22, 61
Mu, 186
Multiplication, 191
  asterisk for, 60

n, 201
Names
  of commands, shortening, 69
  issuing commands by, 50
  of variables, 27–28, 190
Negation, 190
Noise, 135–136
Non–keyboard characters, 54
Norm, 190
Not equal to, 191
Numbers, 187–190
  complex, 131–132, 223
  dimensional values and, 27,
    188–189
  in equations, 26–27
  exponential notation and, 27, 60,
    187, 223
  floating point, 26, 187
  hexadecimal integers and, 26–27,
    188
  imaginary, 26, 187
  numeric format and, 189
  octal integers and, 26, 188
  random, 211
  transcendental, 139
Numerical approximation routines,
  154

Octal integers, 26, 188
Omega, 186
Operating system, 4, 120–121, 196
Operators, 28. *See also*
    Mathematical operators
  calculus, 191–195
  factorial, 146
  vectorization, 168–170
ORIGIN, 187